1001
QUOTATIONS
THAT CONNECT

Also by Craig Brian Larson

750 Engaging Illustrations for Preachers, Teachers, and Writers (Baker, 2002), a compilation of Baker's three previous illustrations books

1001 Illustrations That Connect: Stories, Stats, and News Items for Preaching, Teaching, or Writing (Zondervan, 2008), coedited with Phyllis TenElshof

The Art and Craft of Biblical Preaching (Zondervan, 2004), coedited with Haddon Robinson

Choice Contemporary Stories and Illustrations for Preachers, Teachers, and Writers (Baker, 2000)

Contemporary Illustrations for Preachers, Teachers, and Writers (Baker, 1999)

Hang in There . . . to the Better End (Spire, 1996), originally published under the title *Running the Midnight Marathon* (Revell, 1991)

Illustrations for Preaching and Teaching: From "Leadership Journal" (Baker, 1999)

More Perfect Illustrations for Every Topic and Occasion (Tyndale, 2003), coedited/compiled with Drew Zahn

Movie-Based Illustrations for Preaching and Teaching (Zondervan, 2003), coedited/compiled with Drew Zahn

More Movie-Based Illustrations for Preaching and Teaching (Zondervan, 2004), coedited/compiled with Laurie Quicke

Perfect Illustrations for Every Topic and Occasion (Tyndale, 2002), coedited/compiled with Drew Zahn

Preaching That Connects (Zondervan, 1994), cowritten with Mark Galli

Staying Power (Baker, 2005), originally published under the title *Pastoral Grit* (Bethany House, 1998)

1001 QUOTATIONS THAT CONNECT

Timeless Wisdom for Preaching, Teaching, and Writing

CRAIG BRIAN LARSON
BRIAN LOWERY

GENERAL
EDITORS

ZONDERVAN®

PreachingToday.com
Advancing the Art of Biblical Preaching

ZONDERVAN.com/
AUTHORTRACKER
follow your favorite authors

1001 Quotations That Connect
Copyright © 2009 by Christianity Today International

Requests for information should be addressed to:
Zondervan, *Grand Rapids, Michigan 49530*

ISBN 978-0-310-28036-1

Interior design by Ben Fetterley

Printed in the United States of America

08 09 10 11 12 13 14 • 24 23 22 21 20 19 18 17 16 15 14 13 12 11 10 9 8 7 6 5 4 3 2 1

CONTENTS

INTRODUCTION

One of the most potent arrows in a preacher's quiver is a well-worded quote. The tight bundle of words filled with insight or whimsy can quickly pierce the heart of the listener, producing an "aha" moment, a sense of conviction, or, better yet, life transformation. We have waded through thousands of quotes and gathered the best ones that speak to fundamental issues in the lives of both seekers and Christ-followers.

The quotations have come from the mouths of some of the most influential people of yesterday and today. You will read convincing words from apologists and evangelists, such as C. S. Lewis and Billy Graham, and hear sound bites from celebrities and newsmakers, such as Woody Allen and Ronald Reagan. Fathers and founders, such as Augustine and John Wesley, offer ancient words of wisdom. The passionate words of martyrs and missionaries, such as Dietrich Bonhoeffer, William Carey, and J. Hudson Taylor, will set your heart racing. Poets and mystics, such as Elizabeth Barrett Browning and A. W. Tozer, cast new light on things in life we often pass by. The words of prophets and activists, such as Martin Luther and Dorothy Day, can rattle you, while those of theologians and theorists, such as Karl Barth and Paul Tournier, stand on lofty heights. And always interesting are the keen offerings of writers and preachers, such as Anne Lamott and Peter Marshall.

You will notice that not all quotes by apologists are meant to prove the existence of God or discuss how Jesus is Lord (and not liar or lunatic). Nor do all quotes by missionaries speak of going to the ends of the earth, or capture in creative fashion the essence of our commission, though many do. Finally, you will find in the back of the book three indexes to help you find the quote you need when you need it. You can search by person, topic, or Scripture reference.

This resource celebrates the special gift with words and ideas that few have been given. Some of these quotes can be used to kick-start a sermon. Others may hone a point already well made. Still others may give you the refrain you have desperately looked for during hours of reflection. In the pages that follow, we have handed you 1,001 arrows to add to your quiver, so draw your bow and let fly.

—Craig Brian Larson
editor, PreachingToday.com
Brian Lowery
associate editor, PreachingToday.com

PART 1: CONVINCING WORDS FROM APOLOGISTS AND EVANGELISTS

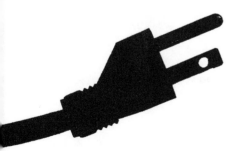

JOHN WILBUR CHAPMAN
AMERICAN EVANGELIST (1859 – 1918)

QUOTATION 1

Anything that dims my vision of Christ, or takes away my taste for Bible study, or cramps me in my prayer life, or makes Christian work difficult, is wrong for me; and I must, as a Christian, turn away from it.

Citation: John Wilbur Chapman, in a personal letter reflecting on the rules to govern a spiritual life

Topics: Bible Study; Devotional Life; Distractions; Focus; Priorities; Spiritual Disciplines

References: Hebrews 12:1 – 13; 1 John 2:15 – 17

QUOTATION 2

It's not the ship in the water but the water in the ship that sinks it. So it's not the Christian in the world but the world in the Christian that constitutes the danger.

Citation: Unknown

Topics: Complacency; Desires; Distractions; Double-mindedness; Holiness; World; Worldliness

References: John 17:11 – 16; Romans 12:2; 1 Corinthians 3:3; Colossians 2:20; Titus 2:12; 1 Peter 5:8 – 11

G. K. CHESTERTON
BRITISH WRITER (1874 – 1936)

QUOTATION 3

Christianity has died many times and risen again, for it has a God who knew his way out of the grave.

Citation: G. K. Chesterton, *The Everlasting Man*

Topics: God's Sovereignty; Jesus Christ; Resurrection; Victory

References: Matthew 16:18; 1 Corinthians 15:50 – 57; 1 Peter 1:3

QUOTATION 4

To be clever enough to get a great deal of money, one must be stupid enough to want it.

Citation: G. K. Chesterton, *A Miscellany of Men*

Topics: Desires; Foolishness; Greed; Materialism; Money; Vices

References: Ecclesiastes 5:10; Matthew 6:24; 19:23 – 24; Luke 12:15 – 21; Philippians 4:11 – 13; 1 Timothy 6:10; Hebrews 13:5

QUOTATION 5

Tradition means giving votes to the most obscure of all classes, our ancestors. It is democracy of the dead.

Citation: G. K. Chesterton, *Orthodoxy*

Topics: Past; Teaching; Tradition

Reference: Hebrews 12:1

QUOTATION 6

To the question, "What is meant by the fall?" I could answer with complete sincerity that, "Whatever I am, I am not myself."

Citation: G. K. Chesterton, *Orthodoxy*

Topics: Depravity; Fall of Humanity; Honesty; Human Condition; Human Nature; Original Sin; Self-worth

References: Genesis 3; Romans 3:10 – 18, 23; 5:12 – 14; Ephesians 4:22 – 24

QUOTATION 7

When I fancied that I stood alone, I was really in the ridiculous position of being backed up by all of Christendom.

Citation: G. K. Chesterton, *Orthodoxy*

Topics: Christian Life; Church; Individualism; Past; Religion; Tradition

References: Matthew 16:18; Romans 12:1 – 2; Philippians 1:27; 2 Thessalonians 2:15; Hebrews 12:1

QUOTATION 8

Certain new theologians dispute original sin, which is the only part of Christian doctrine which can really be proved.

Citation: G. K. Chesterton, *Orthodoxy*

Topics: Depravity; Doctrine; Evil; Fall of Humanity; Human Condition; Original Sin; Sinful Nature; Theology

References: Genesis 3; Romans 3:10–18, 23; 5:12–14; Ephesians 4:22–24; 1 John 1:8

QUOTATION 9

Humility is the mother of giants. One sees great things from the valley; only small things from the peak.

Citation: G. K. Chesterton, *The Hammer of God*

Topics: Arrogance; Humility; Perspective; Pride

References: Proverbs 11:2; 16:18–19; 22:4; 29:23; Micah 6:8; Matthew 18:4; 23:12; Luke 14:10–11; 22:26; Philippians 2:3; James 4:6, 10; 1 Peter 5:5

QUOTATION 10

Hope is the power of being cheerful in circumstances which we know to be desperate.

Citation: G. K. Chesterton, *Heretics*

Topics: Attitudes; Hope; Joy; Power; Trials

References: Psalm 42; Romans 4:18–25

QUOTATION 11

To have a right to do a thing is not at all the same as to be right in doing it.

Citation: G. K. Chesterton, *A Short History of England*

Topics: Decisions; Ethics; Morality; Rights

References: 1 Corinthians 6:12; 10:23–24; Galatians 5:13; 1 Peter 2:16

QUOTATION **12**

Men do not differ much about what things they will call evils; they differ enormously about what evils they will call excusable.

> **Citation:** G. K. Chesterton, *Illustrated London News* (October 23, 1909)
>
> **Topics:** Evil; Excuses; Morality; Tolerance
>
> **References:** Proverbs 20:9; John 3:19–20; 1 Corinthians 6:9–11; Ephesians 4:17–32

QUOTATION **13**

Fallacies do not cease to be fallacies because they become fashions.

> **Citation:** G. K. Chesterton, *Illustrated London News* (April 19, 1930)
>
> **Topics:** Excuses; Morality; Worldliness
>
> **Reference:** 2 Timothy 3:10–17

QUOTATION **14**

If I did not believe in God, I should still want my doctor, my lawyer, and my banker to do so.

> **Citation:** Unknown
>
> **Topics:** Atheism; Belief; Faith; Honesty; Trust
>
> **References:** Psalm 14:1; 53:1; 1 Corinthians 1:25; 3:19; Titus 1:16

QUOTATION **15**

Tolerance is the virtue of the man without convictions.

> **Citation:** Unknown
>
> **Topics:** Complacency; Convictions; Culture; Morality; Postmodernism; Tolerance; Truth
>
> **References:** John 1:17; 14:6; Acts 4:12; Romans 1:16–17; 10:9–10; 2 Timothy 1:8

QUOTATION 16

The point of an open mind, like having an open mouth, is to close it on something solid.

Citation: Unknown

Topics: Knowledge; Maturity; Mind; Spiritual Growth; Teachability; Tolerance; Wisdom

References: Proverbs 2:1–6; 1 John 5:20

QUOTATION 17

The world is not lacking in wonders, but in a sense of wonder.

Citation: Unknown

Topics: Awe; Praise; Reverence; Wonder; Worship

References: Numbers 14:11; Matthew 12:39; 24:3–8; John 2:11

CHARLES COLSON
AMERICAN WRITER, SPEAKER, AND CHIEF COUNSEL FOR PRESIDENT RICHARD NIXON (1931 –)

QUOTATION 18

The pursuit of doctrine for the sake of doctrine can be idolatrous. The gospel will not be demystified. God will not be mocked by the pretensions of those who believe they might fully and certainly know his mind. Was that, after all, not the sin of the Garden?

Citation: Charles Colson, *The Body*

Topics: Doctrine; Knowledge; Mysteries; Theology; Truth

References: Job 38:34–38; 40:1–5; 42:1–6; Romans 11:33–34

QUOTATION 19

If Christians followed the teachings of a benign dead man, their lives would display an innocuous piety. But when Christians stand up for righteousness and justice, they evidence the power of the living God.

Citation: Unknown

Topics: Discipleship; Influence; Justice; Power; Righteousness; Social Action; Social Impact; Testimony; Witness

References: Amos 5:24; Matthew 25:31–46

QUOTATION 20

People who have no fear of God soon have no fear of man, and no respect for human laws and authority.

Citation: Unknown

Topics: Arrogance; Authority; Fear of God; Government; Lawlessness; Morality; Relationships; Respect

Reference: 1 Peter 2:17

QUOTATION 21

Many Christians, like most of the populace, believe the political structures can cure all our ills. The fact is, however, that government, by its very nature, is limited in what it can accomplish. What it does best is perpetuate its own power and bolster its own bureaucracies.

Citation: Unknown

Topics: Focus; Government; Politics; Power; Priorities; World

References: 1 Samuel 8; Psalm 20

ELISABETH ELLIOT
AMERICAN WRITER AND EVANGELIST (1926–)

QUOTATION 22

True faith goes into operation when there are no answers.

Citation: Unknown

Topics: Confusion; Evangelism; Faith; Mysteries; Outreach; Trials; Trust

References: 2 Corinthians 5:7; Philippians 2:12–13; Hebrews 11:1–16

QUOTATION 23

God never does anything to you that isn't for you.

> Citation: Unknown
>
> Topics: Providence; Sanctification; Spiritual Growth; Tests; Trials
>
> Reference: Romans 8:28–31

CHARLES FINNEY
AMERICAN REVIVALIST PREACHER (1792–1875)

QUOTATION 24

A revival is nothing else than a new beginning of obedience to God.

> Citation: Charles Finney, in his lecture "What a Revival of Religion Is"
>
> Topics: Conversion; Obedience; Regeneration; Revival; Transformation
>
> References: 2 Kings 23:1–3; 2 Chronicles 7:11–22; Acts 2:1–13

BILLY GRAHAM
EVANGELIST AND PASTOR (1918–)

QUOTATION 25

Mountaintops are for views and inspiration, but fruit is grown in the valleys.

> Citation: Billy Graham, *Unto the Hills*
>
> Topics: Character; Discouragement; Fruitfulness; Growth; Spiritual Formation; Trials
>
> References: Psalm 119:71; Romans 5:3–5; James 1:2–4; 1 Peter 1:6–7

QUOTATION 26

Heaven is full of answers to prayers for which no one ever bothered to ask.

> Citation: Billy Graham, *Till Armageddon: A Perspective on Suffering*
>
> Topics: Devotional Life; Heaven; Prayer
>
> References: Psalm 91:15; Isaiah 65:24; Luke 11:9; John 15:7

QUOTATION **27**

Today's world is said to be multiplying crises all around us. But we must never forget that, for the gospel, each crisis is an opportunity.

> **Citation:** Billy Graham, addressing the fiftieth anniversary gathering of the National Association of Evangelicals
>
> **Topics:** Evangelism; Missions; Opportunity; Outreach; Tragedy; Trials
>
> **References:** Matthew 9:37; John 4:35; Revelation 3:8

QUOTATION **28**

Courage is contagious. When a brave man takes a stand, the spines of others are stiffened.

> **Citation:** Unknown
>
> **Topics:** Convictions; Courage; Fear; Influence; Leadership
>
> **Reference:** 2 Timothy 1:6–7

QUOTATION **29**

Hot heads and cold hearts never solved anything.

> **Citation:** Unknown
>
> **Topics:** Anger; Attitudes; Community; Compassion; Conflict; Fellowship; Relationships; Temper; Unity
>
> **References:** Ecclesiastes 12:13; Titus 2:12

QUOTATION **30**

When we preach atonement, it is atonement planned by love, provided by love, given by love, finished by love, necessitated because of love. When we preach the resurrection of Christ, we are preaching the miracle of love. When we preach the return of Christ, we are preaching the fulfillment of love.

> **Citation:** Unknown
>
> **Topics:** Atonement; Cross; God's Love; Jesus Christ; Love; Redemption; Resurrection; Salvation; Second Coming
>
> **References:** John 15:12–13; Romans 5:5; 2 Corinthians 5:14

QUOTATION 31

When men are standing at the foot of the cross, there are no racial barriers.

Citation: Unknown

Topics: Acceptance; Division; Fellowship; Injustice; Justice; Racism; Relationships; Unity

References: Matthew 18:21–22; Luke 10:25–37; 23:33–34

QUOTATION 32

The smallest package I ever saw was a man wrapped up wholly in himself.

Citation: Unknown

Topics: Arrogance; Humility; Pride; Self-centeredness; Self-reliance

References: Isaiah 14:13–15; Romans 12:3

QUOTATION 33

It could be that one of the great hindrances to evangelism today is the poverty of our own experience.

Citation: Unknown

Topics: Evangelism; Testimony; Witness

References: Exodus 23:9; John 3:11; 2 Corinthians 1:4

QUOTATION 34

Our world has become a neighborhood without becoming a brotherhood.

Citation: Unknown

Topics: Brotherly Love; Community; Division; Fellowship; Racism; Unity

References: Deuteronomy 5:20; Proverbs 14:21; Luke 6:27–31

FESTO KIVENGERE
UGANDAN BISHOP AND EVANGELIST (1919–88)

QUOTATION 35

The love of Christ was demonstrated through suffering, and those who experience that love can never put it into practice without some cost.

> **Citation:** Festo Kivengere, *I Love Idi Amin*
>
> **Topics:** Christlikeness; Christ's Love; Compassion; Cost; Sacrifice; Self-denial; Suffering; Trials
>
> **Reference:** John 15:9–17

C. S. LEWIS
IRISH WRITER AND APOLOGIST (1898–1963)

QUOTATION 36

Christianity, if false, is of no importance, and, if true, of infinite importance. The one thing it cannot be is moderately important.

> **Citation:** C. S. Lewis, *God in the Dock*
>
> **Topics:** Apathy; Christian Life; Commitment; Complacency; Convictions; Truth
>
> **Reference:** John 14:6; Romans 12:11; 2 Corinthians 5:15; Revelation 3:15–19

QUOTATION 37

If you read history, you will find that the Christians who did most for the present world were just those who thought most of the next.... Aim at heaven and you will get earth "thrown in"; aim at earth and you will get neither.

> **Citation:** C. S. Lewis, *Mere Christianity*
>
> **Topics:** Distractions; Earthly Concerns; Focus; Goals; Heaven; Perspective; Vision
>
> **Reference:** Philippians 3:12–4:1

QUOTATION 38

No man knows how bad he is till he has tried very hard to be good.

>   Citation: C. S. Lewis, *Mere Christianity*
>
>   Topics: Depravity; Evil; Godliness; Human Condition; Human Nature; Sin
>
>   Reference: Romans 7:7–25

QUOTATION 39

The command "Be ye perfect" is not idealistic gas. Nor is it a command to do the impossible. [Jesus] is going to make us into creatures that can obey that command.

>   Citation: C. S. Lewis, *Mere Christianity*
>
>   Topics: Christian Life; Holiness; Sanctification; Spiritual Growth
>
>   References: Matthew 5:48; Philippians 1:6

QUOTATION 40

[Jesus] works on us in all sorts of ways; but above all, he works on us through each other.

>   Citation: C. S. Lewis, *Mere Christianity*
>
>   Topics: Accountability; Community; Fellowship; Relationships; Teachability
>
>   References: Acts 2:42–47; Colossians 3:16

QUOTATION 41

God whispers to us in our well-being; he shouts to us in our suffering.

>   Citation: C. S. Lewis, *The Problem of Pain*
>
>   Topics: Experiencing God; Listening; Pain; Suffering; Trials
>
>   References: 1 Kings 19:12; Proverbs 8:34; Luke 8:15

QUOTATION 42

Prostitutes are in no danger of finding their present life so satisfactory that they cannot turn to God. The proud, the avaricious, the self-righteous, are in that danger.

Citation: C. S. Lewis, *The Problem of Pain*

Topics: Comfort; Complacency; Humility; Materialism; Pride; Salvation

References: Luke 5:27–32; 15:11–32

QUOTATION **43**

Mankind is so fallen that no man can be trusted with unchecked power over his fellows. Aristotle said that some people were only fit to be slaves. I do not contradict him. But I reject slavery because I see no men fit to be masters.

Citation: C. S. Lewis, *Present Concerns*

Topics: Depravity; Fall of Humanity; Human Condition; Human Nature; Power

References: Genesis 6:5; Isaiah 53:6; Galatians 3:28

QUOTATION **44**

Our Lord finds our desires not too strong, but too weak. We are half-hearted creatures, fooling about with drink and sex and ambition when infinite joy is offered us, like an ignorant child who wants to go on making mud pies in a slum because he cannot imagine what is meant by the offer of a holiday at the sea. We are far too easily pleased.

Citation: C. S. Lewis, in the sermon "The Weight of Glory"

Topics: Apathy; Choices; Complacency; Desires; Goals; Indifference; Joy; Pleasure; Satisfaction; Sex

References: Psalms 90:14; 103:5; Isaiah 55:2; 1 Corinthians 2:9; Ephesians 3:20–21; 1 Peter 1:8

QUOTATION **45**

There are only two kinds of people in the end: those who say to God, "Thy will be done," and those to whom God says, "*Thy* will be done."

Citation: C. S. Lewis, *The Great Divorce*

Topics: Arrogance; Decisions; Desires; God's Will; Human Will; Obedience; Rebellion; Self-centeredness; Self-reliance; Stubbornness; Submission

References: Isaiah 14:12–15; Matthew 6:10; Romans 1:18–32; 12:1–2; Galatians 2:20

JOSH MCDOWELL
APOLOGIST, EVANGELIST, AND WRITER (1939 –)

QUOTATION 46

Tolerance says, "You must approve of what I do." Love responds, "I must do something harder: I will love you, even when your behavior offends me."

Tolerance says, "You must agree with me." Love responds, "I must do something harder: I will tell you the truth, because I am convinced the truth will set you free.'"

Tolerance says, "You must allow me to have my way." Love responds, "I must do something harder: I will plead with you to follow the right way, because I believe you are worth the risk."

Tolerance seeks to be inoffensive; love takes risks. Tolerance glorifies division; love seeks unity. Tolerance costs nothing; love costs everything.

> **Citation:** Josh McDowell, *Focus on the Family* magazine
> **Topics:** Cost; Love; Patience; Postmodernism; Tolerance; Truth; Unity
> **References:** 1 Corinthians 13; 1 John 2:15 – 17

F. B. MEYER
BRITISH EVANGELIST AND PASTOR (1847 – 1929)

QUOTATION 47

God has set Eternity in our heart, and man's infinite capacity cannot be filled or satisfied with the things of time and sense.

> **Citation:** F. B. Meyer, *Our Daily Walk*
> **Topics:** Eternal Life; Eternity; Human Condition; Limitations; Satisfaction
> **References:** Psalm 17:15; 1 Peter 1:23; Revelation 7:16

QUOTATION 48

We never test the resources of God until we attempt the impossible.

Citation: Unknown

Topics: Complacency; Courage; God's Sovereignty; God's Strength

References: Matthew 19:26; Luke 1:37

DWIGHT L. MOODY
AMERICAN EVANGELIST (1837–99)

QUOTATION 49

The Christian on his knees sees more than the philosopher on tiptoe.

Citation: Dwight L. Moody, *One Thousand and One Thoughts from My Library*

Topics: Focus; Guidance; Humility; Philosophy; Prayer; Wisdom

References: Psalm 116:17; Matthew 6:9–13; 1 Corinthians 1:18–25; Philippians 4:6

QUOTATION 50

My friends, you are no match for Satan, and when he wants to fight you, just run to your elder Brother, who is more than a match for all the devils in hell.

Citation: Dwight L. Moody, *Jesus the Anointed*

Topics: Jesus Christ; Satan; Spiritual Warfare

References: John 12:31; 2 Thessalonians 2:8; Hebrews 2:14–15

QUOTATION 51

Excuses are the cradle ... that Satan rocks men off to sleep in.

Citation: Dwight L. Moody, in his sermon "Excused"

Topics: Complacency; Evil; Excuses; Satan; Temptation

References: Luke 14:16–24; Romans 1:20

QUOTATION 52

Thank God, our friends are not buried; they are only sown.

Citation: Dwight L. Moody, in his sermon "Jesus Arose: So Shall We Rise"

Topics: Death; Eternal Life; Hope; Resurrection; Second Coming

References: Numbers 23:10; Proverbs 14:32; John 5:28–29;
1 Corinthians 15:35–58

QUOTATION **53**

Law tells me how crooked I am; grace comes along and straightens me out.

Citation: Dwight L. Moody, in an address at Cooper Union (New York)

Topics: Grace; Law; New Covenant; Old Covenant

References: Romans 3:24; 5:15; Titus 3:6–7

QUOTATION **54**

There is not a better evangelist in the world than the Holy Spirit.

Citation: Unknown

Topics: Evangelism; Holy Spirit; Outreach; Witness

References: John 14:15–31; 16:5–16; Acts 1:8

QUOTATION **55**

If I take care of my character, my reputation will take care of itself.

Citation: Unknown

Topics: Character; Holiness; Integrity; Reputation; Spiritual Disciplines

Reference: 1 Peter 2:11–12

QUOTATION **56**

Give me a man who says, "This one thing I do," and not "These fifty things I dabble in."

Citation: Unknown

Topics: Calling; Commitment; Convictions; Dedication; Distractions; Double-mindedness; Focus

Reference: Deuteronomy 6:1–9; Luke 10:38–42

QUOTATION 57

We ought to see the face of God every morning before we see the face of man.

Citation: Unknown

Topics: Bible Study; Devotional Life; Experiencing God; Prayer; Spiritual Disciplines

Reference: Mark 1:35

QUOTATION 58

There are very few who in their hearts do not believe in God, but what they will not do is give him exclusive right of way.

Citation: Unknown

Topics: Discipleship; God's Sovereignty; God's Will; Human Will; Obedience; Submission; Surrender

References: Deuteronomy 8:13 – 14; 2 Timothy 2:4; 1 John 2:15

QUOTATION 59

I'd rather be able to pray than to be a great preacher; Jesus Christ never taught his disciples how to preach, but only how to pray.

Citation: Unknown

Topics: Christlikeness; Prayer; Preaching

References: Matthew 6:9; Luke 18:1 – 8; Ephesians 6:18; Colossians 4:12

QUOTATION 60

Some day you will read in the papers that D. L. Moody, of East Northfield, is dead. Don't you believe a word of it! At that moment I shall be more alive than I am now. I was born of the flesh in 1837. I was born of the Spirit in 1856. That which is born of the flesh may die. That which is born of the Spirit will live forever.

Citation: Unknown

Topics: Death; Eternal Life; Flesh; Heaven; Hope; Jesus Christ; Resurrection; Salvation

References: Psalm 116:15; John 3:36; 11:25 – 26

QUOTATION 61

If you have so much business to attend to that you have no time to pray, depend upon it, you have more business on hand than God ever intended you should have.

Citation: Unknown

Topics: Busyness; Commitment; Prayer; Priorities; Self-discipline; Time; Work

References: 1 Chronicles 16:11; Matthew 26:41; 1 Thessalonians 5:14

QUOTATION 62

It is easier for me to have faith in the Bible than to have faith in D. L. Moody, for Moody has fooled me lots of times.

Citation: Unknown

Topics: Bible; Deceit; Faith; Self-centeredness; Self-examination

References: 2 Corinthians 10:12; Galatians 6:3

QUOTATION 63

I thought when I became a Christian I had nothing to do but just to lay my oars in the bottom of the boat and float along. But I soon found that I would have to go against the current.

Citation: Unknown

Topics: Cost; Persecution; Suffering; Testimony

References: Romans 12:2; Titus 2:12; Hebrews 11:24 – 25

MALCOLM MUGGERIDGE
BRITISH JOURNALIST, WRITER, AND APOLOGIST (1903 – 90)

QUOTATION 64

As man alone, Jesus could not have saved us; as God alone he would not. Incarnate, he could and did.

Citation: Malcolm Muggeridge, *Jesus*

Topics: Atonement; Christmas; Cross; Incarnation; Jesus Christ; Redemption; Salvation

References: John 3:16; Romans 6:23; 1 Timothy 3:16

QUOTATION **65**

I can say that I never knew what joy was like until I gave up pursuing happiness, or cared to live until I chose to die. For these two discoveries I am beholden to Jesus.

Citation: Unknown

Topics: Discipleship; Happiness; Joy; Sacrifice; Self-denial

Reference: Galatians 2:20

QUOTATION **66**

It has been said that when human beings stop believing in God they believe in nothing. The truth is much worse: they believe in anything.

Citation: Unknown

Topics: Atheism; Belief; Deceit; Foolishness; Worldliness

References: Psalms 14:1; 53:1

GEORGE MÜLLER
PRUSSIAN EVANGELIST (1805–98)

QUOTATION **67**

Faith does not operate in the realm of the possible. There is no glory for God in that which is humanly possible. Faith begins where man's power ends.

Citation: Unknown

Topics: Faith; Limitations; Power; Prayer; Self-reliance; Trust

References: Galatians 2:20; 3:3–5; 1 Thessalonians 5:24

QUOTATION 68

The beginning of anxiety is the end of faith, and the beginning of true faith is the end of anxiety.

> **Citation:** Unknown
>
> **Topics:** Anxiety; Faith; Trust; Worry
>
> **References:** Luke 12:25; Philippians 4:6; 1 Peter 5:7

QUOTATION 69

The less we read the Word of God, the less we desire to read it, and the less we pray, the less we desire to pray.

> **Citation:** Unknown
>
> **Topics:** Bible; Bible Study; Complacency; Consequences; Decisions; Desires; Motivation; Prayer; Spiritual Disciplines
>
> **References:** Ephesians 6:18; Colossians 4:2; 1 Peter 3:7

LUIS PALAU
ARGENTINEAN-AMERICAN EVANGELIST (1934–)

QUOTATION 70

Beware of the mind-set in looking to see if the church will meet your needs.... When my family is ready to leave for church, we take certain expectations about what we want to receive and leave them at home with our dog. Consequently, everything we do receive is a blessing.

> **Citation:** Luis Palau, in his sermon "Here's the Church, Here's the People"
>
> **Topics:** Blessings; Church; Perspective; Self-centeredness; Worship
>
> **References:** Ecclesiastes 5:1; John 4:23–24; Hebrews 10:25

QUOTATION 71

When it comes to responding to Jesus, I find it's important to distinguish between reverence, religion, and relationship.

> **Citation:** Unknown

Topics: Christian Life; Conversion; Intimacy; Jesus Christ; Religion; Reverence
References: Matthew 8:18–22; John 6:25–59

QUOTATION 72

It's bad when you fail morally. It's worse when you don't repent.

Citation: Unknown
Topics: Confession; Failure; Morality; Pride; Repentance; Sin
References: Ezekiel 18:30; Joel 2:13–14; Acts 2:38

QUOTATION 73

When you face the perils of weariness, carelessness, and confusion, don't pray for an easier life. Pray instead to be a stronger man or woman of God.

Citation: Unknown
Topics: Limitations; Prayer; Provision; Strength; Trials
Reference: Philippians 4:13

FRANCIS SCHAEFFER
AMERICAN THEOLOGIAN, PHILOSOPHER, AND PRESBYTERIAN PASTOR (1912–84)

QUOTATION 74

There is nothing uglier than an orthodoxy without understanding or without compassion.

Citation: Francis Schaffer, *The God Who Is There*
Topics: Compassion; Doctrine; Gentleness; Hypocrisy; Kindness; Tolerance; Understanding
References: Philippians 4:5; Colossians 3:12–14

QUOTATION **75**

Desire becomes sin when it fails to include the love of God or men. I am to love God enough to be contented.... I am to love men enough not to envy.

Citation: Francis Schaeffer, *True Spirituality*

Topics: Brotherly Love; Contentment; Desires; Envy; Idolatry; Jealousy; Love

References: Psalm 112:10; Proverbs 27:4; 1 Corinthians 13:4

QUOTATION **76**

The inward area is the first place of loss of true Christian life ... and the outward sinful act is the result.

Citation: Francis Schaeffer, *True Spirituality*

Topics: Heart; Purity; Sin; Transformation

Reference: Romans 12:1–2

QUOTATION **77**

We cannot expect the world to believe that the Father sent the Son, that Jesus' claims are true, and that Christianity is true, unless the world sees some reality of oneness of true Christians.

Citation: Francis Schaeffer, *The Mark of the Christian*

Topics: Brotherly Love; Conflict; Division; Friendship; Hypocrisy; Peace; Unity; Witness

References: John 13:34–35; Romans 12:5; Galatians 3:28; Ephesians 4:23

QUOTATION **78**

Christianity is the greatest intellectual system the mind of man has ever touched.

Citation: Francis Schaeffer, in a letter to a close friend

Topics: Knowledge; Mind; Philosophy; Theology; Wisdom; Worldview

Reference: 1 Corinthians 1:18–2:16

QUOTATION **79**

I have come to the conclusion that none of us in our generation feel as guilty about sin as we should or as our forefathers did.

Citation: Francis Schaeffer, in a letter to a college student

Topics: Complacency; Confession; Guilt; Past; Repentance; Shame; Sin

Reference: Romans 3:23

BILLY SUNDAY
AMERICAN EVANGELIST (1862 – 1935)

QUOTATION **80**

What we see as we go through life always depends upon where we stand to look.

Citation: Billy Sunday, in his sermon "Under the Sun"

Topics: Attitudes; Hope; Joy; Life; Perspective; Trust; Vision

References: Psalm 36:2; Isaiah 44:20; Revelation 3:17

QUOTATION **81**

Many a man who tries to talk as if he were standing on a mountain shows by what he says that he is up to his eyes in the mud.

Citation: Billy Sunday, in his sermon "Under the Sun"

Topics: Character; Depravity; False Teachers; Hypocrisy; Integrity; Speech; Witness

Reference: Genesis 11:1 – 9

QUOTATION **82**

There are 256 names given in the Bible for the Lord Jesus Christ, and I suppose this was because he was infinitely beyond all that any one name could express.

Citation: Billy Sunday, in his sermon "Wonderful"

Topics: Bible; Glory; Jesus Christ; Mysteries

References: Isaiah 9:6; Philippians 2:9 – 11; Revelation 19:12

QUOTATION **83**

Listen: I'm against sin. I'll kick it as long as I've got a foot. I'll fight it as long as I've got a fist. I'll butt it as long as I've got a head. I'll bite it as long as I've got a tooth. And when I'm old, fistless, footless, and toothless, I'll gum it till I go home to glory and it goes home to perdition.

Citation: Unknown

Topics: Commitment; Dedication; Perseverance; Sin; Spiritual Warfare; Temptation; Victory; Wholehearted Devotion

References: 2 Chronicles 7:14; Psalm 38:18; Romans 7:23; 2 Corinthians 6:17; 7:1; Ephesians 4:22–24; 1 Peter 1:16; 2:11

QUOTATION **84**

More men fail through lack of purpose than through lack of talent.

Citation: Unknown

Topics: Calling; Failure; Purpose

Reference: 1 Corinthians 10:31

QUOTATION **85**

I sometimes wonder whether the church needs new members one-half as much as she needs the old bunch made over.

Citation: Unknown

Topics: Change; Church; Hypocrisy; Regeneration; Revival; Sanctification; Spiritual Growth; Transformation

References: Deuteronomy 8:13–14; Matthew 19:23; Mark 4:19

QUOTATION **86**

The fellow that has no money is poor. The fellow that has nothing but money is poorer still.

Citation: Unknown

Topics: Materialism; Money; Poor People; Poverty

References: Proverbs 28:20; Matthew 19:23; Mark 4:19; Revelation 3:17

I am a Christian because God says so, and I did what he told me to do, and I stand on God's Word, and if the Book goes down, I'll go with it.

> Citation: Unknown
>
> Topics: Bible; Commitment; Dedication; Faith
>
> References: 2 Chronicles 20:17; Psalms 20:7; 93:5

R. A. TORREY
AMERICAN EVANGELIST (1856 – 1928)

QUOTATION **88**

We are too busy to pray, and so we are too busy to have power. We have a great deal of activity, but we accomplish little; many services but few conversions; much machinery but few results.

> Citation: R. A. Torrey, *How to Obtain Fullness of Power*
>
> Topics: Devotional Life; Distractions; Prayer; Self-discipline
>
> References: Matthew 6:5 – 15; 7:7 – 12; Luke 18:1 – 8

QUOTATION **89**

Oh, men and women, pray through; pray through! Do not just begin to pray and pray a little while and throw up your hands and quit, but pray and pray and pray until God bends the heavens and comes down!

> Citation: R. A. Torrey, *The Power of Prayer*
>
> Topics: Devotional Life; Persistence; Prayer
>
> References: Matthew 6:5 – 15; 7:7 – 12; Luke 18:1 – 8

QUOTATION **90**

The reason why many fail in battle is because they wait until the hour of battle. The reason why others succeed is because they have gained their victory on their knees long before the battle came.

> Citation: Unknown

Topics: Complacency; Preparation; Self-discipline; Spiritual Disciplines; Spiritual Warfare

Reference: Matthew 26:41

GEORGE WHITEFIELD
BRITISH PREACHER AND EVANGELIST (1714–70)

QUOTATION 91

God has condescended to become an author, and yet people will not read his writings. There are very few that ever gave this Book of God, the grand charter of salvation, one fair reading through.

> **Citation:** George Whitefield, in his sermon "Neglect of Christ: The Killing Sin"
>
> **Topics:** Bible; Bible Study; Devotional Life; Experiencing God; Illumination; Revelation
>
> **References:** Psalm 1:1–3; Matthew 22:29; Romans 15:4; 2 Corinthians 3:15; 2 Thessalonians 3:1; 1 John 5:13

QUOTATION 92

God forbid that I should travel with anybody a quarter of an hour without speaking of Christ to them.

> **Citation:** George Whitefield, in his sermon "Jacob's Ladder"
>
> **Topics:** Conversion; Evangelism; Gospel; Opportunity; Testimony
>
> **References:** Psalm 9:11; Isaiah 12:4; Matthew 5:15; 1 Peter 3:15

QUOTATION 93

Young Christians are like little rivulets that make a large noise, and have shallow water; old Christians are like deep water that makes little noise, carries a good load, and gives not way.

> **Citation:** George Whitefield, in his sermon "A Faithful Minister's Parting Blessing"
>
> **Topics:** Aging; Christian Life; Growth; Maturity; Wisdom
>
> **References:** 1 Corinthians 3:2; 14:20; Ephesians 4:14; Hebrews 5:14

QUOTATION 94

A dead ministry will always make a dead people, whereas if ministers are warmed with the love of God themselves, they cannot but be instruments of diffusing that love among others.

Citation: George Whitefield, in a letter to the students of Harvard and Yale

Topics: Complacency; Influence; Kindness; Love; Ministry; Outreach; Passion

References: Leviticus 10:3; Romans 10:14; 1 Corinthians 13:13; 1 Timothy 4:16

QUOTATION 95

I have put my soul, as a blank, into the hands of Jesus Christ my Redeemer, and desired him to write upon it what he pleases. I know it will be his own image.

Citation: George Whitefield, in a personal letter

Topics: Christlikeness; Consecration; Dedication; Sanctification; Soul

References: Genesis 1:27; 5:1; 2 Timothy 2:21; 1 Peter 1:2

QUOTATION 96

The renewal of our natures is a work of great importance. It is not to be done in a day. We have not only a new house to build up, but an old one to pull down.

Citation: Unknown

Topics: Change; Maturity; Regeneration; Revival; Sanctification; Spiritual Growth; Transformation

References: Ephesians 4:17–32

QUOTATION 97

Suffering times are a Christian's best improving times.

Citation: Unknown

Topics: Regeneration; Suffering; Tests; Trials

References: Psalm 66:10; Isaiah 48:10; 2 Corinthians 4:17; 1 Peter 1:7

RAVI ZACHARIAS
INDIAN-BORN PHILOSOPHER, APOLOGIST, AND EVANGELIST (1946–)

QUOTATION 98

In an attempt to be reasonable, man has become irrational. In an attempt to deify himself, he has defaced himself. In an attempt to be free, he has made himself a slave. And like Alexander the Great, he has conquered the world around him but has not yet conquered himself.

> Citation: Ravi Zacharias, in his sermon "The Lostness of Humankind"
>
> Topics: Arrogance; Bondage; Freedom; Idolatry; Self-centeredness; Self-reliance
>
> References: Acts 8:23; Galatians 5:13; 2 Peter 2:19

QUOTATION 99

For man, sin is not just an act. Sin is an attitude. Man is not a sinner because he is a transgressor. He is a transgressor because he is already a sinner.

> Citation: Ravi Zacharias, in his sermon "The Lostness of Humankind"
>
> Topics: Attitudes; Depravity; Heart; Human Condition; Human Nature; Lifestyle; Original Sin; Sin
>
> References: Psalm 52:3; Matthew 15:19; Romans 1:30

QUOTATION 100

By losing morality, we've destroyed essence.

> Citation: Unknown
>
> Topics: Accountability; Ethics; Morality; Purpose
>
> References: Romans 1:18–32

PART 2: HEADLINING WORDS FROM CELEBRITIES AND NEWSMAKERS

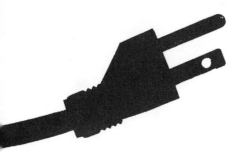

JACK ABRAMOFF

AMERICAN POLITICAL LOBBYIST, ACTIVIST, AND BUSINESSMAN (1959–)

QUOTATION 101

God sent me 1,000 hints that he didn't want me to keep doing what I was doing. But I didn't listen, so he set off a nuclear bomb.

> **Citation:** Jack Abramoff, when reflecting on his role in several political scandals (quoted in *Time* magazine)
>
> **Topics:** Apathy; Arrogance; Complacency; God's Wrath; Listening; Pride; Teachability; Warnings
>
> **Reference:** 2 Samuel 12:7–14

MADELEINE ALBRIGHT

FORMER U.S. SECRETARY OF STATE (1937–)

QUOTATION 102

Not long after September 11, I was on a panel with Elie Wiesel. He asked us to name the unhappiest character in the Bible. Some said Job, because of the trials he endured. Some said Moses, because he was denied entry into the Promised Land. Some said Mary, because she witnessed the crucifixion of her son. Wiesel said he believed the right answer was God, because of the pain he must surely feel in seeing us fight, kill, and abuse each other in the Lord's name.

> **Citation:** Madeline Albright, in a talk given at Yale Divinity School in 2004
>
> **Topics:** God; Pain; Suffering; Violence; War
>
> **Reference:** Genesis 6:6

BUZZ ALDRIN
AMERICAN ASTRONAUT (1930 –)

QUOTATION 103

Bravery comes along as a gradual accumulation of discipline.

> **Citation:** Buzz Aldrin, in an *Esquire* magazine article
>
> **Topics:** Bravery; Character; Courage; Self-control; Self-discipline
>
> **References:** Proverbs 5:23; 10:17; 25:28; 1 Corinthians 16:13; Titus 1:8; Hebrews 3:6; 1 Peter 1:13; 5:8

FRED ALLEN
AMERICAN COMEDIAN (1894 – 1956)

QUOTATION 104

There are many things in life that are more important than money. And they all cost money.

> **Citation:** Unknown
>
> **Topics:** Greed; Materialism; Money; Priorities; Stewardship; Worldliness
>
> **Reference:** 1 Timothy 6:1 – 10

QUOTATION 105

Most of us spend the first six days of each week sowing wild oats; then we go to church on Sunday and pray for a crop failure.

> **Citation:** Unknown
>
> **Topics:** Consequences; Foolishness; Guilt; Lifestyle; Sin
>
> **Reference:** Galatians 6:7 – 8

WOODY ALLEN

AMERICAN FILM DIRECTOR, WRITER, AND ACTOR (1935–)

QUOTATION **106**

I don't want to achieve immortality through my work. I want to achieve it by not dying.

Citation: Unknown

Topics: Eternal and Temporary; Eternal Death; Eternal Life; Immortality; Mortality; Resurrection; Work

References: Psalm 90:12; Isaiah 25:7–8; John 3:16; Romans 6:23; 8:35–39; Hebrews 2:14–15; 9:27

JOAN BAEZ

AMERICAN FOLK SINGER (1941–)

QUOTATION **107**

I don't relate with feminism. I see the whole human race as being broken and terribly in need, not just women.

Citation: Joan Baez, in an interview with *Rolling Stone* magazine

Topics: Brokenness; Feminism; Human Condition; Suffering; Unity

Reference: Galatians 3:28

QUOTATION **108**

The easiest kind of relationship is with ten thousand people. The hardest is with one.

Citation: Unknown

Topics: Accountability; Marriage; Neighbors; Relationships; Spouses

References: Mark 12:31; Ephesians 5:33; Titus 2:4

BRIDGETTE BARDOT
FRENCH ACTRESS AND MODEL (1934 –)

QUOTATION 109

Time will destroy me one day as it destroys everything. But no one else will ever be Bardot. I'm the only Bardot, and my species is unique.

Citation: Bridgette Bardot, in a 1960s interview with *Vogue* magazine

Topics: Arrogance; Beauty; Death; Humanism; Identity; Individualism; Pride; Time

References: Psalm 103:16; Proverbs 31:30

P. T. BARNUM
AMERICAN CIRCUS BUILDER (1810 – 91)

QUOTATION 110

Money is a terrible master but an excellent servant.

Citation: P. T. Barnum, *Art of Money Getting*

Topics: Benevolence; Idolatry; Materialism; Money; Stewardship

Reference: Luke 16:9 – 14

WILLIAM BENNETT
AMERICAN CONSERVATIVE PUNDIT AND POLITICIAN (1943 –)

QUOTATION 111

We have a real problem in this country when it comes to values. We have become the kind of society that civilized countries used to send missionaries to.

Citation: William Bennett, in an interview on *The MacNeil/Lehrer NewsHour*

Topics: Corruption; Culture; Evil; Missions; Morality; Values; Vices; Worldliness

References: Genesis 6:12; Romans 12:2; 2 Timothy 3:1 – 2

HALLE BERRY

AMERICAN ACTRESS (1966 –)

QUOTATION 112

Beauty? Let me tell you something: being thought of as "a beautiful woman" has spared me nothing in life — no heartache, no trouble. Love has been difficult. Beauty is essentially meaningless, and it is always transitory. I can't believe what people do to themselves [to make themselves look beautiful] … and then they end up distorted. Worse, they still have that hole in their soul that led them to change themselves to begin with.

> **Citation:** Halle Berry, in an interview with the *New York Post*
>
> **Topics:** Beauty; Eternal and Temporary; Meaning; Motivation; Perspective; Self-examination; Self-image; Self-worth
>
> **References:** 1 Samuel 16:7; Proverbs 31:30; John 7:24; Galatians 2:6; 1 Peter 3:3 – 5

NAPOLEON BONAPARTE

MILITARY GENERAL AND EMPEROR OF FRANCE (1769 – 1821)

QUOTATION 113

Alexander, Caesar, Charlemagne, and myself founded empires; but on what foundation did we rest the creations of our genius? Upon force. Jesus Christ founded an empire upon love; and at this hour millions of men would die for him.

> **Citation:** Unknown
>
> **Topics:** Government; Jesus Christ; Love; Politics; Power
>
> **Reference:** Matthew 20:28

BONO

IRISH ROCK STAR (1964–)

QUOTATION **114**

Religion to me is almost like when God leaves—and the people devise a set of rules to fill the space.

> **Citation:** Bono, *Bono in His Own Words*
>
> **Topics:** Bible; Bondage; Community; Legalism; Religion; Tradition
>
> **References:** Hosea 6:6; Matthew 9:13; 12:7; James 1:26–27

QUOTATION **115**

Isn't "Love thy neighbor" in the global village so inconvenient? God writes us these lines ... we have to sing them ... take them to the top of the charts, but it's not what the radio is playing, is it?

> **Citation:** Bono, in his address to the Harvard University graduating class of 2001
>
> **Topics:** Brotherly Love; Compassion; Kindness; Mercy; Missions; Social Impact; Social Justice
>
> **Reference:** Matthew 22:39

QUOTATION **116**

The thing that keeps me on my knees is the difference between grace and karma.

> **Citation:** Bono, in *Bono: Conversations with Michka Assaya*
>
> **Topics:** Atonement; Cross; Grace; Jesus Christ; Mercy; Self-reliance
>
> **Reference:** Ephesians 2:8–10

OMAR BRADLEY

U.S. ARMY FIELD COMMANDER
AND GENERAL (1893 – 1981)

QUOTATION 117

We have too many men of science, too few men of God. We have grasped the mystery of the atom and rejected the Sermon on the Mount.... Ours is a world of nuclear giants and ethical infants. We know more about war than we know about peace, more about killing than we know about living.

> **Citation:** Omar Bradley, in his 1948 Armistice Day address
>
> **Topics:** Ethics; Humanism; Knowledge; Lifestyle; Morality; Mysteries; Priorities; Science; Transformation
>
> **References:** Isaiah 59:8; Amos 3:10; Ephesians 4:18

QUOTATION 118

We need to learn to set our course by the stars, not by the lights of every passing ship.

> **Citation:** Unknown
>
> **Topics:** Deceit; Direction; False Teachers; Foolishness; Guidance; Scripture; Truth
>
> **Reference:** 1 John 2:17

DAVID BROWN

AMERICAN MOVIE PRODUCER (1916 –)

QUOTATION 119

The word on the street can make or break you. There is no insurance against word of mouth.

> **Citation:** Unknown
>
> **Topics:** Character; Gossip; Holiness; Integrity; Reputation; Speech; Tongue
>
> **References:** Proverbs 22:1; 1 Corinthians 10:23 – 33

WILLIAM JENNINGS BRYAN

AMERICAN LAWYER, STATESMAN, AND POLITICIAN (1860–1925)

QUOTATION 120

The humblest citizen in all the land, when clad in the armor of a righteous cause, is stronger than all the hosts of error.

Citation: Unknown

Topics: Activism; Humility; Influence; Social Impact; Social Justice

Reference: Proverbs 31:8–9

JEFF BUCKLEY

AMERICAN SINGER (1966–97)

QUOTATION 121

I don't have any allegiance to an organized religion; I have an allegiance to the gifts that I find for myself in those religions.

Citation: Jeff Buckley, quoted in Dimitri Ehrlich's *Inside the Music: Conversations with Contemporary Musicians about Spirituality, Creativity, and Consciousness*

Topics: Religion; Self-centeredness; Self-reliance; Spirituality

Reference: John 13:1–17

WARREN BUFFET

AMERICAN INVESTOR, BUSINESSMAN, AND PHILANTHROPIST (1930–)

QUOTATION 122

If you were a jerk before, you'll be a bigger jerk with a billion dollars.

Citation: Warren Buffet, in a *Forbes* magazine article

Topics: Character; Greed; Lifestyle; Money; Riches; Stewardship

References: Proverbs 22:1; Matthew 19:23–24

DAVID BYRNE
AMERICAN ROCK MUSICIAN (1952–)

QUOTATION 123

I think I might be a workaholic. A lot of it is a way of dealing with other parts of living that I don't feel as comfortable with, such as relating with human beings.

Citation: David Byrne, in an *Independent* magazine article

Topics: Ambition; Conflict; Distractions; Family; Focus; Friendship; Marriage; Recreation; Relationships; Vocation; Work

References: Psalm 119:36; Proverbs 18:1; John 13:34–35; Romans 12:10; 13:8; Philippians 2:3; James 5:5

JIM CARREY
CANADIAN ACTOR AND COMEDIAN (1962–)

QUOTATION 124

I think everybody should get rich and famous and do everything they ever dreamed of so they can see that it's not the answer.

Citation: Jim Carrey, quoted in *Reader's Digest*

Topics: Emptiness; Greed; Money; Purpose; Significance

Reference: Luke 12:15

QUOTATION 125

If we all acted the way we really felt, four out of eight people at a dinner table would be sitting there sobbing.

Citation: Jim Carrey, quoted in a *Third Way* magazine article

Topics: Brokenness; Depression; Emotions; Emptiness; Feelings; Honesty; Sadness

References: Proverbs 15:13; Ecclesiastes 3:1–4; Romans 12:15; 1 Peter 3:8

RAY CHARLES

AMERICAN MUSICIAN (1930 – 2004)

QUOTATION 126

Live every day like it's your last, 'cause one day you're gonna be right.

Citation: Ray Charles, quoted in *Reader's Digest*

Topics: Death; Eternal and Temporary; Eternal Life; Heaven; Hell; Life; Lifestyle; Meaning; Motivation; Perspective; Purpose

References: Psalm 90:12; Luke 12:20; Hebrews 9:27; James 4:14

WINSTON CHURCHILL

BRITISH POLITICIAN AND PRIME MINISTER OF THE UNITED KINGDOM (1874 – 1965)

QUOTATION 127

Destiny, fate, providence seem to me only different ways of expressing the same thing, to wit, that a man's own contribution to his life story is continually dominated by an external superior power.

Citation: Winston Churchill, *Amid These Storms*

Topics: Destiny; Direction; Fate; God's Sovereignty; Guidance; Providence; Provision

References: 2 Chronicles 25:8; Job 26:12; Psalm 62:11; Proverbs 16:9; Romans 16:25

QUOTATION 128

When great causes are on the move in the world … we learn that we are spirits, not animals.

Citation: Winston Churchill, *The Churchill War Papers*

Topics: Human Nature; Motives; Sacrifice; Service; Social Impact; Social Justice

References: Job 32:8; Psalm 8:5; 1 Corinthians 2:11

QUOTATION **129**

The great thing is to get the true picture, whatever it is.

> **Citation:** Winston Churchill, in a note to the chief of the Imperial General staff
> **Topics:** Discernment; Insight; Perspective; Reality; Truth; Vision
> **References:** 1 Kings 3:9; Proverbs 23:23; Isaiah 11:3; John 8:31 – 32

QUOTATION **130**

We make a living by what we get. We make a life by what we give.

> **Citation:** Unknown
> **Topics:** Generosity; Giving; Greed; Money; Sacrifice; Service; Stewardship
> **References:** Micah 6:8; Acts 20:35; 2 Corinthians 9:7; 1 Timothy 6:18 – 19

QUOTATION **131**

Kites rise highest against the wind, not with it.

> **Citation:** Unknown
> **Topics:** Challenges; Difficulties; Overcoming; Perseverance; Struggles; Tests; Trials
> **References:** Job 23:10; Psalm 66:10; Romans 5:3 – 5; James 1:2 – 4; 1 Peter 1:7

BARBER CONABLE
AMERICAN CONGRESSMAN AND PRESIDENT OF THE WORLD BANK (1922 – 2003)

QUOTATION **132**

Hell hath no fury like a vested interest masquerading as a moral principle.

> **Citation:** Unknown
> **Topics:** Deceit; Ethics; Morality; Politics; Power; Self-righteousness; Truth
> **References:** Psalm 101:7; Proverbs 11:18; 26:26; Ephesians 4:22; 5:5

CALVIN COOLIDGE
FORMER U.S. PRESIDENT (1872 – 1933)

QUOTATION **133**

There is no dignity quite so impressive, and no independence quite so important, as living within your means.

Citation: Calvin Coolidge, when explaining his choice to live in a humble two-room suite as vice president of the United States

Topics: Contentment; Greed; Money; Simplicity; Stewardship

References: Ecclesiastes 5:10; 1 Corinthians 4:2; 1 Timothy 6:10

QUOTATION **134**

I have noticed that nothing I never said ever did me any harm.

Citation: Unknown

Topics: Consequences; Decisions; Self-control; Speech; Tongue

References: Proverbs 10:19; Ephesians 4:29 – 32; James 3:1 – 12

BILL COSBY
AMERICAN ACTOR (1937 –)

QUOTATION **135**

I don't know the key to success, but the key to failure is trying to please everybody.

Citation: Unknown

Topics: Calling; Direction; Failure; Focus; Fulfillment; Success; Vocation

References: Proverbs 16:7; Galatians 1:10; 1 Thessalonians 2:4; 4:1 – 12

RUBY DEE
AMERICAN ACTRESS (1924 –)

QUOTATION **136**

The kind of beauty I want most is the hard-to-get kind that comes from within — strength, courage, dignity.

Citation: Unknown

Topics: Beauty; Character; Christlikeness; Courage; Dignity; Integrity; Strength; Transformation; Virtue

Reference: 1 Peter 3:3 – 5

BENJAMIN DISRAELI
BRITISH CONSERVATIVE STATESMAN AND LITERARY FIGURE (1804 – 81)

QUOTATION **137**

The greatest good you can do for another is not just to share your riches, but to reveal to him his own.

Citation: Unknown

Topics: Good Deeds; Leadership; Mentoring; Preaching; Spiritual Perception; Teaching; Vision

References: Psalm 49:20; John 1:15; Romans 8:17; Ephesians 1:3; 4:11 – 16; 1 Thessalonians 2:8

ELIZABETH DOLE
AMERICAN POLITICIAN (1936 –)

QUOTATION **138**

Life is not just a few years to spend on self-indulgence and career advancement. It is a privilege, a responsibility, a stewardship to be lived according to a much higher calling — God's calling. This alone gives true meaning to life.

Citation: Elizabeth Dole, in an address at the National Prayer Breakfast

Topics: Calling; God's Will; Greed; Meaning; Priorities; Responsibility; Self-centeredness; Stewardship; Vocation

References: Matthew 25:14 – 30; 1 Peter 4:10 – 11

DAVE DRAVECKY

AMERICAN SPEAKER, WRITER, AND FORMER PROFESSIONAL BASEBALL PLAYER (1956 –)

QUOTATION **139**

In America, Christians pray for the burden of suffering to be lifted from their backs. In the rest of the world, Christians pray for stronger backs so they can bear their suffering.

Citation: Dave Dravecky, *When You Can't Come Back*

Topics: Overcoming; Pain; Strength; Suffering; Tests; Trials

References: Matthew 10:39; Acts 9:16; 2 Corinthians 4:11

PETER F. DRUCKER

AUSTRIAN-AMERICAN MANAGEMENT CONSULTANT, PROFESSOR, AND WRITER (1909 – 2005)

QUOTATION **140**

What you have to do and the way you have to do it is incredibly simple. Whether you are willing to do it, that's another matter.

Citation: Unknown

Topics: Apathy; Calling; Commitment; Decisions; Dedication; Focus; God's Will; Human Will; Obedience; Rebellion

References: Ecclesiastes 12:13 – 14; Micah 6:8; Matthew 22:37

BOB DYLAN
AMERICAN SINGER-SONGWRITER (1941 –)

QUOTATION 141

Money doesn't talk; it swears.

> **Citation:** Bob Dylan, "It's Alright Ma (I'm Only Bleeding)"
>
> **Topics:** Greed; Materialism; Money; Stewardship; Witness
>
> **Reference:** 1 Timothy 6:10

QUOTATION 142

People seldom do what they believe in. They do what is convenient, then repent.

> **Citation:** Unknown
>
> **Topics:** Belief; Choices; Comfort; Convenience; Convictions; Depravity; Repentance; Self-centeredness
>
> **Reference:** Acts 14:22

DWIGHT D. EISENHOWER
FORMER U.S. PRESIDENT (1890 – 1969)

QUOTATION 143

Peace and justice are two sides of the same coin.

> **Citation:** Unknown
>
> **Topics:** Injustice; Justice; Peace
>
> **Reference:** Isaiah 59:8 – 9

QUOTATION 144

It is better to have one person working with you than having three people working for you.

> **Citation:** Unknown

Topics: Community; Cooperation; Leadership; Relationships; Teamwork

References: 2 Corinthians 8:23; Philippians 4:3; 1 Thessalonians 3:2; Philemon 1–2; 3 John 8

HENRY FORD

AMERICAN BUSINESSMAN AND FOUNDER OF THE FORD MOTOR COMPANY (1863–1947)

QUOTATION 145

You can't build a reputation on what you are going to do.

Citation: Unknown

Topics: Dedication; Determination; Excuses; Goals; Human Will; Leadership; Potential; Promises; Reputation; Success; Vision

References: Proverbs 14:23; Ecclesiastes 10:18; 2 Thessalonians 3:6–15; Revelation 3:1–6

QUOTATION 146

Failure is the opportunity to begin again more intelligently.

Citation: Unknown

Topics: Commitment; Failure; Focus; Opportunity; Perseverance; Perspective; Strength; Success; Teachability

Reference: 2 Corinthians 7:10–11

JOHN WILLIAM GARDNER

AMERICAN BUSINESSMAN AND SECRETARY OF HEALTH, EDUCATION, AND WELFARE (1912–2002)

QUOTATION 147

To sensible men, every day is a day of reckoning.

Citation: Unknown

Topics: Accountability; Calling; Judgment

References: Matthew 12:36; 18:23; Luke 12:20; 1 Peter 4:5

BILL GATES

AMERICAN ENTREPRENEUR AND COFOUNDER OF MICROSOFT (1955–)

QUOTATION 148

In terms of allocation of time resources, religion is not very efficient. There's a lot more I could be doing on a Sunday morning.

> **Citation:** Bill Gates, in a *Time* magazine article
>
> **Topics:** Busyness; Church Attendance; Distractions; Double-mindedness; Focus; Rest; Sabbath; Work; Worldview; Worship
>
> **References:** Exodus 20:8–11; Hebrews 10:24–25

QUOTATION 149

You have to be constantly receptive to bad news, and then you have to act on it. Sometimes I think my most important job as CEO is to listen for bad news. If you don't act on it, your people will eventually stop bringing bad news to your attention. And that's the beginning of the end. The willingness to hear hard truth is vital not only for heads of big corporations but also for anyone who loves the truth. Sometimes the truth sounds like bad news, but it is just what we need.

> **Citation:** Unknown
>
> **Topics:** Insight; Leadership; Preaching; Reality; Teachability; Truth
>
> **Reference:** Romans 3:9–20

MEL GIBSON

AUSTRALIAN ACTOR (1956–)

QUOTATION 150

Evil takes on the form of beauty. It is almost beautiful. It is the great aper of God. But the mask is askew; there is always something wrong. Evil masquerades, but if your antennae are up, you'll detect it.

> **Citation:** Mel Gibson, at a pastors' screening of *The Passion of the Christ*

Topics: Beauty; Deceit; Discernment; Evil; Overcoming; Satan; Spiritual Perception; Spiritual Warfare

References: Matthew 4:8–9; John 8:44; 2 Corinthians 11:14; Ephesians 6:11–12; 1 Timothy 3:7; James 4:7; 1 Peter 5:8; 1 John 4:1

KATHARINE HEPBURN
AMERICAN ACTRESS (1907–2003)

QUOTATION **151**

If you're given a choice between money and sex appeal, take the money. As you get older, the money will become your sex appeal.

> **Citation:** Unknown
>
> **Topics:** Materialism; Money; Relationships; Sex; Worldliness
>
> **References:** Matthew 6:24; 1 John 2:15–17

QUOTATION **152**

I have many regrets, and I'm sure everyone does. The stupid things you do, you regret if you have any sense, and if you don't regret them, maybe you're stupid.

> **Citation:** Unknown
>
> **Topics:** Confession; Conviction of Sin; Foolishness; Guilt; Regrets; Repentance; Self-examination; Shame
>
> **Reference:** Jeremiah 6:15

BILLIE HOLIDAY
AMERICAN JAZZ SINGER (1915–59)

QUOTATION **153**

Sometimes it's worse to win a fight than to lose.

> **Citation:** Unknown
>
> **Topics:** Conflict; Enemies; Maturity; Pride; Victory
>
> **Reference:** 1 Corinthians 6:1–8

BOB HOPE

AMERICAN ACTOR AND COMEDIAN (1903–2003)

QUOTATION 154

Laughter is an instant vacation. Giving is a two-week cruise — with pay.

Citation: Bob Hope, in a *Hemispheres* magazine article

Topics: Generosity; Giving; Happiness; Joy; Laughter

References: Luke 6:38; 2 Corinthians 8:1–15; 9:6–15

LEE IACOCCA

FORMER CHAIRMAN OF CHRYSLER CORPORATION (1924–)

QUOTATION 155

I couldn't care less about what you think of my commercials. What I want to know is, "What kind of car do you drive?"

Citation: Lee Iacocca, when someone complimented him on Chrysler's entertaining commercials

Topics: Fruitfulness; Influence; Obedience; Transformation; Witness

Reference: John 14:15

STEVE JOBS

AMERICAN COFOUNDER AND CEO OF APPLE (1955–)

QUOTATION 156

Remembering that I'll be dead soon is the most important tool I've ever encountered to help me make the big choices in life. Because almost everything — all external expectations, all pride, all fear of embarrassment or failure — these things just fall away in the face of death, leaving only what is truly important.

Citation: Steve Jobs, in his 2005 commencement address to the graduates of Stanford University

Topics: Choices; Death; Distractions; Focus; Goals; Meaning; Motives; Purpose; Vision

Reference: Psalm 90:12

CHARLES KRAUTHAMMER
AMERICAN COLUMNIST AND COMMENTATOR (1950–)

QUOTATION 157

Look outward. You have been rightly taught Socrates' dictum that the unexamined life is not worth living. I would add: The too-examined life is not worth living either.

Citation: Charles Krauthammer, in a *Time* magazine article

Topics: Meaning; Passion; Self-centeredness; Self-examination; Service

References: Lamentations 3:40; Matthew 7:5; 1 Corinthians 11:28; 2 Corinthians 13:5

BARBARA LEE
AMERICAN POLITICIAN (1946–)

QUOTATION 158

An abstinence-until-marriage program is not only irresponsible; it's really inhumane.

Citation: Barbara Lee, after the 2004 International AIDS Conference

Topics: Depravity; Desires; Immorality; Lust; Marriage; Morality; Obedience; Politics; Self-control; Self-discipline; Sex; Sexual Immorality; Values

References: Proverbs 25:28; Romans 13:13; 1 Corinthians 6:12–20; Galatians 5:19–23; Colossians 3:5; 2 Timothy 3:1–2

ABRAHAM LINCOLN
U.S. PRESIDENT (1809–65)

QUOTATION **159**

Faith is not believing that God can, but that God will.

Citation: Abraham Lincoln, *The Collected Works of Abraham Lincoln*
Topics: Belief; Faith; God's Sovereignty; Providence; Provision; Trust
References: Matthew 17:20; Mark 9:23; Hebrews 11:1–2, 6; James 1:5–6

QUOTATION **160**

I can see how it might be possible for a man to look down upon the earth and be an atheist, but I cannot conceive how he could look up into the heavens and say there is no God.

Citation: Abraham Lincoln, in a conversation with Captain Gilbert J. Greene, a young printer in the 1800s
Topics: Atheism; Belief; Creation; Revelation
Reference: Psalm 19:1

QUOTATION **161**

Character is like a tree and reputation like its shadow. The shadow is what we think of it; the tree is the real thing.

Citation: Unknown
Topics: Character; Godliness; Integrity; Reputation; Self-examination; Truth; Witness
References: 1 Samuel 18:30; Proverbs 22:1; Ecclesiastes 7:1

DOUGLAS MACARTHUR
U.S. ARMY GENERAL (1880–1964)

QUOTATION **162**

A man doesn't grow old because he has lived a certain number of years; he grows old when he deserts his ideals.

Citation: Douglas MacArthur, in his retirement address before Congress

Topics: Aging; Character; Commitment; Compromise; Convictions

Reference: Titus 2:2–3

JAMES MACKINTOSH
SCOTTISH POLITICIAN AND HISTORIAN (1765–1832)

QUOTATION 163

It is right to be contented with what we have, never with what we are.

Citation: Unknown

Topics: Apathy; Character; Complacency; Contentment; Holiness; Sanctification

References: Proverbs 15:18; Philippians 1:27; Hebrews 13:5

STEVE MARTIN
AMERICAN COMEDIAN AND ACTOR (1945–)

QUOTATION 164

Before you criticize a man, walk a mile in his shoes. That way, when you do criticize him, you'll be a mile away and have his shoes.

Citation: Unknown

Topics: Criticism; Judging Others; Relationships

References: Matthew 5:38–42; Luke 6:29–31; Acts 11:2; Romans 14:10; James 4:11–12

GROUCHO MARX
AMERICAN COMEDIAN AND FILM STAR (1890–1977)

QUOTATION 165

I find television very educating. Every time somebody turns on the set, I go into the other room and read a book.

Citation: Unknown

Topics: Distractions; Entertainment; Self-discipline; Technology; Television; Wisdom

References: Matthew 8:19; Romans 12:2; Colossians 3:2

HENRI MATISSE
FRENCH ARTIST (1869 – 1954)

QUOTATION **166**

There are flowers everywhere for those who want to see them.

Citation: Henri Matisse, *Matisse on Art*

Topics: Awe; Beauty; Creation; Distractions; Focus; Joy; Perspective; Thanksgiving; Vision

Reference: Ephesians 5:20

JOHN MCCAIN
ARIZONA SENATOR AND FORMER POW (1936 –)

QUOTATION **167**

In the past, I've been able to overcome my fears because of an acute sense of an even greater fear — that of feeling remorse. You can live with pain. You can live with embarrassment. Remorse is an awful companion. And whatever the unwelcome consequences of courage, they are unlikely to be worse than the discovery that you are less than you pretend to be.

Citation: John McCain, in a *FastCompany* magazine article

Topics: Character; Consequences; Courage; Fear; Hypocrisy; Integrity; Past; Regrets; Repentance; Self-examination

References: Genesis 4:7; Psalm 106:3; Proverbs 21:3; 1 Corinthians 16:13; 2 Corinthians 8:21

MARILYN MONROE

AMERICAN ACTRESS (1926–62)

QUOTATION **168**

Hollywood is a place where they'll pay you a thousand dollars for a kiss and fifty cents for your soul.

Citation: Marilyn Monroe, *My Story*

Topics: Immorality; Priorities; Sex; Soul; Worldliness

Reference: 1 John 2:15–17

QUOTATION **169**

A career is a wonderful thing, but you can't snuggle up to it on a cold night.

Citation: Unknown

Topics: Ambition; Career; Community; Individualism; Loneliness; Marriage; Relationships; Work

Reference: Genesis 2:18

HENRY MOORE

BRITISH SCULPTOR (1898–1986)

QUOTATION **170**

The secret of life is to have a task, something you do your entire life, something you bring everything to, every minute of the day for your whole life. And the most important thing is: It must be something you cannot possibly do.

Citation: Henry Moore, in a conversation with poet Donald Hall about the meaning of life

Topics: Calling; Challenges; Commitment; Convictions; Dedication; Goals; Meaning; Ministry; Motivation; Motives; Purpose; Vision; Vocation

References: 1 Corinthians 10:31; 2 Corinthians 5:9–11; Philippians 3:13–14

ANDREW NICCOL
AMERICAN SCREENWRITER, PRODUCER, AND DIRECTOR (1964–)

QUOTATION 171

It's gotten to the point that our ability to manufacture fraud now exceeds our ability to detect it.

Citation: Andrew Niccol, in the *New York Times* article "Perfect Model: Gorgeous, No Complaints, Made of Pixels"

Topics: Deceit; Discernment; False Teachers; Hypocrisy; Spiritual Perception; Truth

Reference: 1 Thessalonians 5:21

RICHARD NIXON
U.S. PRESIDENT (1913–94)

QUOTATION 172

Going through the necessary soul-searching of deciding whether to fight a battle or to run away from it is far more difficult than the battle itself.

Citation: Unknown

Topics: Decisions; Guidance; Honesty; Self-examination

Reference: John 15:20

CHARLIE PARKER
AMERICAN JAZZ SAXOPHONIST AND COMPOSER (1920–55)

QUOTATION 173

If you don't live it, it won't come out of your horn.

Citation: Unknown

Topics: Character; Hypocrisy; Integrity; Outreach; Preaching; Witness

References: Matthew 12:34–35; 15:8; Luke 6:45

GEORGE S. PATTON JR.

U.S. ARMY GENERAL (1885–1945)

QUOTATION 174

Courage is fear holding on a minute longer.

> **Citation:** Unknown
> **Topics:** Commitment; Courage; Dedication; Fear; Overcoming; Perseverance
> **Reference:** Philippians 1:20

PRINCE PHILIP

DUKE OF EDINBURGH (1921–)

QUOTATION 175

Freedom can be destroyed as easily by making a mockery of it as it can by its retraction.

> **Citation:** Prince Philip, when speaking to a hostile university audience
> **Topics:** Foolishness; Freedom; Perspective
> **Reference:** Romans 1:18–32

RONALD REAGAN

U.S. PRESIDENT (1911–2004)

QUOTATION 176

I don't pay much attention to critics. The world is divided into two kinds of people: those who can and those who criticize.

> **Citation:** Ronald Reagan, quoted in a *New Yorker* article
> **Topics:** Criticism; Enemies; Judging Others; Overcoming; Perspective
> **Reference:** Exodus 16:7–12

It's hard, when you're up to your armpits in alligators, to remember you came here to drain the swamp.

Citation: Ronald Reagan, at the White House reception for women appointees of the administration

Topics: Calling; Change; Character; Commitment; Dedication; Distractions; Enemies; Focus; Goals; Influence; Leadership

Reference: Matthew 5:10–12

VANESSA REDGRAVE
AMERICAN ACTRESS (1937–)

QUOTATION **178**

Integrity is so perishable in the summer months of success.

Citation: Unknown

Topics: Character; Double-mindedness; Holiness; Integrity; Eternal and Temporary; Prosperity; Success; Temptation

Reference: Deuteronomy 8:1–18

CONDOLEEZZA RICE
U.S. SECRETARY OF STATE (1954–)

QUOTATION **179**

There is nothing wrong with holding an opinion and holding it passionately. But at those times when you're absolutely sure that you are right, go find somebody who disagrees. Don't allow yourself the easy course of the constant "amen" to everything that you say.

Citation: Condoleezza Rice, when giving advice to new CBS anchorwoman Katie Couric

Topics: Accountability; Character; Community; Leadership; Teachability

References: Proverbs 18:24; 27:17; Matthew 12:36; Galatians 6:2; Ephesians 4:15–16; James 5:16

FRED ROGERS

AMERICAN EDUCATOR, MINISTER, AND TELEVISION HOST (1928–2003)

QUOTATION 180

Life is deep and simple, and what our society gives us is shallow and complicated.

Citation: Fred Rogers, in an interview shortly before he died

Topics: Discernment; False Teachers; Life; Morality; Wisdom

References: Mark 1:9–15; 12:28–31; John 6:29; 2 Corinthians 11:3; Galatians 5:6; Ephesians 3:16–21; 1 John 4:7–8

WILL ROGERS

CHEROKEE-AMERICAN COWBOY, COMEDIAN, HUMORIST, AND SOCIAL COMMENTATOR (1879–1935)

QUOTATION 181

Common sense isn't as common as it used to be.

Citation: Unknown

Topics: Depravity; Foolishness; Wisdom; Worldliness

References: Psalm 49:13; Proverbs 14:8; Ecclesiastes 10:1

QUOTATION 182

Don't let yesterday use up too much of today.

Citation: Unknown

Topics: Change; Forgiveness; Past; Perspective; Present; Transformation

References: Psalm 90:12; Ephesians 5:15–16

QUOTATION **183**

Live so that you wouldn't be ashamed to sell the family parrot to the town gossip.

Citation: Unknown

Topics: Character; Holiness; Hypocrisy; Integrity; Reputation; Respect; Testimony; Witness

References: Job 5:21; Proverbs 22:1; Ecclesiastes 7:1; Romans 12:17; 2 Corinthians 8:18–24; Ephesians 4:1–6; Philippians 2:14–16

QUOTATION **184**

Half our life is spent trying to find something to do with the time we have rushed through life trying to save.

Citation: Unknown

Topics: Calling; Choices; Life; Meaning; Purpose; Time; Vocation

References: Psalm 90:12; Ecclesiastes 3:1–11; Ephesians 5:15–16

ELEANOR ROOSEVELT
U.S. FIRST LADY (1884–1962)

QUOTATION **185**

No one can make you feel inferior without your consent.

Citation: Unknown

Topics: Enemies; Identity; Overcoming; Self-image; Self-worth; Significance; Spiritual Warfare

Reference: 1 Timothy 4:12

FRANKLIN ROOSEVELT
U.S. PRESIDENT (1882–1945)

QUOTATION **186**

I doubt if there is a problem — political or economic — that will not melt before the fire of a spiritual awakening.

Citation: Franklin Roosevelt, in a speech to the National Council of Churches

Topics: Holy Spirit; Problems; Renewal; Revival; Spirituality

References: James 4:10; 1 Peter 5:5–6

THEODORE ROOSEVELT
U.S. PRESIDENT (1858–1919)

QUOTATION 187

Far better is it to dare mighty things, to win glorious triumphs, even though checkered by failure, than to rank with those poor spirits who neither enjoy much nor suffer much, because they live in the gray twilight that knows not victory or defeat.

Citation: Theodore Roosevelt, when reflecting on building the Panama Canal

Topics: Apathy; Calling; Complacency; Courage; Ministry; Planning; Risk; Victory

References: Deuteronomy 31:6; Philippians 1:28; Hebrews 11; Revelation 3:16

QUOTATION 188

It is better to be faithful than famous.

Citation: Unknown

Topics: Eternal and Temporary; Faithfulness; Perspective; Priorities; Success

References: Psalm 132:12; Luke 19:17; Revelation 2:10

ANTONIN SCALIA
U.S. SUPREME COURT JUSTICE (1936–)

QUOTATION 189

God assumed from the beginning that the wise of the world would view Christians as fools ... and he has not been disappointed.... If I have brought any message today, it is this: Have the courage to have your wisdom regarded as stupidity. Be fools for Christ. And have the courage to suffer the contempt of the sophisticated world.

Citation: Antonin Scalia, speaking to the Knights of Columbus Council in Baton Rouge, Louisiana

Topics: Commitment; Convictions; Foolishness; Jesus Christ; Persecution; Reputation; Trials; Wisdom; World

References: Romans 1:21–23; 1 Corinthians 1:18–31; 2:14; 3:18–20; 4:10

BROOKE SHIELDS
AMERICAN ACTRESS (1965–)

QUOTATION 190

When I felt there was nothing I could do to help myself, knowing that I was prayed for was often the only thing that stood between me and despair.

Citation: Brooke Shields, in her *Guideposts* magazine article "What Friends Are For"

Topics: Brotherly Love; Community; Despair; Fellowship; Hope; Intercession; Prayer; Trials

References: Matthew 7:7–8; Luke 18:1–8; Ephesians 6:18; Philippians 4:6; 1 Thessalonians 5:17; Hebrews 4:14–16; James 5:13

MARGARET THATCHER
BRITISH PRIME MINISTER (1925–)

QUOTATION 191

Being powerful is like being a lady. If you have to tell people you are, you aren't.

Citation: Margaret Thatcher, in a *Forbes* article

Topics: Character; Hypocrisy; Integrity; Power; Witness

Reference: 1 Peter 2:11–12

QUOTATION **192**

When Christians meet ... their purpose is not—or should not be—to ascertain what is the mind of the majority, but what is the mind of the Holy Spirit—something which may be quite different.

Citation: Margaret Thatcher, in a *Saturday Evening Post* article

Topics: Direction; Discernment; God's Will; Guidance; Holy Spirit; Human Will; Illumination; Insight; Spiritual Perception; Submission; Teachability

Reference: Acts 15:1–21

LILY TOMLIN
AMERICAN ACTRESS AND COMEDIAN (1939–)

QUOTATION **193**

For fast-acting relief, try slowing down.

Citation: Unknown

Topics: Busyness; Recreation; Sabbath; Time; Work; Worry

Reference: Psalm 127:1–2

HARRY S. TRUMAN
U.S. PRESIDENT (1884–1972)

QUOTATION **194**

It takes courage to face a duelist with a pistol. . . . But it takes still greater and far higher courage to face friends with a grievance.

Citation: Harry Truman, in a speech at the State Capitol, Raleigh, North Carolina

Topics: Accountability; Admonishment; Conflict; Confrontation; Courage; Fear; Rebuke; Relationships

Reference: Matthew 18:15–18

BARBARA WALTERS

AMERICAN JOURNALIST, WRITER, AND MEDIA PERSONALITY (1929–)

QUOTATION 195

Show me someone who never gossips, and I'll show you someone who isn't interested in people.

Citation: Unknown

Topics: Compassion; Gossip; Kindness; Slander; Speech; Tongue

Reference: James 3:1–12

JOHN WAYNE

AMERICAN ACTOR (1907–79)

QUOTATION 196

Courage is being scared to death and saddling up anyway.

Citation: Unknown

Topics: Commitment; Courage; Determination; Fear; Perseverance; Self-control; Self-discipline; Tests; Trials

References: Deuteronomy 31:6; Joshua 1:7; Acts 4:13; Philippians 1:20; Hebrews 13:6

DANIEL WEBSTER

STATESMAN AND U.S. SECRETARY OF STATE (1782–1852)

QUOTATION 197

There is nothing so powerful as truth—and often nothing so strange.

Citation: Daniel Webster, *The Murder of Captain Joseph White*

Topics: Bible; Mysteries; Power; Preaching; Scripture; Truth

References: 1 Corinthians 1:18–2:16

MAE WEST

AMERICAN ACTRESS AND PLAYWRIGHT (1892–1980)

QUOTATION 198

When choosing between two evils, I always like to try the one I've never tried before.

Citation: Unknown

Topics: Depravity; Desires; Evil; Human Nature; Sin; Temptation

Reference: Romans 1:30; Ephesians 4:19

TOM WHITTAKER

AMERICAN MOUNTAINEER AND FIRST DISABLED PERSON TO CLIMB TO THE SUMMIT OF MOUNT EVEREST (1949–)

QUOTATION 199

One of the things that really attracts me about mountaineering is its total pointlessness. So I've dedicated my life to it.

Citation: Tom Whittaker, in a *Time* magazine article

Topics: Commitment; Dedication; Meaning; Motivation; Priorities; Purpose; Values; Vision

References: Ecclesiastes 1:2; 12:13–14; Ephesians 5:15–16; Philippians 3:7–11

ANNE WIDDECOMBE

BRITISH CONSERVATIVE POLITICIAN AND MEMBER OF PARLIAMENT (1947–)

QUOTATION 200

Let's face it—we are not a happier society as a result of the liberalization of the seventies. We have record rates of divorce, record rates of suicide, record rates of teenage pregnancy, record rates of youth crime, record rates of underage sex. We should invite people to recognize that the Great Experiment has failed. You cannot have happiness without restraint.

Citation: Anne Widdecombe, in the British newspaper *Telegraph*

Topics: Culture; Depravity; Divorce; Family; Happiness; Human Condition; Immorality; Morality; Self-control; Sexual Immorality

References: Jeremiah 31:31 – 34; 1 Thessalonians 4:3 – 8

WOODROW WILSON
U.S. PRESIDENT (1822 – 1903)

QUOTATION 201

I would rather fail in a cause that someday will triumph than to win in a cause that I know someday will fail.

Citation: Unknown

Topics: Abortion; Failure; Overcoming; Perseverance; Perspective; Success; Victory

References: Job 17:9; Galatians 6:9; Hebrews 12:1

OPRAH WINFREY
AMERICAN MEDIA PERSONALITY (1954 –)

QUOTATION 202

I believe that every single event in life happens in an opportunity to choose love over fear.

Citation: Unknown

Topics: Choices; Fear; Life; Love; Opportunity

Reference: 1 John 4:7 – 21

PART 3: ANCIENT WORDS FROM FATHERS AND FOUNDERS

ST. AMBROSE
BISHOP OF MILAN AND CHURCH FATHER (c. 338–397)

QUOTATION 203

A possession ought to belong to the possessor, not the possessor to the possession.

> **Citation:** Unknown
>
> **Topics:** Greed; Idolatry; Lust; Materialism; Money; Temptation
>
> **References:** Isaiah 5:8; James 5:3

QUOTATION 204

The church's foundation is unshakable and firm against the assaults of the raging sea. Waves lash at the church but do not shatter it. Although the elements of this world constantly batter and crash against her, she offers the safest harbor of salvation for all in distress.

> **Citation:** Unknown
>
> **Topics:** Church; Influence; Overcoming; Persecution; Salvation; Strength; Victory; World
>
> **References:** Matthew 16:18–19; Romans 16:20

ST. ATHANASIUS
PATRIARCH OF ALEXANDRIA AND CHURCH FATHER (c. 293–373)

QUOTATION 205

[Jesus] became what we are that he might make us what he is.

> **Citation:** Unknown
>
> **Topics:** Advent; Christlikeness; Christmas; Glory; Incarnation; Jesus Christ
>
> **References:** John 1:1–18; 17:11–26; Galatians 2:20; Philippians 2:1–11

ST. AUGUSTINE
BISHOP OF HIPPO AND CHURCH FATHER (354–430)

QUOTATION 206

The peace of the rational soul is the ordered arrangement of knowledge and action.

> **Citation:** St. Augustine, *The City of God*
> **Topics:** Knowledge; Peace; Social Action; Soul; Wisdom
> **References:** Psalm 119:165; Isaiah 26:3; Matthew 5:9; John 14:27; Romans 8:6

QUOTATION 207

Trust the past to God's mercy, the present to God's love, and the future to his providence.

> **Citation:** St. Augustine, *The City of God*
> **Topics:** Faith; Future; God's Love; Mercy; Past; Present; Providence; Provision; Trust
> **References:** 2 Samuel 7:28; Psalms 20:7; 52:8; 62:8; John 14:1

QUOTATION 208

Total abstinence is easier than perfect moderation.

> **Citation:** St. Augustine, *On the Good of Marriage*
> **Topics:** Addictions; Drugs; Drunkenness; Flesh; Self-control; Self-discipline; Sex; Sexual Immorality; Temptation
> **References:** Genesis 2:24; Psalm 51; Romans 13:13; 1 Corinthians 6:18

QUOTATION 209

No man has a right to lead such a life of contemplation as to forget in his own ease the service due to his neighbor; nor has any man a right to be so immersed in active life as to neglect the contemplation of God.

> **Citation:** St. Augustine, *Of the Dress and Habits of the Christian*
> **Topics:** Christian Life; Devotional Life; Self-examination; Service; Spiritual Disciplines
> **References:** Deuteronomy 22:1; Psalm 46:10; Matthew 22:39; Luke 3:11; James 1:22

QUOTATION **210**

Seeing women when you go out is not forbidden, but it is sinful to desire them or to wish them to desire you, for it is not by touch or passionate feeling alone, but by one's gaze also, that lustful desires mutually arise. And do not say that your hearts are pure if there is immodesty of the eye, because the unchaste eye carries the message of an impure heart.

> **Citation:** St. Augustine, *The Rule of St. Augustine*
>
> **Topics:** Desires; Lust; Purity; Self-control; Sex; Sexual Immorality; Sin; Temptation; Thoughts
>
> **References:** Job 31:1; Proverbs 6:25–26; Matthew 5:28; 1 Corinthians 6:18; Colossians 3:5; 1 John 2:16

QUOTATION **211**

There are many sheep without, many wolves within.

> **Citation:** St. Augustine, *Tractates on the Gospel of John*
>
> **Topics:** Church; Discipleship; Division; Enemies; False Teachers; Spiritual Warfare
>
> **References:** Matthew 7:15; 10:16; 2 Peter 2:1; 3 John 9–10

QUOTATION **212**

The confession of evil works is the first beginning of good works.

> **Citation:** St. Augustine, *Tractates on the Gospel of John*
>
> **Topics:** Confession; Evil; Forgiveness; Good Deeds; Repentance; Righteousness
>
> **References:** Leviticus 5:5; Psalm 32:5; Proverbs 28:13; James 5:16; 1 John 1:9

QUOTATION **213**

Do not seek to understand in order that you may believe, but believe so that you may understand.

> **Citation:** St. Augustine, *Tractates on the Gospel of John*
>
> **Topics:** Belief; Doubt; Faith; Unbelief; Understanding
>
> **References:** Genesis 15:6; John 20:29; Romans 3:22; 1 Corinthians 1:20

QUOTATION 214

God judged it better to bring good out of evil than not to permit any evil to exist.

> **Citation:** St. Augustine, *Handbook of Faith, Hope, and Love*
>
> **Topics:** Evil; God's Sovereignty; Providence; Redemption; Spiritual Warfare; Theodicy
>
> **References:** Genesis 2:9; 50:20; Romans 8:28

QUOTATION 215

There is no love without hope, no hope without love, and neither hope nor love without faith.

> **Citation:** St. Augustine, *The Distinction between Faith and Hope, and the Mutual Dependence of Faith, Hope, and Love*
>
> **Topics:** Christian Life; Faith; Hope; Love; Peace
>
> **References:** Romans 12:12; 1 Corinthians 13:13; Colossians 1:5; 1 Thessalonians 1:3; Hebrews 11:1

QUOTATION 216

It is human to err; it is devilish to remain willfully in error.

> **Citation:** St. Augustine, *Sermons*
>
> **Topics:** Disobedience; Human Condition; Sin; Stubbornness; Teachability
>
> **References:** Hosea 11:1–2; James 4:17; 1 John 3:6–9

QUOTATION 217

What you are must always displease you, if you would attain that which you are not.

> **Citation:** St. Augustine, *Sermons*
>
> **Topics:** Complacency; Human Condition; Indifference; Spiritual Growth
>
> **References:** 2 Corinthians 5:17; Ephesians 4:20–24; Colossians 3:5–7; James 3:11–12; 1 Peter 1:14

QUOTATION **218**

Our Lord came down from life to suffer death;
the Bread came down, to hunger;
the Way came down, on the way to weariness;
the Fount came down, to thirst.

> **Citation:** St. Augustine, *Sermons*
>
> **Topics:** Advent; Atonement; Christmas; Cross; Incarnation; Jesus Christ; Redemption; Salvation
>
> **References:** Matthew 1:1–23; Luke 1:26–38; 2:1–20; John 1:1–18

QUOTATION **219**

He so loved us that, for our sake,
He was made man in time,
    although through him all times were made.
He was made man, who made man.
He was created of a mother whom he created.
He was carried by hands that he formed.
He cried in the manger in wordless infancy, he the Word,
    without whom all human eloquence is mute.

> **Citation:** St. Augustine, *Sermons*
>
> **Topics:** Advent; Christmas; Christ's Love; Incarnation; Jesus Christ
>
> **References:** Matthew 1:1–23; Luke 1:26–38: 2:1–20; John 1:1–18

QUOTATION **220**

It is not the pain but the purpose that makes the martyr.

> **Citation:** St. Augustine, *Contra Crescon*
>
> **Topics:** Courage; Martyrdom; Motives; Purpose
>
> **References:** Psalm 44:22; Matthew 10:39; 16:24; Acts 7:54–60; 2 Corinthians 4:11; Revelation 2:10

QUOTATION **221**

God became a man for this purpose: since you, a human being, could not reach God, but you can reach other humans, you might now reach God through a man. And so the man Christ Jesus became the mediator of God and human beings.

God became a man so that following a man—something you are able to do—you might reach God, which was formerly impossible to you.

Citation: St. Augustine, *Commentary on Psalm 134*

Topics: Advent; Christmas; Discipleship; Experiencing God; Incarnation; Reconciliation

References: Matthew 1:18–25; Luke 2:1–20; John 1:1–14; 3:16; 17:3; Romans 8:34; Hebrews 7:25

QUOTATION **222**

Since it is God we are speaking of, you do not understand it. If you could understand it, it would not be God.

Citation: Unknown

Topics: Experiencing God; Faith; God; Incarnation; Knowledge; Mysteries

References: Psalm 139:6; Isaiah 55:8–9

QUOTATION **223**

Habit, if not resisted, soon becomes necessity.

Citation: Unknown

Topics: Addictions; Character; Desires; Habits; Needs; Self-control; Temptation

References: Proverbs 11:6; John 8:34; Romans 7:25; Hebrews 12:1

QUOTATION **224**

The Holy Scriptures are our letters from home.

Citation: Unknown

Topics: Bible; Bible Study; Devotional Life; Guidance; Revelation

References: Psalm 119:105–112; 2 Timothy 3:16

QUOTATION 225

Idolatry is worshiping anything that ought to be used, or using anything that is meant to be worshiped.

Citation: Unknown

Topics: Double-mindedness; Humanism; Idolatry; Worldliness; Worship

References: Exodus 20:3–5; Romans 1:21–23

QUOTATION 226

Christ is not valued at all, unless he is valued above all.

Citation: Unknown

Topics: Commitment; Devotion; Discipleship; Focus; Jesus Christ; Priorities; Worship

Reference: Matthew 10:37–39

QUOTATION 227

A good conscience is the palace of Christ; the temple of the Holy Ghost; the paradise of delight; the standing Sabbath of the saints.

Citation: Unknown

Topics: Conscience; Holiness; Holy Spirit; Righteousness

References: Genesis 20:5; Job 27:6; Acts 24:16; 1 Timothy 1:5

QUOTATION 228

God has promised forgiveness to your repentance, but he has not promised tomorrow to your procrastination.

Citation: Unknown

Topics: Apathy; Commitment; Forgiveness; Procrastination; Urgency

References: Proverbs 14:23; Ecclesiastes 10:18; 2 Corinthians 6:2;
1 Thessalonians 5:14; 2 Thessalonians 3:6–15

QUOTATION 229

God loves each one of us as if there were only one of us to love.

Citation: Unknown

Topics: Experiencing God; God's Love; Worth

References: John 3:16; 1 John 3:1–3; 3:16

WILLIAM BOOTH

BRITISH PREACHER AND FOUNDER OF THE SALVATION ARMY (1829–1912)

QUOTATION 230

I seemed to hear a voice sounding in my ears, "Where can you go and find such heathen as these, and where is there so great a need for your labours?"

Citation: William Booth, in a letter to his wife, Catherine, after seeing some of East London's gin palaces

Topics: Calling; Evangelism; Evil; Lostness; Mission; Motivation; Outreach; Witness

References: Proverbs 20:1; Matthew 9:12; Luke 19:10

QUOTATION 231

God help me ... to cultivate a spirit of self-denial and to yield myself a prisoner of love to the Redeemer of the world.

Citation: William Booth, in a mission statement written at age twenty

Topics: Calling; Dedication; Evangelism; Mission; Obedience; Outreach; Sacrifice; Self-denial; Submission; Vision

References: Psalms 5:3; 88:13; Romans 13:11–12

QUOTATION 232

While women weep, as they do now, I'll fight; while little children go hungry, I'll fight; while men go to prison, in and out, in and out, as they do now, I'll fight; while there is a drunkard left, while there is a poor lost girl upon the streets, where there remains one dark soul without the light of God, I'll fight! I'll fight to the very end!

Citation: William Booth, in his final public speech

Topics: Calling; Commitment; Compassion; Dedication; Injustice; Justice; Persistence; Poverty; Social Action; Social Justice

References: Proverbs 22:9; Isaiah 32:7; Matthew 19:21

QUOTATION **233**

Work as if everything depended upon your work, and pray as if everything depended upon your prayer.

Citation: Unknown

Topics: Calling; Commitment; Intercession; Ministry; Prayer; Vocation; Work

References: Joshua 24:15; Ezra 7:23; Romans 1:9

QUOTATION **234**

Faith and works should travel side by side, step answering to step, like the legs of men walking. First faith, and then works; and then faith again, and then works again—until you can scarcely distinguish which is one and which is the other.

Citation: Unknown

Topics: Christian Life; Faith; Godliness; Good Deeds

References: Matthew 5:16; James 2:17–18; 1 Peter 2:12

ELIAS BOUDINOT

AMERICAN LAWYER AND STATESMAN (1740–1821)

QUOTATION **235**

Were you to ask me to recommend the most valuable book in the world, I should fix on the Bible as the most instructive, both to the wise and ignorant. Were you to ask me for one, affording the most rational and pleasing entertainment to the inquiring mind, I should repeat, it is the Bible; and the most interesting history, I should still urge you to look into your Bible. I would make it, in short, the Alpha and Omega of knowledge.

Citation: Elias Boudinot, *The Age of Revelation*

Topics: Bible; Bible Study; Devotional Life; Knowledge; Revelation; Wisdom
References: Joshua 1:8; 2 Timothy 3:14–17

QUOTATION **236**

To have a God who is almighty, all wise, all good and merciful to go to as your constant friend, as your continual benefactor, as your safeguard and guide, it should — it must — sweeten every bitter drought of life.

Citation: Elias Boudinot, in a personal letter (as seen in James H. Hutson's *The Founders on Religion*)
Topics: Attributes of God; Experiencing God; Hope; Joy; Mercy; Peace; Provision
References: John 14:15–31; 16:5–16

ST. JOHN CHRYSOSTOM
ARCHBISHOP OF CONSTANTINOPLE AND CHURCH FATHER (349–407)

QUOTATION **237**

We must not mind insulting men, if by respecting them we offend God.

Citation: St. John Chrysostom, *Six Books on the Priesthood*
Topics: Accountability; Courage; Fear
Reference: Acts 5:29

QUOTATION **238**

When facing the Evil One, you must never lay down your arms; you must never take any sleep if you want to remain forever unhurt. You must do one of two things: either take off your armor and so fall and perish, or stand always armed and watchful.

Citation: St. John Chrysostom, *Six Books on the Priesthood*
Topics: Evil; Responsibility; Satan; Spiritual Warfare; Victory
References: Ephesians 6:10–20; 1 Peter 5:8–11

QUOTATION 239

Even if we stand at the very summit of virtue, it is by mercy that we shall be saved.

Citation: Unknown

Topics: Atonement; Grace; Jesus Christ; Justification; Mercy; Redemption; Righteousness; Salvation; Virtue

Reference: Romans 3:9–20

BENJAMIN FRANKLIN
U.S. FOUNDING FATHER, WRITER, POLITICIAN, AND INVENTOR (1706–90)

QUOTATION 240

The soul of man is immortal, and will be treated with justice in another life respecting its conduct in this.

Citation: Benjamin Franklin, in a letter to Ezra Stiles (as seen in James H. Hutson's *The Founders on Religion*)

Topics: Afterlife; Consequences; Eternal Death; Eternal Life; Final Judgment; Heaven; Hell; Soul

Reference: 2 Corinthians 5:10

QUOTATION 241

If men are so wicked as we now see with religion, what would they be if without it?

Citation: Benjamin Franklin, in a personal letter (as seen in James H. Hutson's *The Founders on Religion*)

Topics: Depravity; Human Condition; Human Nature; Religion; Secularism; Transformation

Reference: Matthew 5:13–16

ALEXANDER HAMILTON

U.S. FOUNDING FATHER, ARMY OFFICER, LAWYER, AND POLITICIAN (c. 1755 – 1804)

QUOTATION 242

The sacred rights of mankind are not to be rummaged for among old parchments or musty records. They are written as with a sunbeam, in the whole volume of human nature, by the hand of divinity itself; and can never be erased or obscured by mortal power.

Citation: Alexander Hamilton, in his paper "The Farmer Refuted"

Topics: Injustice; Justice; Purpose; Rights; Worth

References: Amos 5:24; Micah 6:8; Matthew 23:23

HIPPOLYTUS OF ROME

THEOLOGIAN AND PROLIFIC RELIGIOUS WRITER (c. 170 – c. 236)

QUOTATION 243

A heavenly light more brilliant than all others sheds its radiance everywhere, and he who was begotten before the morning star and all the stars of heaven, Christ, mighty and immortal, shines upon all creatures more brightly than the sun.

Citation: Unknown

Topics: Awe; Beauty; Glory; Illumination; Jesus Christ; Revelation

Reference: John 8:12

ST. IRENAEUS
BISHOP OF LYONS AND CHURCH FATHER (c. 130–200)

QUOTATION 244

There is no need to look anywhere else for truth which we can easily obtain from the church. The apostles have, as it were, deposited this truth in all its fullness in this depository, so that whoever wants to may draw from this water of life. This is the gate of life; all others are thieves and robbers.

Citation: St. Irenaeus, *Against Heresies*

Topics: Bible; Church; Direction; False Teachers; Guidance; Heresy; Truth

References: 1 Timothy 3:15; 2 Timothy 3:16

QUOTATION 245

This is the Creator: in respect of his love, our Father; in respect of his power, our Lord; in respect of his wisdom, our Maker and Designer.

Citation: St. Irenaeus, *Against Heresies*

Topics: Creator; God's Love; God's Sovereignty; Mercy

Reference: Revelation 4:11

QUOTATION 246

It is God's intention that he should be seen, and the vision of God is the acquisition of immortality—and the immortality brings man near to God.

Citation: St. Irenaeus, *Against Heresies*

Topics: Experiencing God; God; Immortality; Revelation; Vision

Reference: John 17:24–26

QUOTATION 247

Where the church is, there is the Spirit of God; and where the Spirit of God is, there is the church and every kind of grace.

Citation: St. Irenaeus, *Against Heresies*

Topics: Church; Community; Fellowship; Grace; Holy Spirit; Kindness; Spiritual Gifts

References: Acts 2:1–4; 1 Corinthians 12:4–31

JOHN JAY

U. S. FOUNDING FATHER AND FIRST CHIEF JUSTICE OF THE U.S. SUPREME COURT (1745–1829)

QUOTATION 248

Among the strange things of this world, nothing seems stranger than that men pursuing happiness should knowingly quit the right and take a wrong road, and frequently do what their judgments neither approve nor prefer. Yet so is the fact; and this fact points strongly to the necessity of our being healed, or restored, or regenerated by a power more energetic than any of those which properly belong to the human mind.

Citation: John Jay, in a letter (as seen in James H. Hutson's *The Founders on Religion*)

Topics: Depravity; Foolishness; Happiness; Healing; Limitations; Joy; Meaning; Purpose; Redemption

Reference: Romans 1:20–32

THOMAS JEFFERSON

U.S. PRESIDENT, FOUNDING FATHER, AND PRINCIPAL AUTHOR OF THE DECLARATION OF INDEPENDENCE (1743–1826)

QUOTATION 249

Prayers to heaven, the only contribution of old age.

Citation: Thomas Jefferson, in a letter (as seen in James H. Hutson's *The Founders on Religion*)

Topics: Aging; Intercession; Prayer

Reference: Luke 2:36–37

ST. JEROME
PRIEST AND CHURCH FATHER (345–420)

QUOTATION 250

A friend is long sought, hardly found, and with difficulty kept.

> **Citation:** St. Jerome, in his letter to Rufinus the Monk
>
> **Topics:** Brotherly Love; Community; Fellowship; Friendship; Relationships
>
> **References:** Proverbs 27:10; James 2:23

QUOTATION 251

I beg you, my dearest brother, to live among these [sacred books], to meditate on them, to know nothing else, to seek nothing else. Does not this seem to you to be a little bit of heaven here on earth?

> **Citation:** St. Jerome, in one of his many letters to the church
>
> **Topics:** Bible; Bible Study; Spiritual Disciplines; Teachability
>
> **Reference:** 2 Timothy 2:15

ST. LEO (THE GREAT)
FIRST POPE OF THE ROMAN CATHOLIC CHURCH (440–461)

QUOTATION 252

[The] eternal Son of the eternal Father was born of the Holy Spirit and the Virgin Mary.... Humility was assumed by majesty, weakness by strength, mortality by eternity; and to pay the debt that we had incurred, an inviolable nature was united to a nature that can suffer.

> **Citation:** St. Leo (the Great), in a letter (often called "Tome of Leo") to Flavian, patriarch of Constantinople
>
> **Topics:** Atonement; Christmas; Humility; Incarnation; Jesus Christ; Redemption; Salvation; Virgin Birth
>
> **References:** Matthew 1:18; Luke 1:35

ORIGEN

SCHOLAR, THEOLOGIAN, AND CHURCH FATHER (c. 185 – c. 254)

QUOTATION 253

Virtue is not virtue if it be untested and unexamined.

Citation: Origen, *Homilia in Numeros*

Topics: Character; Holiness; Temptation; Trials; Virtue

References: Genesis 22:1 – 2; Matthew 4:1

QUOTATION 254

Jesus, my feet are dirty. Come even as a slave to me, pour water into your bowl, come and wash my feet. In asking such a thing, I know I am overbold, but I dread what was threatened when you said to me, "If I do not wash your feet I have no fellowship with you." Wash my feet then, because I long for your companionship.

Citation: Unknown

Topics: Jesus Christ; Humility; Self-examination; Service

References: Mark 10:43 – 44; Luke 22:27; John 13:4 – 8; Philippians 2:7

WILLIAM PENN

U.S. FOUNDER OF THE PROVINCE OF PENNSYLVANIA (1644 – 1718)

QUOTATION 255

They that soar too high often fall hard; which makes a low and level dwelling preferable. The tallest trees are most in the power of the winds, and ambitious men of the blasts of fortune.

Citation: William Penn, *Some Fruits of Solitude*

Topics: Ambition; Arrogance; Humility; Lifestyle; Pride

References: 2 Chronicles 26:16; Proverbs 11:2; 16:18; Luke 22:26

QUOTATION 256

Right is right, even if everyone is against it; and wrong is wrong, even if everyone is for it.

Citation: Unknown

Topics: Character; Convictions; Integrity; Morality; Opposition; Persecution

Reference: Isaiah 5:20

PHILIP JAKOB SPENER
GERMAN THEOLOGIAN AND "FATHER OF PIETISM" (1635–1705)

QUOTATION 257

The more at home the Word of God is among us, the more we shall bring about faith and its fruits.

Citation: Philip Jakob Spener, *Pious Longings*

Topics: Bible; Bible Study; Devotional Life; Spiritual Formation; Spiritual Growth

References: Joshua 1:8; 1 Peter 2:2

TERTULLIAN
CHURCH FATHER (c. 155–230)

QUOTATION 258

God's purpose and promises to man are for the benefit not of the soul alone but of the soul and the flesh.

Citation: Tertullian, *The Resurrection of the Body*

Topics: Promises; Purpose; Resurrection; Sanctification; Transformation

Reference: 1 Corinthians 6:12–20

QUOTATION **259**

The Devil is opposed to the truth in many ways. He has sometimes even attempted to destroy it by defending it.

Citation: Unknown

Topics: Deceit; Devil; Evil; Satan; Spiritual Warfare; Temptation; Truth

References: Matthew 4:1 – 11; Acts 15:1 – 21

QUOTATION **260**

It is an image of the Trinity as a plant, with the Father as a deep root, the Son as the shoot that breaks forth into the world, and the Spirit as that which spreads beauty and fragrance.

Citation: Unknown

Topics: God; Holy Spirit; Jesus Christ; Theology; Trinity

References: Genesis 1:26 – 27; Luke 3:16; John 4:23 – 24

QUOTATION **261**

The blood of the martyrs is the seed of the church.

Citation: Unknown

Topics: Church; Martyrdom; Sacrifice

Reference: Acts 8:1 – 3

QUOTATION **262**

Nothing that is God's is obtainable by money.

Citation: Unknown

Topics: Eternal and Temporary; Greed; Materialism; Money

References: Matthew 6:19; Mark 4:19; Acts 8:18 – 22; James 5:3

QUOTATION **263**

Truth does not blush.

Citation: Unknown

Topics: Boldness; Courage; Revelation; Truth

References: Proverbs 12:19; Zechariah 8:16; Ephesians 4:25

GEORGE WASHINGTON
U.S. PRESIDENT (1732–99)

QUOTATION 264

Labor to keep alive in your breast that little spark of celestial fire called conscience.

Citation: George Washington, in a "rules of conduct" document he composed as a child

Topics: Accountability; Character; Conscience; Morality

Reference: 1 Peter 3:21

QUOTATION 265

Providence has at all times been my only dependence, for all other resources seem to have failed us.

Citation: George Washington, in a speech during America's struggle to establish itself as an independent nation

Topics: God's Sovereignty; Guidance; Limitations; Providence; Provision

Reference: Proverbs 3:5–6

JOHN WESLEY
BRITISH THEOLOGIAN AND EARLY LEADER OF METHODIST MOVEMENT (1703–91)

QUOTATION 266

Good men avoid sin from the love of virtue; wicked men avoid sin from a fear of punishment.

Citation: John Wesley, *The Almost Christian*

Topics: Consequences; God's Wrath; Judgment; Obedience; Punishment; Righteousness; Sin; Virtue

References: Deuteronomy 26:16; Proverbs 11:19, 21

QUOTATION **267**

When I was young, I was sure of everything. In a few years, having been mistaken a thousand times, I was not half so sure of most things as I was before. At present, I am hardly sure of anything but what God has revealed to man.

Citation: John Wesley, in response to a critical letter in the *London Magazine*

Topics: Bible; Confidence; Knowledge; Limitations; Mysteries; Revelation; Wisdom

References: Job 32:8; Hosea 14:9; Matthew 24:35

QUOTATION **268**

I am a Bible-bigot. I follow it in all things, both great and small.

Citation: John Wesley, written in his personal journal

Topics: Bible; Commitment; Convictions; Dedication; Focus; Influence

References: Deuteronomy 17:19; Psalm 111:7; Matthew 5:18

QUOTATION **269**

Do all the good you can, by all the means you can, in all the ways you can, in all the places you can, to all the people you can, as long as ever you can.

Citation: John Wesley, part of his personal motto

Topics: Benevolence; Calling; Dedication; Godliness; Good Deeds; Holiness; Ministry; Outreach; Spiritual Gifts; Vocation

References: Matthew 5:16; 1 Timothy 6:18; Hebrews 10:24; 1 Peter 2:12

QUOTATION **270**

The lowest and worst have a claim to our courtesy.

Citation: John Wesley, in his sermon "On Pleasing All Men"

Topics: Compassion; Humility; Kindness; Mercy; Poor People; Service; Social Justice

References: Deuteronomy 15:7; Proverbs 19:17; Matthew 25:40

Self-denial of all kinds is the very life and soul of piety.

> **Citation:** John Wesley, in his sermon "On Redeeming the Time"
>
> **Topics:** Arrogance; Pride; Sacrifice; Self-denial
>
> **References:** Mark 8:34; Romans 8:13; Galatians 5:24

JOHN WITHERSPOON
AMERICAN CLERGYMAN AND SIGNER OF THE DECLARATION OF INDEPENDENCE (1723–94)

QUOTATION **272**

It is only the fear of God that can deliver us from the fear of man.

> **Citation:** Unknown
>
> **Topics:** Courage; Experiencing God; Fear; Fear of God
>
> **References:** Proverbs 1:7; Galatians 1:10

RABBI ZUSYA
RABBI AND TEACHER (c. 1719–1800)

QUOTATION **273**

In the world to come I shall not be asked, "Why were you not Moses?" I shall be asked, "Why were you not Zusya?"

> **Citation:** Unknown
>
> **Topics:** Ambition; Calling; Fulfillment; Goals; Identity in Christ; Mission; Purpose; Self-worth; Vocation
>
> **References:** Ephesians 6:7–8; Colossians 3:23–24; 1 Peter 4:10

PART 4: PASSIONATE WORDS FROM MARTYRS AND MISSIONARIES

DIETRICH BONHOEFFER
GERMAN THEOLOGIAN, PASTOR, AND MARTYR (1906–45)

QUOTATION **274**

I think God is nearer to suffering than to happiness, and to find God in this way gives peace and rest and a strong and courageous heart.

Citation: Dietrich Bonhoeffer, in a letter to his twin sister, Sabine

Topics: Courage; Encouragement; Experiencing God; Happiness; Joy; Rest; Strength; Suffering

References: Matthew 5:11; 10:39; Acts 5:41; Romans 8:17; 2 Corinthians 4:11

QUOTATION **275**

Only he who believes is obedient, and only he who is obedient believes.

Citation: Dietrich Bonhoeffer, *The Cost of Discipleship*

Topics: Belief; Commitment; Discipleship; Obedience

Reference: Romans 1:5

QUOTATION **276**

To deny oneself is to be aware only of Christ and no more of self, to see only him who goes before and no more the road which is too hard for us. Once more, all that self-denial can say is: "He leads the way, keep close to him."

Citation: Dietrich Bonhoeffer, *The Cost of Discipleship*

Topics: Commitment; Discipleship; Sacrifice; Self-denial; Self-discipline; Selflessness; Submission; Wholehearted Devotion

References: Micah 6:8; Matthew 16:24–26; Romans 12:2; Galatians 2:20; 2 Timothy 1:7; Hebrews 12:1

QUOTATION **277**

Though we all have to enter upon discipleship alone, we do not remain alone.

Citation: Dietrich Bonhoeffer, *The Cost of Discipleship*

Topics: Brotherly Love; Community; Fellowship; Relationships

Reference: Hebrews 10:24–25

QUOTATION 278

[Disciples] see that for all the jollity on board, the ship is beginning to sink. The world dreams of progress, of power, and of the future. But the disciples meditate on the end, the last judgment, and the coming of the kingdom. To such heights the world cannot rise.

Citation: Dietrich Bonhoeffer, *The Cost of Discipleship*

Topics: Discipleship; Final Judgment; God's Wrath; Kingdom; Perspective; Power; Second Coming; Worldliness

References: 2 Corinthians 5:9–11; Revelation 20

QUOTATION 279

The Incarnation is the ultimate reason why the service of God cannot be divorced from the service of man.

Citation: Dietrich Bonhoeffer, *The Cost of Discipleship*

Topics: Incarnation; Jesus Christ; Mission; Outreach; Service

References: Matthew 25:31–46; Galatians 6:9–10

QUOTATION 280

The right way to approach God is to stretch out our hands and ask of One who we know has the heart of a Father.

Citation: Dietrich Bonhoeffer, *The Cost of Discipleship*

Topics: God as Father; Humility; Intercession; Prayer

Reference: Matthew 6:9

QUOTATION 281

Earthly possessions dazzle our eyes and delude us into thinking that they can provide security and freedom from anxiety. Yet all the time they are the very source of all anxiety.

Citation: Dietrich Bonhoeffer, *The Cost of Discipleship*

Topics: Materialism; Money; Perspective; Self-reliance; Worry

Reference: Matthew 6:25–34

QUOTATION 282

A prison cell, in which one waits, hopes, does various unessential things, and is completely dependent on the fact that the door of freedom has to be opened "from the outside," is not a bad picture of Advent.

Citation: Dietrich Bonhoeffer, in a letter written from prison to his fiancée, Maria von Wedemeyer

Topics: Advent; Christmas; Dependence; Hope; Limitations; Jesus Christ; Redemption; Salvation

References: Matthew 26:64; Luke 12:40; 1 Corinthians 4:5

QUOTATION 283

Christian brotherhood is not an ideal which we must realize; it is rather a reality created by God in Christ in which we may participate.

Citation: Dietrich Bonhoeffer, *Life Together*

Topics: Brotherly Love; Community; Fellowship; Relationships

Reference: Galatians 3:27–28

QUOTATION 284

He who can no longer listen to his brother will soon no longer be listening to God, either.

Citation: Dietrich Bonhoeffer, *Life Together*

Topics: Accountability; Community; Fellowship; Listening; Obedience; Relationships; Teachability

References: Proverbs 15:31; Luke 8:15; James 1:19

QUOTATION 285

I can no longer condemn or hate a brother [or sister] for whom I pray, no matter how much trouble he causes me. His face that hitherto may have been strange and intolerable to me is transformed through intercession into the countenance of a brother for whom Christ died.

Citation: Dietrich Bonhoeffer, *Life Together*

Topics: Anger; Enemies; Hatred; Intercession; Prayer

Reference: Matthew 5:44

QUOTATION **286**

It is not necessary that we should discover new ideas in our meditation. It is sufficient, and far more important, if the Word, as we read and understand it, penetrates and dwells within us.

Citation: Dietrich Bonhoeffer, *Life Together*

Topics: Bible; Bible Study; Change; Illumination; Maturity; Spiritual Growth; Teachability; Transformation

References: Joshua 1:8; Psalm 119:15

QUOTATION **287**

In a world where success is the measure and justification of all things, the figure of him who was sentenced and crucified remains a stranger.

Citation: Dietrich Bonhoeffer, *Ethics*

Topics: Cross; Failure; Sacrifice; Self-denial; Success

Reference: Isaiah 53:1 – 12

QUOTATION **288**

The hungry need bread and the homeless need a roof; the dispossessed need justice and the lonely need fellowship; the undisciplined need order and the slaves need freedom. To allow the hungry to remain hungry would be blasphemy against God and one's neighbor, for what is nearest to God is precisely the need of one's neighbor.

Citation: Dietrich Bonhoeffer, *Ethics*

Topics: Brotherly Love; Compassion; Good Deeds; Kindness; Needs; Neighbors; Social Impact; Social Justice

Reference: Matthew 25:31 – 46

QUOTATION **289**

It is not only what is said that matters, but also the man who says it.

Citation: Dietrich Bonhoeffer, *Ethics*

Topics: Character; Ethics; Integrity; Speech; Truth; Words

References: Matthew 7:29; Luke 21:33

QUOTATION 290

The cross of Christ destroyed the equation "religion equals happiness."

Citation: Dietrich Bonhoeffer, in a sermon preached in Spain

Topics: Cross; Happiness; Pain; Religion; Sacrifice; Self-denial; Tests; Trials

References: Acts 14:22; 1 Corinthians 1:17; Galatians 6:14; Ephesians 2:16; Philippians 1:29; Colossians 2:14

QUOTATION 291

One act of obedience is better than one hundred sermons.

Citation: Unknown

Topics: Character; Evangelism; Example; Good Deeds; Obedience; Preaching

Reference: 1 Corinthians 11:1

QUOTATION 292

As high as God is above man, so high are the sanctity, the rights, and the promise of marriage above the sanctity, the rights, and the promise of love. It is not your love that sustains the marriage, but from now on, the marriage that sustains your love.

Citation: Dietrich Bonhoeffer, *A Wedding Sermon from Prison*

Topics: Commitment; Devotion; Love; Marriage; Romance; Spouses

References: Ephesians 5:21–33; Titus 2:4

ST. BONIFACE
GERMAN MISSIONARY (c. 672–754)

QUOTATION 293

In her voyage across the ocean of this world, the church is like a great ship being pounded by the waves of life's different stresses. Our duty is not to abandon ship but to keep her on course.

Citation: St. Boniface, in a letter to Cuthbert, archbishop of Canterbury

Topics: Church; Commitment; Community; Dedication; Focus; Purpose

References: Acts 2:42–47; Ephesians 4:2–6; 2 Timothy 4:3–5; Hebrews 10:25

WILLIAM CAREY

BRITISH MISSIONARY TO INDIA (1761 – 1834)

QUOTATION **294**

Expect great things from God; attempt great things for God.

> Citation: William Carey, in his sermon "Expect Great Things, Attempt Great Things"
>
> Topics: Courage; God; Mission; Risk; Trust
>
> References: 1 Samuel 17:45 – 47; Matthew 7:7 – 8

QUOTATION **295**

To know the will of God, we need an open Bible and an open map.

> Citation: Unknown
>
> Topics: Bible; Calling; Devotional Life; Direction; God's Will; Guidance; Human Will; Teachability
>
> Reference: Romans 12:1 – 2

QUOTATION **296**

When I am gone, say nothing about Dr. Carey. Speak about Dr. Carey's Savior.

> Citation: William Carey, while on his deathbed
>
> Topics: Death; Humility; Jesus Christ; Redemption; Salvation; Savior
>
> References: Romans 15:17; Philippians 3:20; 2 Peter 1:11

QUOTATION **297**

God has a sovereign right to dispose of us as he pleases; we ought to acquiesce in all that God does with us and to us.

> Citation: William Carey, in a letter to Andrew Murray after a fire in Carey's warehouse in India had destroyed twenty years worth of work in manuscripts and other translation materials
>
> Topics: God's Sovereignty; Submission; Trials
>
> References: Psalm 46:10; Romans 8:28

We must not be contented with praying, without exerting ourselves in the use of means for the obtaining of those things we pray for.

Citation: William Carey, *An Enquiry into the Obligation of Christians to Use Means for the Conversion of the Heathens*

Topics: Calling; Prayer; Responsibility

References: Matthew 6:5–15; 7:7–12; Luke 11:1–13; 18:1–8

AMY CARMICHAEL
IRISH MISSIONARY TO INDIA (1867–1951)

QUOTATION **299**

We will have eternity to celebrate the victories, but only a few hours before sunset to win them.

Citation: Amy Carmichael, *Things as They Are*

Topics: Calling; Eternal Life; Eternal and Temporary; Mission; Outreach; Victory; Witness

Reference: John 9:4

QUOTATION **300**

Certain it is that the reason there is so much shallow living—much talk but little obedience—is that so few are prepared to be, like the pine on the hilltop, alone in the wind for God.

Citation: Unknown

Topics: Calling; Commitment; Convictions; Sacrifice; Strength; Suffering; Witness

References: Matthew 8:18–22; Luke 14:25–35

QUOTATION **301**

You cannot pull people uphill who do not want to go; you can only point up.

Citation: Unknown

Topics: Evangelism; Leadership; Mentoring; Witness

Reference: 1 Timothy 4

QUOTATION **302**

God always answers us in the deeps, never in the shallows of our soul.

> **Citation:** Unknown
>
> **Topics:** Experiencing God; Pain; Prayer; Soul; Suffering
>
> **References:** 1 Kings 19:12; Proverbs 8:34; Ezekiel 43:2

QUOTATION **303**

To look up into a dark sky and see it suddenly open as lightning plays across it, to see in one revealing flash deep into the kingdoms of light, is to know what prayer most truly is. There is mystery, but beyond that darkness is not a deeper darkness, but light—kingdoms of light.

> **Citation:** Amy Carmichael, *Learning of God*
>
> **Topics:** God's Sovereignty; Light; Mysteries; Prayer
>
> **References:** Job 5:9; Romans 8:26–27; 11:33–34

THOMAS COKE
WELSH BISHOP AND MISSIONARY (1747–1814)

QUOTATION **304**

Our instructions will be always barren, if they be not watered with our tears and prayers.

> **Citation:** Unknown
>
> **Topics:** Devotional Life; Intercession; Knowledge; Prayer
>
> **Reference:** Acts 20:31

JIM ELLIOT

AMERICAN MISSIONARY TO ECUADOR
AND MARTYR (1927–56)

QUOTATION 305

I must not think it strange if God takes in youth those whom I would have kept on earth until they were older. God is peopling eternity, and I must not restrict him to old men and women.

> **Citation:** Unknown
>
> **Topics:** Death; Eternal Life; Eternity; God's Sovereignty; Heaven; Life; Mysteries; Providence
>
> **Reference:** Isaiah 40:13–14

ST. IGNATIUS OF ANTIOCH

THIRD PATRIARCH OF ANTIOCH, CHURCH FATHER,
AND MARTYR (35–107)

QUOTATION 306

Let fire and cross; let the crowds of wild beasts; let tearings … let shatterings of the whole body; and let all the evil torments of the Devil come upon me: only let me attain to Jesus Christ.

> **Citation:** St. Ignatius, *The Epistle of Ignatius to the Romans*
>
> **Topics:** Commitment; Dedication; Devil; Enemies; Evil; Martyrdom; Overcoming; Pain; Persecution; Satan; Spiritual Warfare; Suffering; Tests; Trials
>
> **Reference:** Philippians 3:7–11

QUOTATION 307

It is not that I want merely to be called a Christian, but actually to *be* one. Yes, if I prove to be one, then I can have the name.

> **Citation:** St. Ignatius, *The Epistle of Ignatius to the Romans*
>
> **Topics:** Christlikeness; Discipleship; Wholehearted Devotion
>
> **References:** Acts 11:26; 1 Peter 4:16

QUOTATION **308**

I am God's wheat. May I be ground by the teeth of the wild beasts until I become the fine white bread that belongs to Christ.

> **Citation:** St. Ignatius, in one of his prayers
>
> **Topics:** Persecution; Sanctification; Suffering; Tests; Trials
>
> **References:** Job 23:10; Isaiah 48:10; 1 Peter 1:7

QUOTATION **309**

Be mild at their anger, humble at their boastings, to their blasphemies return your prayers, to their error your firmness in the faith; when they are cruel, be gentle; not endeavoring to imitate their ways, let us be their brethren in all kindness and moderation: but let us be followers of the Lord; for who was ever more unjustly used, more destitute, more despised?

> **Citation:** St. Ignatius, concerning the church's response to its enemies
>
> **Topics:** Attitudes; Christlikeness; Enemies; Gentleness; Kindness; Mercy; Persecution; Suffering
>
> **Reference:** 1 Peter 2:21–23

E. STANLEY JONES
AMERICAN MISSIONARY TO INDIA (1884–1973)

QUOTATION **310**

If you don't make up your mind, your unmade mind will unmake you.

> **Citation:** E. Stanley Jones, *The Way to Power and Poise*
>
> **Topics:** Calling; Choices; Commitment; Complacency; Convictions; Decisions; Direction; Double-mindedness; Purpose
>
> **References:** Deuteronomy 30:15; Joshua 24:15; Mark 10:21; James 1:8

QUOTATION 311

Faith is not merely your holding on to God; it is God holding on to you.

Citation: Unknown

Topics: Faith; God; Providence; Provision; Trust

References: Psalm 37:5; Isaiah 50:10; John 5:24; 1 Thessalonians 5:24

QUOTATION 312

There is nothing holy but a holy person; there is nothing unholy but an unholy person. Holy persons gathered together make a holy place, not the other way around.

Citation: E. Stanley Jones, *Mastery*

Topics: Church; Community; Holiness

Reference: 1 Corinthians 1:2

QUOTATION 313

The cross is the key. If I lose this key, I fumble. The universe will not open to me. But with the key in my hand I know I hold his secret.

Citation: E. Stanley Jones, *Christ at the Round Table*

Topics: Cross; Jesus Christ; Meaning; Mysteries

Reference: Galatians 6:14

ADONIRAM JUDSON SR.
AMERICAN MISSIONARY TO BURMA (1788 – 1850)

QUOTATION 314

The motto of every missionary, whether preacher, printer, or schoolmaster, ought to be "Devoted for life."

Citation: Adoniram Judson, in a letter to Rufus Anderson, corresponding secretary, American Board of Commissioners for Foreign Missions

Topics: Calling; Commitment; Dedication; Lifestyle; Mission; Missions

Reference: Colossians 4:17

QUOTATION 315

The future is as bright as the promises of God.

> **Citation:** Adoniram Judson, while serving time in a Burmese jail
>
> **Topics:** Future; God's Promises; Hope; Perspective; Trust
>
> **Reference:** 2 Peter 1:4

QUOTATION 316

I am not tired of my work, neither am I tired of the world; yet when Christ calls me home, I shall go with the gladness of a boy bounding away from school.

> **Citation:** Unknown
>
> **Topics:** Commitment; Death; Eternal Life; Work
>
> **Reference:** Philippians 1:20–26

ERIC LIDDELL
SCOTTISH MISSIONARY TO CHINA (1902–45)

QUOTATION 317

Circumstances may appear to wreck our lives and God's plans, but God is not helpless among the ruins. Our broken lives are not lost or useless. God's love is still working. He comes in and takes the calamity and uses it victoriously, working out his wonderful plan of love.

> **Citation:** Eric Liddell, *The Disciplines of the Christian Life*
>
> **Topics:** God's Love; God's Sovereignty; Sanctification; Suffering; Tragedy; Trials
>
> **References:** Proverbs 3:5–6; Ecclesiastes 3:11; John 13:7; Romans 8:28

QUOTATION 318

Have a great aim — have a high standard — make Jesus your ideal ... make him an ideal not merely to be admired but also to be followed.

> **Citation:** Unknown
>
> **Topics:** Commitment; Direction; Goals; Imitation of Christ; Jesus Christ
>
> **References:** Colossians 3:1–4; Hebrews 12:2

DAVID LIVINGSTONE
SCOTTISH MISSIONARY TO AFRICA (1813–73)

QUOTATION **319**

The noblest thing a man can do is just humbly to receive, and then go amongst others and give.

Citation: Unknown

Topics: Benevolence; Brotherly Love; Compassion; Giving; Good Deeds; Humility; Service; Stewardship

References: Matthew 10:8; John 13:14; Romans 12:8

QUOTATION **320**

All that I am I owe to Jesus Christ, revealed to me in his divine book.

Citation: Unknown

Topics: Bible; Christlikeness; Jesus Christ; Revelation

References: Deuteronomy 8:3; Psalm 119:103; 1 Corinthians 15:10; 1 Peter 2:2

QUOTATION **321**

Anxiety, sickness, suffering, or danger, now and then, with a foregoing of the common conveniences and charities of this life, may make us pause, and cause the spirit to waver, and the soul to sink; but let this be only for a moment. All these are nothing when compared with the glory which shall hereafter be revealed in, and for, us.

Citation: David Livingstone, in an address at Cambridge University

Topics: Doubt; Glory; Healing; Pain; Resurrection; Skepticism; Suffering; Tests; Trials; Trust; Worry

Reference: Romans 8:18

QUOTATION **322**

People talk of the sacrifice I have made in spending so much of my life in Africa. Can that be called a sacrifice which is simply paid back as a small part of a great debt owing to our God, which we can never repay? It is emphatically no sacrifice. Say rather it is a privilege.

Citation: David Livingstone, in an address at Cambridge University

Topics: Evangelism; Missions; Opportunity; Outreach; Sacrifice; Self-denial; Service; Thanksgiving; Worship

Reference: 2 Corinthians 5:20

ST. JUSTIN MARTYR
APOLOGIST AND MARTYR (100 – 165)

QUOTATION 323

We pray for our enemies; we seek to persuade those who hate us without cause to live conformably to the goodly precepts of Christ, that they may become partakers with us of the joyful hope of blessings from God, the Lord of all.

Citation: St. Justin Martyr, *First Apology*

Topics: Compassion; Enemies; Intercession; Mercy; Prayer

Reference: Luke 6:27 – 31

QUOTATION 324

You can kill us but not hurt us.

Citation: St. Justin Martyr, *First Apology*

Topics: Enemies; Eternal Life; Evil; God's Sovereignty; Heaven; Hope; Martyrdom; Persecution; Victory

Reference: John 11:25 – 26

QUOTATION 325

Wherein is it possible for us, wicked and impious creatures, to be justified, except in the only Son of God? O sweet reconciliation! O untraceable ministry! O unlooked-for blessing! That the wickedness of many should be hidden in one godly and righteous man, and the righteousness of one justify a host of sinners!

Citation: Unknown

Topics: Atonement; Grace; Jesus Christ; Justification; Mercy; Reconciliation; Redemption; Righteousness; Salvation

Reference: 2 Corinthians 5:21

Though we are beheaded, and crucified, and exposed to beasts and chains and fire and all other forms of torture, it is plain that we do not forsake the confession of our faith, but the more things of this kind which happen to us the more are there others who become believers and truly religious through the name of Jesus.

Citation: Unknown

Topics: Enemies; Evangelism; Evil; Influence; Martyrdom; Overcoming; Persecution; Spiritual Warfare; Strength; Suffering

Reference: 1 Peter 5:6–11

JOHN R. MOTT

AMERICAN MISSIONARY AND LEADER OF THE YMCA AND WORLD STUDENT CHRISTIAN FEDERATION (1865–1955)

QUOTATION **327**

There is no subject more inspiring than the subject of world missions. No subject more broadening; it embraces all mankind. No subject more deepening; it takes us down to the very depths of the designs of God. Surely no subject more elevating. I can think of nothing that so lifts a man out of himself.

Citation: John R. Mott, in an address at Princeton Theological Seminary

Topics: Evangelism; Humility; Individualism; Missions; Self-centeredness; Witness

Reference: Matthew 28:18–20

QUOTATION **328**

The greatest hindrances to the evangelization of the world are those within the church.

Citation: John R. Mott, *The Evangelization of the World in This Generation*

Topics: Church; Evangelism; Missions; Outreach

References: Matthew 28:18–20; Acts 15:1–21

I never knew a man to overcome a bad habit gradually.

> **Citation:** Unknown
>
> **Topics:** Conversion; Maturity; Repentance; Sanctification; Self-denial; Spiritual Growth
>
> **Reference:** Luke 19:8 – 9

D. T. NILES

SRI LANKAN MISSIONARY AND THEOLOGIAN (1908 – 70)

QUOTATION **330**

Hurry means that we gather impressions but have no experiences, that we collect acquaintances but make no friends, that we attend meetings but experience no encounter. We must recover eternity if we are to find time, and eternity is what Jesus came to restore. For without it, there can be no charity.

> **Citation:** D. T. Niles, at Scotland's Warrack Lectures (1958)
>
> **Topics:** Busyness; Distractions; Eternity; Priorities; Recreation; Sabbath; Solitude; Spiritual Disciplines
>
> **References:** Ecclesiastes 3:11; Galatians 5:22 – 23; Ephesians 3:16 – 19; 5:15 – 16; Philippians 4:6 – 7

ST. PATRICK

IRISH MISSIONARY AND PATRON SAINT OF IRELAND (387 – 461)

QUOTATION **331**

> God's might to direct me,
> God's power to protect me,
> God's wisdom for learning,
> God's eye for discerning,
> God's ear for my hearing,
> God's Word for my clearing.

Citation: St. Patrick, in his poem "The Guardsman's Cry"

Topics: Bible; Devotional Life; Direction; God's Sovereignty; Guidance; Power; Providence; Provision; Wisdom

References: Psalms 23:5; 31:19; Isaiah 25:9; Matthew 23:37

QUOTATION 332

I was like a stone lying in deep mud, but he that is mighty lifted me up and placed me on top of the wall.

Citation: St. Patrick, *Declaration*

Topics: Atonement; Deliverance; Grace; Jesus Christ; Redemption; Worth

Reference: Psalm 40:2

LEONARD RAVENHILL
BRITISH EVANGELIST (1907–94)

QUOTATION 333

We never pray for folks we gossip about, and we never gossip about the folk for whom we pray!

Citation: Leonard Ravenhill, *Why Revival Tarries*

Topics: Caring; Gossip; Intercession; Judging Others; Prayer; Relationships; Tongue; Words

References: Ephesians 6:18; Colossians 1:3; 1 Timothy 2:1; 5:13; James 5:16

QUOTATION 334

A man may study because his brain is hungry for knowledge, even Bible knowledge. But he prays because his soul is hungry for God.

Citation: Unknown

Topics: Bible; Bible Study; Experiencing God; Prayer; Soul; Spiritual Disciplines

References: Psalms 63:1–8; 105:3–4

ROBERT E. SPEER
AMERICAN MISSION LEADER (1867 – 1947)

QUOTATION 335

If one can be certain that his principles are right, he need not worry about the consequences.

> **Citation:** Unknown
>
> **Topics:** Character; Consequences; Convictions; Dedication; Integrity; Motives; Witness
>
> **Reference:** Romans 12:7

QUOTATION 336

I do not see any disloyalty to the past in believing that God means the future to be better than it. Unless the past has made ready for a better future, the past was a bad past.

> **Citation:** Robert E. Speer, *Honoring the Past*
>
> **Topics:** Future; Hope; Past; Redemption; Vision
>
> **Reference:** Philippians 3:12 – 4:1

J. HUDSON TAYLOR
BRITISH MISSIONARY TO CHINA (1832 – 1905)

QUOTATION 337

God had looked for a man weak enough, and he found me.

> **Citation:** J. Hudson Taylor, when asked why he was used of the Lord so greatly in China
>
> **Topics:** Calling; Mission; Missions; Self-worth; Strength; Weakness
>
> **References:** 1 Samuel 15:29; 1 Corinthians 1:26 – 31; 2 Corinthians 12:8 – 10

QUOTATION 338

God's work, done in God's way, will never lack God's supply.

> **Citation:** Unknown
>
> **Topics:** Calling; God; Mission; Missions; Provision; Work
>
> **References:** Matthew 6:33; Philippians 4:19

QUOTATION 339

Do not have your concert first, then tune your instrument afterwards. Begin the day with the Word of God and prayer, and get first of all in harmony with him.

> **Citation:** Unknown
>
> **Topics:** Bible; Devotional Life; Experiencing God; Prayer; Self-discipline; Spiritual Disciplines
>
> **References:** Psalm 5:3; 1 Timothy 4:7

QUOTATION 340

I look upon foreign missionaries as the scaffolding around a rising building. The sooner it can be dispensed with, the better; or rather, the sooner it can be transferred to other places, to serve the same temporary use, the better.

> **Citation:** Hudson Taylor, in a letter to his parents about his work in China
>
> **Topics:** Focus; Ministry; Missions; Outreach; Vision
>
> **References:** Psalm 22:27; Isaiah 55:5; Mark 4:30–32

QUOTATION 341

I am more than ever convinced that if we were to take the direction of our Master and the assurances he gave to his first disciples more fully as our guide, we should find them to be just as suited to our times as to those in which they were originally given.

> **Citation:** J. Hudson Taylor, *The Call to Service*
>
> **Topics:** Great Commission; Ministry; Teachability; Trust
>
> **References:** Matthew 5:13–16; 28:16–20

QUOTATION 342

It is a solemn and most momentous truth that our every act in this present life—and our every omission too—has a direct and important bearing both on our own future welfare, and on that of others.

Citation: J. Hudson Taylor, *The Call to Service*

Topics: Community; Evangelism; Missions; Witness

References: Matthew 7:13–29; Galatians 6:9–10

QUOTATION 343

Do not Christians often really feel, and also act, as though it was incumbent upon them to *begin* with, "Give us this day our daily bread," virtually concluding with, "If consistent with this, may thy name be hallowed too"?

Citation: J. Hudson Taylor, *The Call to Service*

Topics: Greed; Humility; Prayer; Priorities; Worship

References: Matthew 6:5–15; Luke 11:1–13

SAMUEL ZWEMER
AMERICAN MISSIONARY TO ARABIC COUNTRIES (1867–1952)

QUOTATION 344

The unoccupied fields of the world await those who are willing to be lonely for the sake of Christ.

Citation: Samuel Zwemer, *The Unoccupied Mission Fields of Africa and Asia*

Topics: Calling; Christian Life; Commitment; Loneliness; Missions

References: Matthew 9:35–38; Luke 10:1–2

PART 5: ILLUMINATING WORDS
FROM POETS AND MYSTICS

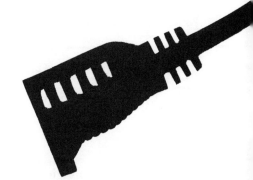

ABBA AGATHON
DESERT FATHER (THIRD CENTURY AD)

QUOTATION 345

There is no labor greater than praying to God. For every time a man wants to pray, his enemies, the demons, try to prevent him; for they know that nothing obstructs them so much as prayer to God.

Citation: Abba Agathon, when asked by his brethren which activity requires the greatest effort

Topics: Prayer; Satan; Self-discipline; Spiritual Warfare

References: Matthew 7:7 – 12; Luke 18:1 – 8

QUOTATION 346

If an angry man raises the dead, God is still displeased with his anger.

Citation: Unknown

Topics: Anger; Obedience; Perfection

References: Matthew 7:21 – 23; Luke 16:10; 1 Corinthians 13; 1 Timothy 3:1 – 13

DANTE ALIGHIERI
ITALIAN POET (1265 – 1321)

QUOTATION 347

O conscience, upright and stainless, how bitter a sting to thee is a little fault!

Citation: Dante Alighieri, *The Divine Comedy*

Topics: Conscience; Guilt; Purity; Sin

References: Romans 7:7 – 25; 1 Corinthians 8:9 – 13

ST. ANTHONY OF EGYPT
EGYPTIAN SAINT AND DESERT FATHER (251 – 356)

QUOTATION **348**

A time is coming when men will go mad, and when they see someone who is not mad, they will attack him, saying, "You are mad; you are not like us."

Citation: St. Anthony, *Sayings of the Desert Fathers*

Topics: Character; Conflict; Division; Persecution; World

Reference: 2 Timothy 4:3 – 5

JOHANN SEBASTIAN BACH
GERMAN COMPOSER AND MUSICIAN (1685 – 1750)

QUOTATION **349**

Where there is devotional music, God with his grace is always present.

Citation: J. S. Bach, written in the margins of his Bible next to 2 Chronicles 5:13 – 14

Topics: Devotional Life; Grace; Music; Praise; Worship

References: Psalms 92; 95; 98; 1 Corinthians 14:26; Ephesians 5:19; Colossians 3:16

QUOTATION **350**

The aim and final end of all music should be none other than the glory of God and the refreshment of the soul.

Citation: Unknown

Topics: Entertainment; God's Glory; Music; Praise; Purpose; Worship

References: Psalms 92; 95; 98; 1 Corinthians 10:31; 14:26; Ephesians 5:19; Colossians 3:16

ST. BERNARD OF CLAIRVAUX
FRENCH ABBOT (1090 – 1153)

QUOTATION 351

There are four stages of growth in Christian maturity: (1) Love of self for self's sake; (2) Love of God for self's sake; (3) Love of God for God's sake; (4) Love of self for God's sake.

> **Citation:** Unknown
>
> **Topics:** Christian Life; Christlikeness; Love; Maturity; Spiritual Growth
>
> **References:** 1 Corinthians 13; Ephesians 4:15; Philippians 2:1 – 11

QUOTATION 352

What we love we shall grow to resemble.

> **Citation:** Unknown
>
> **Topics:** Change; Christlikeness; Growth; Holiness; Love; Sanctification
>
> **References:** Deuteronomy 6:1 – 9; Matthew 22:34 – 40; Mark 12:28 – 31

QUOTATION 353

It is no great thing to be humble when you are brought low; but to be humble when you are praised is a great and rare attainment.

> **Citation:** Unknown
>
> **Topics:** Arrogance; Humility; Perspective; Praise; Pride
>
> **References:** Matthew 18:1 – 6; Mark 10:35 – 45

WENDELL BERRY
AMERICAN POET AND WRITER (1934 –)

QUOTATION 354

Don't own so much clutter that you will be relieved to see your house catch fire.

> **Citation:** Unknown

Topics: Materialism; Money; Possessions; Simplicity
Reference: Proverbs 13:4

WILLIAM BLAKE
BRITISH POET (1757 – 1827)

QUOTATION 355

It is easier to forgive an enemy than to forgive a friend.

> **Citation:** William Blake, Jerusalem: The Emanation of the Giant Albion
> **Topics:** Enemies; Forgiveness; Friendship; Mercy; Relationships
> **References:** Matthew 18:15 – 35; 2 Corinthians 2:5 – 11

QUOTATION 356

A truth that's told with bad intent beats all the lies you can invent.

> **Citation:** William Blake, in his poem "The Pickering Manuscript"
> **Topics:** Character; Deceit; Hostility; Malice; Motives; Truth
> **References:** 1 Corinthians 13:1 – 8; Philippians 1:12 – 30

QUOTATION 357

Great things are done when men and mountains meet.

> **Citation:** Unknown
> **Topics:** Obstacles; Overcoming; Prayer; Trust
> **References:** Matthew 17:14 – 23; 21:18 – 22; Mark 11:20 – 25

ST. BONAVENTURE
ITALIAN MYSTIC, THEOLOGIAN, AND PHILOSOPHER (1221–74)

QUOTATION 358

Something may appear to be good, but in reality it destroys some greater good and opens the door for more obvious evils.

> **Citation:** Unknown
>
> **Topics:** Evil; Sin; Temptation
>
> **References:** Matthew 23:27; 2 Corinthians 5:12; 10:7

QUOTATION 359

When you are too sure of yourself, you are less on guard against the Enemy. Be alert, therefore, for the Devil, who, if he can claim even one hair of your head, will lose no time in making a braid of it.

> **Citation:** Unknown
>
> **Topics:** Arrogance; Devil; Evil; Foolishness; Overconfidence; Pride
>
> **References:** Ephesians 6:12; James 4:7; 1 Peter 5:8

ELIZABETH BARRETT BROWNING
VICTORIAN POET (1806–61)

QUOTATION 360

Earth's crammed with heaven, and every common bush afire with God; but only he who sees takes off his shoes—the rest sit round it and pluck blackberries.

> **Citation:** Elizabeth Barrett Browning, *Aurora Leigh*
>
> **Topics:** Awe; Creation; Creator; Discernment; Distractions; Experiencing God; Heaven; Holiness; Vision; Worship
>
> **References:** Exodus 3:5; Romans 1:20

ST. JOHN CASSIAN
SCYTHIAN THEOLOGIAN AND MYSTIC (c. 360–435)

QUOTATION **361**

It is a bigger miracle to be patient and refrain from anger than it is to control the demons which fly through the air.

Citation: Unknown

Topics: Anger; Demons; Patience; Self-control

References: Genesis 4:1–8; Exodus 20:13; Proverbs 29:8; Matthew 5:21–26

EDGAR DEGAS
FRENCH ARTIST (1834–1917)

QUOTATION **362**

A painting requires a little mystery, some vagueness, some fantasy. When you always make your meaning perfectly plain, you end up boring people.

Citation: Unknown

Topics: Knowledge; Mind; Mysteries

Reference: Matthew 13:1–23

EMILY DICKINSON
AMERICAN POET (1830–86)

QUOTATION **363**

The soul should always stand ajar.

Citation: Emily Dickinson, in her poem "The Soul Should Always Stand Ajar"

Topics: Discernment; Soul; Spiritual Perception; Vulnerability

References: Deuteronomy 6:5; 1 Chronicles 22:19; Proverbs 24:14; Matthew 22:37; Mark 12:30; Luke 10:27

To live is so startling, it leaves but little room for other occupations.

> **Citation:** Emily Dickinson, in a letter to a friend, T. W. Higginson
>
> **Topics:** Awe; Life; Meaning; Purpose; Wonder
>
> **Reference:** Luke 10:38–42

JOHN DONNE
BRITISH POET (1572–1631)

QUOTATION **365**

O what a giant is man when he fights against himself, and what a dwarf when he needs or exercises his own assistance for himself.

> **Citation:** John Donne, *Devotions upon Emergent Occasions*
>
> **Topics:** Overcoming; Pride; Self-centeredness; Suffering
>
> **References:** Job 15:20; Psalm 107:17; Proverbs 13:15; Romans 2:9

QUOTATION **366**

Sleep with clean hands, either kept clean all day by integrity or washed clean at night by repentance.

> **Citation:** John Donne, in a sermon for Lent
>
> **Topics:** Confession; Integrity; Prayer; Repentance; Sleep
>
> **References:** Isaiah 1:15–17; Acts 22:16; 2 Corinthians 7:1

JOHANNES ECKHART
GERMAN THEOLOGIAN, PHILOSOPHER, AND MYSTIC (c. 1260–c. 1328)

QUOTATION **367**

God is like a person who clears his throat while hiding and so gives himself away.

> **Citation:** Unknown

Topics: Experiencing God; Incarnation; Mysteries; Revelation

References: Psalm 19; John 1:1–18; Romans 1:18–20

T. S. ELIOT
BRITISH POET (1888–1965)

QUOTATION 368

Tradition itself is not enough; it must be perpetually criticized and brought up to date under the supervision of what I call orthodoxy.

Citation: T. S. Eliot, *After Strange Gods*

Topics: Guidance; Orthodoxy; Religion; Tradition; Truth

Reference: 2 Timothy 3:10–4:8

QUOTATION 369

And the end of all our exploring
Will be to arrive where we started
And know the place for the first time.

Citation: T. S. Eliot, "Little Gidding"

Topics: Doctrine; Eternal Life; Knowledge; Meaning; Revelation; Searching; Significance; Theology

Reference: Revelation 21:1–7; 22:1–6

QUOTATION 370

Where is the life we have lost in living?
Where is the wisdom we have lost in knowledge?
Where is the knowledge we have lost in information?

Citation: T. S. Eliot, "Choruses from The Rock"

Topics: Knowledge; Mind; Technology; Wisdom

Reference: Philippians 1:3–11

QUOTATION **371**

You, have you built well, have you forgotten the cornerstone?
Talking of right relations of men, but not of relations of men to God.

Citation: T. S. Eliot, "Choruses from The Rock"

Topics: Commitment; Dedication; Double-mindedness; Priorities; Worldliness

References: Psalm 118:22; Isaiah 28:16; 1 Peter 2:4–12

QUOTATION **372**

The church must be forever building, and always decaying, and always being restored.

Citation: T. S. Eliot, "Choruses from The Rock"

Topics: Change; Church; Culture; Influence; Transformation

References: Matthew 5:13–16; 28:16–20; Revelation 3:1–6

QUOTATION **373**

I had far rather walk, as I do, in daily terror of eternity, than feel that this was only a child's game in which all the contestants would get equally worthless prizes in the end.

Citation: Unknown

Topics: Eternity; Fear of God; Final Judgment; Holy Spirit; Lifestyle; Meaning; Purpose; Rewards

References: Matthew 7:13–29; 25:14–30; Galatians 6:16–26

RALPH WALDO EMERSON
AMERICAN POET AND ESSAYIST (1803–82)

QUOTATION **374**

People wish to be settled; only as far as they are unsettled is there any hope for them.

Citation: Ralph Waldo Emerson, in his essay "Circles"

Topics: Apathy; Change; Comfort; Complacency; Convenience; Repentance; Security; Transformation

References: Proverbs 27:1; 1 Corinthians 15:34; Ephesians 5:15–16; Hebrews 11:8–19

QUOTATION 375

Money often costs too much.

Citation: Unknown

Topics: Greed; Idolatry; Materialism; Money; Stewardship

References: Matthew 6:19–24; Hebrews 13:5

QUOTATION 376

Do not go where the path may be. Go instead where there is no path, and leave a trail.

Citation: Unknown

Topics: Courage; Fear; Influence; Leadership; Vision

References: 1 Samuel 17:20–32; Daniel 6:1–23; 2 Timothy 1:3–12

QUOTATION 377

What lies behind us and what lies before us are tiny matters compared to what lies within us.

Citation: Unknown

Topics: Character; Focus; Hope; Overcoming; Strength

References: John 14:17; Romans 8:9; 1 Corinthians 3:16

QUOTATION 378

Unless you try to do something beyond what you have already mastered, you will never grow.

Citation: Unknown

Topics: Goals; Growth; Risk; Teachability

References: 1 Corinthians 9:25; Hebrews 6:1; 2 Peter 3:18

It is easy in the world to live after the world's opinion. It is easy in solitude to live after one's own. But the great man is he who, in the midst of the crowd, keeps with perfect sweetness the independence of his character.

Citation: Unknown

Topics: Character; Integrity; Lifestyle; Strength; Worldliness

References: Psalm 57:7; Matthew 5:13; 10:22; Luke 1:6

ST. EPHREM
SYRIAN THEOLOGIAN AND MYSTIC (FOURTH CENTURY AD)

QUOTATION **380**

A blossom is the beginning of fruit bearing, and submission the beginning of humility.

Citation: Unknown

Topics: Humility; Pride; Submission

References: Matthew 18:1–6; Mark 10:35–45; Ephesians 5:21; James 3:13–18

EVAGRIUS OF PONTUS
CAPPADOCIAN MONK AND ASCETIC (c. 345–399)

QUOTATION **381**

The further the soul advances, the greater are the adversaries against which it must contend.

Citation: Unknown

Topics: Enemies; Evil; Satan; Soul; Spiritual Warfare; Temptation

Reference: Ephesians 6:10–20

QUOTATION **382**

Blessed are you, if the struggle grows fierce against you at the time of prayer.

Citation: Unknown

Topics: Blessings; Prayer; Spiritual Warfare; Suffering

References: Romans 7:23; Ephesians 6:12; 1 Timothy 1:18–19

FREDERICK W. FABER
BRITISH HYMN WRITER AND THEOLOGIAN (1814–63)

QUOTATION 383

God is whispering to us well-nigh incessantly. Whenever the sounds of the world die out in the soul, or sink low, then we hear these whisperings of God. He is always whispering to us, only we do not always hear, because of the noise, hurry, and distraction which life causes as it rushes on.

Citation: Unknown

Topics: Busyness; Distractions; Experiencing God; Hearing God; Listening; Sabbath; Solitude; Spiritual Disciplines; Spiritual Perception

References: 1 Kings 19:11–13; Psalms 37:7; 46:10; 131:1–2; Isaiah 30:15; Lamentations 3:26

FRANÇOIS FÉNELON
FRENCH ROMAN CATHOLIC THEOLOGIAN, POET, WRITER, AND MYSTIC (1651–1715)

QUOTATION 384

Self-denial has its place in a Christian's life, but God doesn't ask you to choose what is most painful to you. If you followed this path, you would soon ruin your health, reputation, business, and friendships.

Self-denial consists of bearing patiently all those things that God allows to pass into your life. If you don't refuse anything that comes in God's order, you are tasting of the cross of Jesus Christ.

Citation: François Fénelon, *The Seeking Heart*

Topics: Fasting; Patience; Sacrifice; Self-denial; Suffering

References: Matthew 16:24–26; 2 Corinthians 1:5–7; 1 Peter 1:6–7

QUOTATION 385

Learn to sabotage every plan your self-nature presents to you.... When you are faithful in this way, it is almost as good for your body as it is for your spirit and soul.

Citation: François Fénelon, *The Seeking Heart*

Topics: God's Will; Human Will; Pride; Sacrifice; Self-denial; Self-centeredness; Submission

References: 1 Corinthians 9:24–27; 10:33; James 4:7

QUOTATION 386

How free you are when you do all things simply to the glory of God.... There is nothing simpler or more faithful than learning to accept the will of God apart from your personal taste—your likes and dislikes and impulses.

Citation: François Fénelon, *The Seeking Heart*

Topics: God's Glory; God's Will; Human Will; Obedience; Submission

References: Psalm 90:12; 1 Corinthians 7:29–31; 10:31; Ephesians 5:15–16

QUOTATION 387

You must violently resist the tides of the world. Violently give up all that holds you back from God. Violently turn your will over to God to do his will alone.

Citation: François Fénelon, *The Seeking Heart*

Topics: God's Will; Human Will; Passion; Submission; Worldliness

References: Matthew 5:29–30; 11:12; Colossians 3:2; 2 Timothy 2:4; Titus 2:12; 1 John 2:15

QUOTATION 388

When the torrential floods of daily business sweep you away, just let yourself be carried off with no regret. Don't you know you will find God in this torrent, too?

Citation: François Fénelon, *The Seeking Heart*

Topics: Busyness; Experiencing God; Peace; Trust; Work

Reference: Philippians 2:12–13

QUOTATION **389**

I would have every minister of the gospel address his audience with the zeal of a friend, with the generous energy of a father, and with the exuberant affection of a mother.

> **Citation:** Unknown
>
> **Topics:** Affection; Compassion; Friendship; Passion; Preaching
>
> **References:** Matthew 5:13–16; Luke 8:16–18; 10:25–37

QUOTATION **390**

There is but one way in which God should be loved, and that is to take no step except with him and for him, and to follow, with a generous self-abandonment, everything which he requires.

> **Citation:** François Fénelon, *The Many Aspects of Self-Denial: Full of Self, Empty of God*
>
> **Topics:** Commitment; Discipleship; God's Will; Guidance; Self-denial; Wholehearted Devotion
>
> **References:** Deuteronomy 6:5; Matthew 22:37; Mark 12:30; Luke 10:27

QUOTATION **391**

We are not masters of our own feeling, but we are by God's grace masters of our consent.

> **Citation:** François Fénelon, in a letter to persons struggling with challenges
>
> **Topics:** Decisions; God's Will; Human Will; Self-control; Temptation
>
> **References:** Proverbs 1:10; 1 Corinthians 10:13; Ephesians 6:13

QUOTATION **392**

Don't worry about the future—worry quenches the work of grace within you. The future belongs to God. He is in charge of all things. Never second-guess him.

> **Citation:** Unknown
>
> **Topics:** Future; God's Sovereignty; Grace; Submission; Trust; Worry
>
> **References:** Proverbs 3:5; Matthew 6:25; Luke 21:34; 1 Peter 5:7

RICHARD J. FOSTER
AMERICAN THEOLOGIAN, WRITER, AND MYSTIC (1942–)

QUOTATION 393

Our Adversary majors in three things: noise, hurry, and crowds. If he can keep us engaged in "muchness" and "manyness," he will rest satisfied.

Citation: Richard J. Foster, *Celebration of Discipline*

Topics: Busyness; Distractions; Focus; Sabbath; Satan; Solitude; Spiritual Disciplines; Spiritual Warfare; Temptation; World

Reference: Luke 10:38–42

QUOTATION 394

Goals are discovered, not made.

Citation: Richard J. Foster, *Celebration of Discipline*

Topics: Direction; Goals; Guidance; Planning; Vision

References: Matthew 6:10; 26:39; Mark 14:36; Luke 22:42

QUOTATION 395

The desperate need today is not for a greater number of intelligent people, or gifted people, but for deep people.

Citation: Richard J. Foster, *Celebration of Discipline*

Topics: Bible Study; Devotional Life; Spiritual Disciplines; Spiritual Formation

Reference: 1 Corinthians 2:6–16

QUOTATION 396

For the Christian, the bottom line can never be the bottom line.

Citation: Richard J. Foster, *Money, Sex, and Power*

Topics: Business; Love of Money; Materialism; Priorities

References: Proverbs 16:8; 22:16; Matthew 16:26

QUOTATION 397

Love is not communicated in the big event but in the small acts of kindness.

Citation: Richard J. Foster, *Money, Sex, and Power*

Topics: Compassion; Kindness; Love; Marriage; Service

References: Romans 12:10; 1 Corinthians 13:4; Ephesians 4:32

QUOTATION 398

Too many of us allow the late news to dictate what we think about when we go to bed.

Citation: Richard J. Foster, in an interview with *Christianity Today*

Topics: Devotional Life; Focus; Media; Prayer; Thoughts; Worldview

References: 1 Chronicles 16:11; Ephesians 6:18

ROBERT FROST
AMERICAN POET (1874 – 1963)

QUOTATION 399

Home is the place where, when you have to go there, they have to take you in.

Citation: Robert Frost, in his poem "The Death of the Hired Man"

Topics: Community; Family; Hospitality; Love; Security

References: Psalm 133:1; Matthew 18:21; Luke 15:22

QUOTATION 400

I never dared be radical when young for fear it would make me conservative when old.

Citation: Robert Frost, in his poem "Precaution"

Topics: Courage; Passion; Perspective

References: Ecclesiastes 9:10; Amos 6:1

In three words I can sum up everything I've learned about life: it goes on.

Citation: Unknown

Topics: Hope; Life; Patience; Perseverance; Perspective

References: Job 17:9; Ecclesiastes 7:8; Hebrews 10:36

JOHN GAY
BRITISH POET (1685 – 1732)

QUOTATION **402**

Shadow owes its birth to light.

Citation: John Gay, "The Persian, the Sun, and the Cloud"

Topics: Evil; Goodness; Hope; Perspective; Theodicy

Reference: Genesis 3:1 – 8

ST. GREGORY OF NYSSA
CAPPADOCIAN BISHOP AND MYSTIC (c. 335 – 394)

QUOTATION **403**

The soul, slipping at every point from what cannot be grasped, becomes dizzy and perplexed and returns once again to what is connatural to it, content now to know merely this about the Transcendent: that it is completely different from the nature of the things that the soul knows.

Citation: St. Gregory, in his commentary on Ecclesiastes

Topics: Experiencing God; God; Limitations; Mysteries; Soul

References: Deuteronomy 29:29; Job 11:7; Psalm 97:2; Isaiah 55:8 – 9

QUOTATION **404**

The one limit of virtue is the absence of a limit.

Citation: St. Gregory, *The Life of Moses*

Topics: Character; Goodness; Limitations; Integrity; Maturity; Spiritual Growth; Virtue

References: Jeremiah 32:17; Matthew 17:20; Ephesians 3:16–21

QUOTATION 405

He who gives you the day will also give you the things necessary for the day.

Citation: St. Gregory, in his sermon "The Lord's Prayer"

Topics: Blessings; Daily Bread; Faith; God's Sovereignty; Needs; Provision; Trust

References: Matthew 6:25–34; Philippians 4:19

NATHANIEL HAWTHORNE
AMERICAN WRITER (1804–64)

QUOTATION 406

Our Creator would never have made such lovely days, and have given us the deep hearts to enjoy them, above and beyond all thought, unless we were meant to be immortal.

Citation: Nathaniel Hawthrone, *The Old Manse*

Topics: Creation; Creator; Eternal Life; Eternity; Heaven; Hope; Immortality; Joy; Pleasure; Resurrection; Worth

Reference: Psalm 16:11; Ecclesiastes 3:11

GEORGE HERBERT
BRITISH POET (1593–1633)

QUOTATION 407

God strikes with his finger, and not with his arm.

Citation: George Herbert, in his poem "Jacula Prudentum"

Topics: Gentleness; God's Sovereignty; Grace; Mercy; Power

References: Psalm 18:35; Isaiah 40:11; 2 Corinthians 10:1

QUOTATION **408**

Death used to be an executioner, but the gospel has made him just a gardener.

> Citation: Unknown
>
> Topics: Death; Eternal Life; Gospel; Hope; Resurrection
>
> References: John 11:25–26; 1 Corinthians 15:50–57; Hebrews 2:14–15

VICTOR HUGO
FRENCH POET AND WRITER (1802–85)

QUOTATION **409**

There is one spectacle greater than the sea: that is the sky. There is one spectacle greater than the sky: that is the interior of the soul.

> Citation: Victor Hugo, *Les Misérables*
>
> Topics: Awe; Beauty; Creation; Mysteries; Soul; Worth
>
> References: Genesis 1:27; Job 32:8; Ecclesiastes 12:7

QUOTATION **410**

To lie a little is not possible; whoever lies, lies a whole lie.

> Citation: Victor Hugo, *Les Misérables*
>
> Topics: Deceit; Lying; Speech; Tongue; Vices
>
> References: Leviticus 19:11; Psalm 101:7; Proverbs 12:19; Colossians 3:9

ST. IGNATIUS OF LOYOLA
SPANISH ROMAN CATHOLIC PRIEST AND MYSTIC (1491–1556)

QUOTATION **411**

The Devil cannot take from the soul the light of faith: he, however, removes the light of consideration, so that the soul may not reflect on what it believes.

> Citation: St. Ignatius of Loyola, *Spiritual Exercises, Meditation I*

Topics: Ignorance; Light; Prayer; Reflection; Satan; Soul; Spiritual Blindness

References: Psalm 119:148; Matthew 13:19; Mark 4:15; 2 Corinthians 4:4; 2 Timothy 2:7

QUOTATION 412

Teach us, Lord, to serve you as you deserve, to give and not to count the cost, to fight and not to heed the wounds, to toil and not to seek for rest, to labor and not to ask for any reward save that of knowing that we do your will.

Citation: St. Ignatius of Loyola, from his recorded prayers

Topics: Commitment; Cost; Discipleship; Rewards; Service; Submission

References: Deuteronomy 10:12; Psalm 2:11; Acts 20:19; Ephesians 6:7; Hebrews 12:28

ST. JOHN OF THE CROSS
SPANISH MYSTIC (1542–91)

QUOTATION 413

What does it profit you to give God one thing if he asks of you another? Consider what it is God wants, and then do it. You will as a result better satisfy your heart than with that toward which you yourself are inclined.

Citation: St. John of the Cross, *The Collected Works of St. John of the Cross*

Topics: Calling; Disobedience; God's Will; Hearing God; Human Will; Obedience; Submission

References: 1 Samuel 15:22; Matthew 23:23–24; Acts 13:22

QUOTATION 414

If an experience fails to engender humility, charity, mortification, holy simplicity, and silence ... of what value is it?

Citation: St. John of the Cross, *Ascent of Mt. Carmel*

Topics: Godliness; Holiness; Humility; Love; Spiritual Disciplines

Reference: 1 Timothy 4:7

QUOTATION 415

Faith and love are like the blind man's guides. They will lead you along a path unknown to you, to the place where God is hidden.

> Citation: St. John of the Cross, *The Spiritual Canticle*
> Topics: Experiencing God; Faith; Love; Mysteries
> References: 1 Corinthians 13:13; Galatians 5:6

QUOTATION 416

The soul enters the night of spirit in order to journey to God in pure faith, which is the means whereby the soul is united to God.

> Citation: St. John of the Cross, *Dark Night of the Soul*
> Topics: Faith; Pain; Purity; Soul; Suffering; Tests
> References: Hebrews 11; James 1:2–4

KIMBERLY JOHNSON
AMERICAN POET (1971–)

QUOTATION 417

Never ruin an apology with an excuse.

> Citation: Unknown
> Topics: Confession; Excuses; Reconciliation
> References: Matthew 18:15–18; 1 John 1:8

SAMUEL JOHNSON
BRITISH POET (1709–84)

QUOTATION 418

There can be no friendship without confidence, and no confidence without integrity.

> Citation: Samuel Johnson, *The Idler*

Topics: Brotherly Love; Character; Community; Friendship; Integrity; Relationships

Reference: Proverbs 17:9

QUOTATION **419**

He that would pass the latter part of his life with honor and decency, must, when he is young, consider that he shall one day be old; and remember, when he is old, that he has once been young.

Citation: Samuel Johnson, *The Rambler*

Topics: Aging; Maturity; Perspective; Self-examination; Time

References: Psalm 92:12; Ecclesiastes 12:1; Ephesians 5:15 – 16

THOMAS à KEMPIS
ROMAN CATHOLIC MONK AND WRITER (c. 1380 – 1471)

QUOTATION **420**

Those who stand highest in the esteem of men are most exposed to grievous peril, since they often have too great a confidence in themselves.

Citation: Thomas à Kempis, *The Imitation of Christ*

Topics: Arrogance; Pride; Self-centeredness; Self-righteousness

Reference: Proverbs 16:18

QUOTATION **421**

Be not angry that you cannot make others as you wish them to be, since you cannot make yourself as you wish to be.

Citation: Thomas à Kempis, *The Imitation of Christ*

Topics: Brotherly Love; Compassion; Judging Others; Leadership; Mercy; Patience; Spiritual Growth

Reference: Matthew 7:1 – 5

QUOTATION **422**

A humble peasant who serves God is much more pleasing to him than an arrogant academic who neglects his own soul to consider the course of the stars.

Citation: Thomas à Kempis, *The Imitation of Christ*
Topics: Arrogance; Humility; Knowledge; Mind; Pride; Work
References: James 4:6; 1 Peter 5:5

QUOTATION **423**

If the works of God could easily be grasped by human understanding, they could not be called wonderful or too great for words.

Citation: Thomas à Kempis, *The Imitation of Christ*
Topics: Experiencing God; God; God's Glory; Mysteries
References: Psalms 8:3 – 5; 40:5; 139:14; Ecclesiastes 3:11; Isaiah 55:8 – 9

QUOTATION **424**

Jesus now has many lovers of his heavenly kingdom, but few bearers of his cross.

Citation: Thomas à Kempis, *The Imitation of Christ*
Topics: Cross; Discipleship; Jesus Christ; Kingdom; Persecution; Suffering
References: Matthew 10:38; 16:24; Mark 10:21

QUOTATION **425**

If thou bear the cross cheerfully, it will bear thee.

Citation: Thomas à Kempis, *The Imitation of Christ*
Topics: Christian Life; Cross; Discipleship
References: Matthew 10:38; 1 Corinthians 1:18; Galatians 6:14

QUOTATION **426**

For a little reward men make a long journey; for eternal life many will scarce lift a foot once from the ground.

Citation: Thomas à Kempis, *The Imitation of Christ*

Topics: Eternal Life; Rewards; Values

References: Matthew 13:44; 16:26; Luke 18:28 – 30; John 3:36

WILLIAM LAW
BRITISH WRITER AND MYSTIC (1686 – 1761)

QUOTATION 427

Where did we come up with this concept of "spare time," anyway? Is there any time for which we aren't accountable to God? Is there any time during which God doesn't care what you are doing? No Christian has ever had spare time. You may have spare time from labor or necessity, you may stop working and refresh yourself, but no Christian ever had time off from living like a Christian.

Citation: William Law, *A Practical Treatise upon Christian Perfection*

Topics: Christian Life; Entertainment; Responsibility; Rest; Sabbath; Work

References: Psalm 90:12; 1 Corinthians 7:29 – 31; Ephesians 5:15 – 16

QUOTATION 428

If we look to God to supply half our happiness, we can only love him with half our hearts.

Citation: William Law, *A Practical Treatise upon Christian Perfection*

Topics: God; Joy; Love; Wholehearted Devotion

References: Deuteronomy 6:5; 10:12; Isaiah 61:10; 1 Peter 1:8

QUOTATION 429

If you attempt to talk with a dying man about sports or business, he is no longer interested. He now sees other things as more important. People who are dying recognize what we often forget, that we are standing on the brink of another world.

Citation: William Law, *A Practical Treatise upon Christian Perfection*

Topics: Death; Distractions; Eternal Death; Eternal Life; Heaven; Hell; Life; Perspective; Priorities

References: Matthew 16:26; Luke 21:34; Colossians 3:2

BROTHER LAWRENCE
FRENCH MONK AND MYSTIC (c. 1610–91)

QUOTATION **430**

What can God have that gives him greater satisfaction than that a thousand times a day all his creatures should thus pause to withdraw and worship him in the heart.

> **Citation:** Brother Lawrence, *The Practice of the Presence of God*
>
> **Topics:** Devotional Life; Praise; Prayer; Self-discipline; Thanksgiving; Worship
>
> **References:** Psalm 95:6; Matthew 4:10; John 4:23–24; Revelation 14:7

QUOTATION **431**

Let us give our thoughts completely to knowing God. The more one knows him, the more one wants to know him, and since love is measured commonly by knowledge, then, the deeper and more extensive knowledge shall be, so love will be greater, and, if love is great, we shall love him equally in suffering and consolation.

> **Citation:** Brother Lawrence, *The Practice of the Presence of God*
>
> **Topics:** Commitment; Experiencing God; Knowledge; Love
>
> **References:** Proverbs 1:7; Hosea 6:6

QUOTATION **432**

Pain is only intolerable when seen in a distorted light. But when we know it is the hand of a loving God that shapes it all, and that it is our Father who gives us the cup of sorrow to drink, there is no distortion and so no unbearable burden.

> **Citation:** Brother Lawrence, *The Practice of the Presence of God*
>
> **Topics:** Pain; Perspective; Suffering; Tests; Trials; Trust
>
> **References:** Deuteronomy 8:5; Job 5:17; 2 Corinthians 4:17; Hebrews 12:11

1001 QUOTATIONS THAT CONNECT

QUOTATION **433**

The most holy practice, the nearest to daily life, and the most essential for the spiritual life, is the practice of the presence of God, that is to find joy in his divine company and to make it a habit of life, speaking humbly and conversing lovingly with him at all times, every moment, without rule or restriction, above all at times of temptation, distress, dryness, and revulsion, and even of faithlessness and sin.

> **Citation:** Brother Lawrence, *The Practice of the Presence of God*
>
> **Topics:** Fellowship; Prayer; Presence of God; Temptation
>
> **References:** Isaiah 43:2; John 15:4; Ephesians 6:18; 1 Thessalonians 5:17 – 18

QUOTATION **434**

When we are in doubt, God will never fail to give light when we have no other plan than to please him and to act in love for him.

> **Citation:** Brother Lawrence, *The Practice of the Presence of God*
>
> **Topics:** Direction; Doubt; Guidance; Illumination; Love
>
> **References:** Judges 6:17; Matthew 11:3; John 20:25

QUOTATION **435**

We cannot avoid the dangers and the reefs of which this life is full, without the real and constant help of God. Let us ask him for it without ceasing. But how can we ask him without being with him? And how can we be with him without often thinking of him? And how can we often think of him without forming a holy habit of doing so?

> **Citation:** Brother Lawrence, *The Practice of the Presence of God*
>
> **Topics:** Devotional Life; Experiencing God; Godliness; Guidance; Pain; Prayer; Suffering
>
> **References:** 1 Chronicles 16:11; Isaiah 43:2; Ephesians 6:18; 1 Thessalonians 5:17 – 18

QUOTATION **436**

Let us thus think often that our only business in this life is to please God.

> **Citation:** Brother Lawrence, *The Practice of the Presence of God*

Topics: Christian Life; Goals; Pleasing God

References: Deuteronomy 10:12; Micah 6:8; Mark 12:33; 1 Thessalonians 4:1–12

RAMON LLULL
SPANISH WRITER, PHILOSOPHER, AND MYSTIC (c. 1233–1315)

QUOTATION **437**

He who loves not, lives not.

Citation: Unknown

Topics: Life; Love; Risk; Self-denial

Reference: 1 John 4:7–8

EDWIN MARKHAM
AMERICAN POET (1852–1940)

QUOTATION **438**

We have committed the Golden Rule to memory; let us now commit it to life.

Citation: Unknown

Topics: Brotherly Love; Compassion; Golden Rule; Good Deeds; Kindness; Lifestyle

Reference: Matthew 7:12

THOMAS MERTON
ROMAN CATHOLIC WRITER AND MYSTIC (1915–68)

QUOTATION **439**

Hell can be described as a perpetual alienation from our true being, our true self, which is in God.

Citation: Thomas Merton, *New Seeds of Contemplation*

Topics: Alienation; Eternal Death; Eternal Life; Final Judgment; Hell

Reference: Psalm 62:1

QUOTATION **440**

Every moment of every event of every man's life on earth plants something in his soul.

Citation: Thomas Merton, *New Seeds of Contemplation*

Topics: Christian Life; Influence; Soul; Sowing and Reaping

Reference: Psalm 23:3

QUOTATION **441**

Go into the desert not to escape other men but in order to find them in God.

Citation: Thomas Merton, *New Seeds of Contemplation*

Topics: Brotherly Love; Experiencing God; Self-discipline; Solitude

Reference: Luke 1:80

QUOTATION **442**

It is not that someone else is preventing you from living happily; you yourself do not know what you want. Rather than admit this, you prefer that someone is keeping you from exercising your liberty. Who is this? It is you yourself.

Citation: Thomas Merton, *New Seeds of Contemplation*

Topics: Freedom; Joy; Self-examination

References: Isaiah 61:1; Romans 8:21; 2 Corinthians 3:17

QUOTATION **443**

The common life can either make one more of a person or less of a person, depending on whether it is truly common life or merely life in a crowd.

Citation: Thomas Merton, *New Seeds of Contemplation*

Topics: Community; Fellowship; Individualism

References: Acts 2:42–47; 4:34–35

QUOTATION **444**

The Devil is not afraid to preach the will of God provided he can preach it his own way.

Citation: Thomas Merton, *New Seeds of Contemplation*
Topics: Devil; Evil; God's Will; Satan; Spiritual Warfare; Temptation
Reference: Luke 4:9–13

QUOTATION **445**

People are in a hurry to magnify themselves by imitating what is popular — and too lazy to think of anything better.

Citation: Thomas Merton, *New Seeds of Contemplation*
Topics: Creativity; Pride; Self-discipline; Self-exaltation
Reference: Luke 16:15

QUOTATION **446**

To hope is to risk frustration. Therefore, make up your mind to risk frustration.

Citation: Thomas Merton, *New Seeds of Contemplation*
Topics: Convictions; Decisions; Hope; Risk
Reference: Hebrews 11:1

QUOTATION **447**

Love does not give money; it gives itself. If it gives itself first — and a lot of money too — that is all the better. But first it must sacrifice itself.

Citation: Thomas Merton, *Run to the Mountain: The Journals of Thomas Merton*
Topics: Compassion; Giving; Love; Sacrifice; Tithing
References: Matthew 19:21; 1 Corinthians 10:24; Philippians 2:4

QUOTATION **448**

As soon as you are really alone, you are with God.

Citation: Thomas Merton, *Thoughts in Solitude*

1001 QUOTATIONS THAT CONNECT

Topics: Experiencing God; Intimacy; Listening; Meditation; Prayer; Rest; Solitude; Spiritual Disciplines; Worship

References: Psalm 131:2; Jeremiah 29:13; Mark 1:35; Luke 5:16; James 4:8

QUOTATION **449**

Not all men are called to be hermits, but all men need enough silence and solitude in their lives to enable the deep inner voice of their own true self to be heard at least occasionally.

Citation: Thomas Merton, *The Silent Life*

Topics: Devotional Life; Growth; Solitude; Spiritual Disciplines

References: Ecclesiastes 3:7; Amos 5:13; James 1:19

QUOTATION **450**

People don't want to hear any more words. In our mechanical age, all words have become alike.... To say, "God is love," is like saying, "Eat Wheaties."

Citation: Thomas Merton, *The Spring of Contemplation*

Topics: Character; Christlikeness; Evangelism; Example; Godliness; Integrity; Lifestyle; Words; Worldliness

References: Ecclesiastes 10:12; Romans 12:2; 1 Corinthians 11:1; 1 Timothy 4:12; 2 Timothy 3:1 – 2

QUOTATION **451**

To consider persons and events and situations only in the light of their effect upon myself is to live on the doorstep of hell.

Citation: Thomas Merton, *No Man Is an Island*

Topics: Evil; Narcissism; Self-centeredness; Self-exaltation

References: Romans 14:21; 1 Corinthians 10:24; Philippians 2:4

MICHELANGELO
ITALIAN RENAISSANCE ARTIST AND POET (1475–1564)

QUOTATION 452

A true work of art is but a shadow of divine perfection.

Citation: Unknown

Topics: Art; Awe; Beauty; Creation; Creativity; God

References: Deuteronomy 32:4; Psalm 18:30; Ecclesiastes 3:14; Matthew 5:48

QUOTATION 453

Do not fret, for God did not create us to abandon us.

Citation: Unknown

Topics: Creation; Creator; Fear; Guidance; Hope; Presence of God; Security; Trust

References: Matthew 28:20; Hebrews 13:5–6

ABBOT MOSES
DESERT FATHER (TENTH CENTURY AD)

QUOTATION 454

They who are conscious of their own sins have no eyes for the sins of their neighbors.

Citation: Unknown

Topics: Judging Others; Self-examination; Sin

Reference: Matthew 7:1–5

OGDEN NASH
AMERICAN POET (1902–71)

QUOTATION 455

I do not like to get the news because there has never been an era when so many things have been going right for so many of the wrong persons.

> **Citation:** Ogden Nash, The Face Is Familiar
>
> **Topics:** God's Sovereignty; Jealousy; Mysteries; World
>
> **References:** Psalms 7; 12; 13; Habakkuk 1:1–4, 12–17; 3

QUOTATION 456

There is only one way to achieve happiness on this terrestrial ball, and that is to have either a clear conscience or none at all.

> **Citation:** Unknown
>
> **Topics:** Character; Conscience; Guilt; Joy; Purity
>
> **References:** Psalm 40:12; Romans 2:15; 1 Timothy 1:18–19

QUOTATION 457

To keep your marriage brimming,
With love in the loving cup,
Whenever you're wrong admit it,
Whenever you're right, shut up.

> **Citation:** Unknown
>
> **Topics:** Humility; Love; Marriage; Teachability
>
> **References:** Luke 22:42; 1 Corinthians 7:1–7; Hebrews 5:8

WATCHMAN NEE
CHINESE WRITER AND MYSTIC (1903 – 72)

QUOTATION **458**

Alone I cannot serve the Lord effectively, and he will spare no pains to teach me this. He will bring things to an end, allowing doors to close and leaving me ineffectively knocking my head against a wall until I realize that I need the help of the Body as well as of the Lord.

> **Citation:** Watchman Nee, *Normal Christian Life*
>
> **Topics:** Accountability; Church; Community; Fellowship; Individualism; Relationships
>
> **References:** Romans 12:4; 1 Corinthians 12:12; Ephesians 4:12

QUOTATION **459**

God will answer all our questions in one way and one way only—namely, by showing us more of his Son.

> **Citation:** Watchman Nee, *Normal Christian Life*
>
> **Topics:** Christlikeness; Jesus Christ; Maturity; Questions; Revelation
>
> **References:** Matthew 3:17; 16:7; Colossians 3:1 – 17

QUOTATION **460**

I have never met a soul who has set out to satisfy the Lord and has not been satisfied himself.

> **Citation:** Watchman Nee, *Normal Christian Life*
>
> **Topics:** Calling; Contentment; Joy; Obedience; Satisfaction
>
> **References:** Psalm 91:14 – 16; Proverbs 13:25; Isaiah 58:10 – 11

QUOTATION **461**

To have God do his own work through us, even once, is better than a lifetime of human striving.

> **Citation:** Unknown

Topics: Calling; God's Will; Human Will; Service; Submission; Work
References: Matthew 6:10; 26:39; 1 Timothy 4:8 – 10

QUOTATION **462**

Our prayers lay the track down on which God's power can come. Like a mighty locomotive, his power is irresistible, but it cannot reach us without rails.

Citation: Unknown
Topics: Devotional Life; Experiencing God; Intercession; Power; Prayer
References: Psalm 91:15; Isaiah 58:9; Matthew 21:22

KATHLEEN NORRIS
AMERICAN POET AND ESSAYIST (1947 –)

QUOTATION **463**

Perfection, in a Christian sense, means becoming mature enough to give ourselves to others.

Citation: Kathleen Norris, *Amazing Grace*
Topics: Growth; Holiness; Maturity; Perfection; Sacrifice; Servanthood
References: Matthew 5:48; 19:21; John 13:1 – 17

HENRI J. M. NOUWEN
DUTCH-AMERICAN ROMAN CATHOLIC PRIEST, MYSTIC, AND WRITER (1932 – 96)

QUOTATION **464**

The mystery of ministry is that we have been chosen to make our own limited and very conditional love the gateway for the unlimited and unconditional love of God.

Citation: Henri J. M. Nouwen, *In the Name of Jesus*
Topics: Brotherly Love; Compassion; God's Love; Ministry; Unconditional Love
References: John 15:9 – 17; Romans 12:9 – 21; 1 Corinthians 13; 1 John 3:11 – 24; 4:7 – 21

QUOTATION 465

The temptation of power is greatest when intimacy is a threat.

Citation: Henri J. M. Nouwen, *In the Name of Jesus*

Topics: Accountability; Community; Intimacy; Power; Pride

References: Romans 12:10; Philippians 2:1–11

QUOTATION 466

Prayer is not a pious decoration of life but the breath of human existence.

Citation: Henri J. M. Nouwen, *The Wounded Healer*

Topics: Christian Life; Prayer; Spiritual Growth

References: Matthew 6:5–15; 7:7–12; Luke 11:1–13; 18:1–8

QUOTATION 467

Conversion is the individual equivalent of revolution.

Citation: Henri J. M. Nouwen, *The Wounded Healer*

Topics: Calling; Change; Conversion; Growth; Rebirth; Sanctification

Reference: Romans 6; 8; 1 Corinthians 6:9–11; Colossians 3:1–17

QUOTATION 468

For a compassionate man nothing human is alien: no joy and no sorrow, no way of living and no way of dying.

Citation: Henri J. M. Nouwen, *The Wounded Healer*

Topics: Brotherly Love; Caring; Compassion; Death; Empathy; Joy; Pain; Perspective; Suffering

Reference: 2 Corinthians 1:1–11

QUOTATION 469

The emptiness of the past and the future can never be filled with words but only by the presence of a man.

Citation: Henri J. M. Nouwen, *The Wounded Healer*

Topics: Brotherly Love; Community; Future; Hope; Incarnation; Ministry; Past
References: Ecclesiastes 4:9 – 12; 2 Corinthians 1:1 – 11

QUOTATION **470**

A man can keep his sanity and stay alive as long as there is at least one person who is waiting for him.

Citation: Henri J. M. Nouwen, *The Wounded Healer*
Topics: Brotherly Love; Community; Compassion; Family; Hope; Marriage; Peace
Reference: Ecclesiastes 4:9 – 12

QUOTATION **471**

Hope prevents us from clinging to what we have and frees us to move away from the safe place and enter unknown and fearful territory.

Citation: Henri J. M. Nouwen, *The Wounded Healer*
Topics: Change; Courage; Growth; Hope; Risk; Trust
References: 1 Samuel 17:20 – 32; Daniel 6:1 – 23; Romans 4:18; Colossians 1:3 – 8; 2 Timothy 1:3 – 12; Hebrews 6:18 – 20

QUOTATION **472**

A Christian community is … a healing community not because wounds are cured and pains are alleviated, but because wounds and pains become openings or occasions for a new vision.

Citation: Henri J. M. Nouwen, *The Wounded Healer*
Topics: Brotherly Love; Church; Community; Fellowship; Healing; Pain; Suffering; Vision; Vulnerability
References: Acts 2:42 – 47; 2 Corinthians 1:1 – 11; Galatians 6:1 – 10

QUOTATION **473**

The great illusion of leadership is to think that man can be led out of the desert by someone who has never been there.

Citation: Henri J. M. Nouwen, *The Wounded Healer*

Topics: Empathy; Leadership; Ministry; Pain; Suffering

References: Isaiah 48:10; Jeremiah 3:15; John 15:16; Acts 20:28

QUOTATION 474

Wealth takes away the sharp edges of our moral sensitivities and allows a comfortable confusion about sin and virtue.

Citation: Henri J. M. Nouwen, *Gracias*

Topics: Character; Comfort; Materialism; Money; Morality; Virtue; Wealth

References: Deuteronomy 8:13 – 14; Matthew 19:23; Mark 4:19; 1 Timothy 6:9

QUOTATION 475

Songs, good feelings, beautiful liturgies, nice presents, big dinners, and sweet words do not make Christmas. Christmas is saying yes to a hope based on God's initiative, which has nothing to do with what I think or feel. Christmas is believing that the salvation of the world is God's work and not mine.

Citation: Henri J. M. Nouwen, in an article in the *New Oxford Review*

Topics: Christmas; Hope; Incarnation; Providence; Redemption; Salvation

References: Matthew 1:18 – 25; Luke 2:1 – 20; John 1:1 – 18

QUOTATION 476

The desire for solitude is often the first sign of prayer.

Citation: Henri J. M. Nouwen, *Making All Things New*

Topics: Prayer; Solitude; Spiritual Disciplines

References: Matthew 6:6; 14:23; Luke 22:41

ABBA POEMEN

DESERT FATHER (THIRD CENTURY AD)

QUOTATION 477

A man may seem to be silent, but if his heart is condemning others, he is babbling ceaselessly. But there may be another who talks from morning till night yet he is truly silent; that is, he says nothing that is not profitable.

Citation: Unknown

Topics: Judging Others; Tongue; Words

References: Matthew 7:1 – 5; Luke 6:37 – 42

ALEXANDER POPE
BRITISH POET (1688 – 1744)

QUOTATION **478**

Satan now is wiser than of yore,
And tempts by making rich, not by making poor.

Citation: Alexander Pope, Moral Essays

Topics: Materialism; Money; Poverty; Satan; Temptation; Wealth

References: Deuteronomy 8:7 – 18; Haggai 1:6; Luke 12:21; James 5:3

CARL SANDBURG
AMERICAN POET, HISTORIAN, AND NOVELIST (1878 – 1967)

QUOTATION **479**

Love your neighbor as yourself; but don't take down the fence.

Citation: Carl Sandburg, *The People, Yes*

Topics: Brotherly Love; Community; Discernment; Relationships

References: Matthew 5:43 – 44; 22:38 – 40; Mark 12:30 – 31; Luke 10:27;
Romans 13:9; Galatians 5:14; James 2:8

QUOTATION **480**

When a nation goes down, or a society perishes, one condition may always be
found: they forgot where they came from. They lost sight of what had brought
them along.

Citation: Carl Sandburg, *Remembrance Rock*

Topics: Focus; Foolishness; Past

Reference: Deuteronomy 6:1 – 25

QUOTATION **481**

There is an eagle in me that wants to soar, and there is a hippopotamus in me that wants to wallow in the mud.

Citation: Unknown

Topics: Character; Depravity; Desires; Human Condition; Human Nature; Temptation; Tests

References: Romans 7:15–25; 8:3–13; 2 Corinthians 5:17; Galatians 5:13–24; Ephesians 2:3; Colossians 2:11–13

QUOTATION **482**

Life is like an onion: you peel it off one layer at a time, and sometimes you weep.

Citation: Unknown

Topics: Pain; Suffering; Tears; Tests; Trials

References: Psalms 4; 10; 13; 27; Jeremiah 9:1–2; Lamentations 2:11; James 1:2–18; 1 Peter 3:8–22; 4:12–19

QUOTATION **483**

Time is the coin of your life. It is the only coin you have, and only you can determine how it will be spent. Be careful lest you let other people spend it for you.

Citation: Unknown

Topics: Discernment; Focus; Guidance; Life; Lifestyle; Opportunity; Time

References: Psalm 39; Ecclesiastes 12:13–14

ST. SERAPHIM OF SAROV
RUSSIAN MONK AND MYSTIC (1759–1864)

QUOTATION **484**

God is a fire that warms and kindles the heart and inward parts. Hence, if we feel in our hearts the cold which comes from the Devil—for the Devil is cold—let us call on the Lord. He will come to warm our hearts with perfect love, not only for him but also for our neighbor, and the cold of him who hates the good will flee before the heat of his countenance.

Citation: Unknown

Topics: Devil; Evil; Experiencing God; God's Love

References: 2 Timothy 2:22–26; James 4:7; 1 Peter 5:8–11; 1 John 4:7–8

QUOTATION **485**

Have peace in your heart, and thousands will be saved around you.

Citation: Unknown

Topics: Compassion; Example; Missions; Outreach; Peace

References: Luke 1:78–79; Romans 8:6; 14:17; Galatians 5:22–23

ST. TERESA OF ÁVILA
SPANISH MYSTIC (1515–82)

QUOTATION **486**

Many people neglect the task that lies at hand and are content with having wished to do the impossible.

Citation: St. Teresa of Ávila, *Interior Castle*

Topics: Complacency; Courage; Goals; Responsibility; Work

References: Matthew 10:42; 25:14–30

QUOTATION **487**

Souls without prayer are like people whose bodies or limbs are paralyzed: they possess feet and hands but they cannot control them.

Citation: St. Teresa of Ávila, *Interior Castle*

Topics: Maturity; Power; Prayer; Self-control

References: Matthew 7:7; Ephesians 6:18; James 5:13

A. W. TOZER

AMERICAN PREACHER, WRITER, AND MYSTIC (1897–1963)

QUOTATION **488**

An honest man with an open Bible and a pad and pencil is sure to find out what is wrong with him very quickly.

> Citation: A. W. Tozer, *Formula for a Burning Heart*
>
> Topics: Bible; Devotional Life; Humility; Self-examination; Teachability
>
> References: Psalms 19:7–14; 119:105–112; 2 Timothy 3:14–17; 2 Peter 1:12–21

QUOTATION **489**

Being made in [God's] image we have within us the capacity to know him. In our sins we lack only the power.

> Citation: A. W. Tozer, *The Pursuit of God*
>
> Topics: Experiencing God; Human Condition; Human Nature; Knowledge; Sin; Worth
>
> References: Genesis 1:26–31; 2:4–25; 3; Romans 5:12–21

QUOTATION **490**

A new world will arise out of the religious mists when we approach our Bible with the idea that it is not only a book which was once spoken, but a book which is *now speaking*.

> Citation: A. W. Tozer, *The Pursuit of God*
>
> Topics: Bible; Bible Study; Revelation; Revival; Spiritual Disciplines
>
> References: Psalms 19:7–14; 119:105–112; 2 Timothy 3:14–17; 2 Peter 1:12–21

QUOTATION **491**

Faith is a gaze of a soul upon a saving God.

> Citation: A. W. Tozer, *The Pursuit of God*

Topics: Christian Life; Experiencing God; Faith; Salvation

References: Psalms 14; 28; Daniel 6:26–27; Ephesians 3:14–21; Hebrews 11:1–3

QUOTATION 492

A fairly accurate description of the human race might be furnished … by taking the Beatitudes, turning them wrong side out and saying, "Here is your human life and conduct."

Citation: A. W. Tozer, *The Pursuit of God*

Topics: Human Condition; Lifestyle; Sin; Worldview

Reference: Matthew 5:1–12

QUOTATION 493

Always the most revealing thing about the church is her idea of God, just as her most significant message is what she says about him or leaves unsaid, for her silence is often more eloquent than her speech.

Citation: A. W. Tozer, *The Knowledge of the Holy*

Topics: Church; Doctrine; God; Knowing God; Theology

References: Ephesians 1:16–23; 3:16–21

QUOTATION 494

We cover our deep ignorance with words, but we are ashamed to wonder, we are afraid to whisper mystery.

Citation: A. W. Tozer, *The Knowledge of the Holy*

Topics: Awe; Knowledge; Mysteries; Theology; Wonder

Reference: Ecclesiastes 5:1–7

QUOTATION 495

[God] needs no one, but when faith is present he works through anyone.

Citation: A. W. Tozer, *The Knowledge of the Holy*

Topics: Faith; God; Ministry

Reference: Galatians 5:6; Colossians 1:3–8; 1 Thessalonians 1:3

QUOTATION **496**

Life is a short and fevered rehearsal for a concert we cannot stay to give. Just when we appear to have attained some proficiency we are forced to lay our instruments down.

Citation: A. W. Tozer, *The Knowledge of the Holy*

Topics: Death; Eternal and Temporary; Life

Reference: James 4:14–17

QUOTATION **497**

The whole outlook of mankind might be changed if we could all believe that we dwell under a friendly sky and that the God of heaven, though exalted in power and majesty, is eager to be friends with us.

Citation: A. W. Tozer, *The Knowledge of the Holy*

Topics: Compassion; Experiencing God; Friendship with God; God's Glory; Mercy

Reference: Romans 1:18–32

QUOTATION **498**

To fear and not be afraid—that is the paradox of faith.

Citation: A. W. Tozer, *The Knowledge of the Holy*

Topics: Awe; Christian Life; Experiencing God; Faith; Fear; Power

References: Psalm 27; 1 Peter 2:17; 1 John 4:18

QUOTATION **499**

Modern mankind can go anywhere, do everything and be completely curious about the universe. But only a rare person now and then is curious enough to want to know God.

Citation: A. W. Tozer, *Renewed Day by Day*

Topics: Curiosity; Knowing God; Technology

References: Proverbs 2:3–5; 23:23; John 8:31–32; Ephesians 1:17; Philippians 3:10; 2 Peter 1:5

JOHANN WOLFGANG VON GOETHE
GERMAN WRITER AND POET (1749 – 1832)

QUOTATION **500**

The glorious fact is not that the past is sullied, dirty, or unclean, but that the future is unsullied.

Citation: Unknown

Topics: Eternal Life; Forgiveness; Future; Heaven; Hope; Promises; Reconciliation; Sin

References: Romans 3:9 – 26; 5:1 – 11; Revelation 21:1 – 7; 22:1 – 6

QUOTATION **501**

Take what you have inherited from your fathers and work to make it your own.

Citation: Unknown

Topics: Maturity; Spiritual Growth; Teachability; Tradition

Reference: Hebrews 12:1 – 2

QUOTATION **502**

None are more hopelessly enslaved than those who falsely believe they are free.

Citation: Unknown

Topics: Bondage; Deceit; Freedom; Sin

References: John 8:31 – 47; Romans 1:21 – 23; Galatians 5:1, 13; 1 Peter 2:16

QUOTATION **503**

Things which matter most must never be at the mercy of things which matter least.

Citation: Unknown

Topics: Distractions; Priorities; Values

Reference: Matthew 6:19 – 34

WILLIAM WORDSWORTH
BRITISH POET (1770 – 1850)

QUOTATION 504

Faith is a passionate intuition.

> **Citation:** William Wordsworth, "The Excursion"
>
> **Topics:** Belief; Christian Life; Faith
>
> **References:** Romans 4; Hebrews 11

QUOTATION 505

Wisdom is oftentimes nearer when we stoop than when we soar.

> **Citation:** William Wordsworth, "The Excursion"
>
> **Topics:** Humility; Pride; Wisdom
>
> **References:** Proverbs 11:2; Luke 14:7 – 11; John 13:1 – 17; James 3:13 – 18

PART 6: RATTLING WORDS FROM PROPHETS AND ACTIVISTS

HENRY WARD BEECHER

AMERICAN MINISTER, SOCIAL REFORMER, AND ABOLITIONIST (1813 – 87)

QUOTATION 506

The world is to be cleaned by somebody, and you are not called of God if you are ashamed to scrub.

> **Citation:** Henry Ward Beecher, in his sermon "Scope and Function of a Christian Life"
>
> **Topics:** Calling; Great Commission; Humility; Influence; Ministry; Outreach; Servanthood; Service
>
> **References:** Mark 13:34; John 13:1 – 17; Galatians 6:2

QUOTATION 507

"I can forgive, but I cannot forget," is only another way of saying, "I cannot forgive."

> **Citation:** Unknown
>
> **Topics:** Anger; Enemies; Forgiveness; Grace; Hatred; Mercy
>
> **References:** Mark 11:25; Luke 17:4; Colossians 3:13

CATHERINE BOOTH

BRITISH MOTHER OF THE SALVATION ARMY (1829 – 90)

QUOTATION 508

What the law tried to do by a restraining power from without, the gospel does by an inspiring power from within.

> **Citation:** Catherine Booth, in her essay "The Fruits of Union with Christ"
>
> **Topics:** Bondage; Freedom; Gospel; Holy Spirit; Jesus Christ; Law; Rebirth; Regeneration
>
> **References:** Matthew 5:17; John 3:3 – 8; Romans 7:4; Galatians 3:19 – 29

If we are to better the future, we must disturb the present.

> **Citation:** Unknown
>
> **Topics:** Change; Complacency; Culture; Future; Influence; Present; Transformation
>
> **References:** Ecclesiastes 3:2–8; Matthew 10:34; Luke 12:35

JOHN CALVIN
FRENCH THEOLOGIAN AND REFORMER (1509–64)

QUOTATION **510**

For (such is our innate pride) we always seem to ourselves just, and upright, and wise, and holy, until we are convinced, by clear evidence, of our injustice, vileness, folly, and impurity.

> **Citation:** John Calvin, *Institutes of the Christian Religion*
>
> **Topics:** Arrogance; Depravity; Human Condition; Humility; Perception; Pride; Self-examination; Sin; Vices
>
> **References:** Romans 3:9–26; 5:12–21

QUOTATION **511**

But herein appears the shameful ingratitude of men. Though they have in their own persons a factory where innumerable operations of God are carried on, and a magazine stored with treasures of inestimable value, instead of bursting forth in his praise, as they are bound to do, they, on the contrary, are the more inflated and swelled with pride.

> **Citation:** John Calvin, *Institutes of the Christian Religion*
>
> **Topics:** Depravity; Human Condition; Human Nature; Humility; Ingratitude; Potential; Praise; Pride; Vices; Worth
>
> **Reference:** Romans 1:18–32

QUOTATION 512

When once the light of Divine Providence has illumined the believer's soul, he is relieved and set free, not only from the extreme fear and anxiety which formerly oppressed him, but from all care. For as he justly shudders at the idea of chance, so he can confidently commit himself to God.

> **Citation:** John Calvin, *Institutes of the Christian Religion*
>
> **Topics:** Bondage; Fear; Freedom; God's Sovereignty; Hope; Illumination; Peace; Providence; Provision
>
> **References:** Matthew 10:29–31; Hebrews 4:14–16; 1 John 4:18

QUOTATION 513

Reason, by which man discerns between good and evil and by which he understands and judges, is a natural gift; it could not be entirely destroyed. But being partly weakened and partly corrupted, a shapeless ruin is all that remains.

> **Citation:** John Calvin, *Institutes of the Christian Religion*
>
> **Topics:** Evil; Human Condition; Knowledge; Limitations; Mind; Reason
>
> **Reference:** Romans 7:7–25

QUOTATION 514

We have one kind of intelligence of earthly things, and another of heavenly things.

> **Citation:** John Calvin, *Institutes of the Christian Religion*
>
> **Topics:** Illumination; Insight; Knowledge; Mind; Wisdom
>
> **References:** Matthew 6:22–24; Luke 11:34–36; 1 Corinthians 2:6–16; 1 John 2:15–17

QUOTATION 515

Is it faith to understand nothing and merely submit your convictions implicitly to the church? Faith consists not in ignorance, but in knowledge—knowledge not of God merely, but of the divine will.

> **Citation:** John Calvin, *Institutes of the Christian Religion*

Topics: Convictions; Faith; God's Will; Ignorance; Illumination; Insight; Knowledge; Revelation; Wisdom

Reference: Philippians 1:9–11

QUOTATION 516

I call it not humility, so long as we think there is any good remaining in us. Those who have joined together two things, to think humbly of ourselves before God and yet hold our own righteousness in some estimation, have ... a pernicious hypocrisy.

Citation: John Calvin, *Institutes of the Christian Religion*

Topics: Arrogance; Humility; Hypocrisy; Pride; Self-reliance; Self-righteousness

References: Matthew 23:25–28; Mark 12:38–39; Luke 20:45–46; Romans 7:24

QUOTATION 517

There is nothing which God more abominates than when men endeavor to cloak themselves by submitting signs and external appearance for integrity of heart.

Citation: John Calvin, *Institutes of the Christian Religion*

Topics: Character; Holiness; Hypocrisy; Integrity

References: 1 Samuel 16:7; Matthew 23:25–28; Mark 12:38–39; Luke 20:45–46

QUOTATION 518

Sacraments, therefore, are exercises which confirm our faith in the Word of God; and because we are carnal, they are exhibited under carnal objects, that thus they may train us in accommodation to our sluggish capacity, as nurses lead children by the hand.

Citation: John Calvin, *Institutes of the Christian Religion*

Topics: Baptism; Bible; Direction; Faith; Guidance; Limitations; Lord's Supper; Sacraments

References: Matthew 26:17–30; Mark 14:12–16; Luke 22:7–13

QUOTATION 519

There is no nation so barbarous, no people so savage, that they do not have a pervasive belief that there is a God....

There has been no region since the beginning of the world, no city, no home, that could exist without religion; this fact in itself points to a sense of divinity inscribed in the hearts of all people.

> **Citation:** John Calvin, *Institutes of the Christian Religion*
>
> **Topics:** Belief; Christian Life; Experiencing God; Faith; God; Religion
>
> **Reference:** Romans 1:18–32

QUOTATION 520

The human heart has so many crannies where vanity hides, so many holes where falsehood lurks, is so decked out with deceiving hypocrisy, that it often dupes itself.

> **Citation:** John Calvin, *Institutes of the Christian Religion*
>
> **Topics:** Deceit; Depravity; Evil; Heart; Hypocrisy; Sinful Nature
>
> **References:** Proverbs 20:9; Isaiah 64:6; Jeremiah 17:9–10; 2 Timothy 3:13; Titus 3:3; 1 John 1:8

QUOTATION 521

For those to whom [God] is Father, the church may also be Mother.

> **Citation:** John Calvin, *Institutes of the Christian Religion*
>
> **Topics:** Church; Community; Fellowship; Guidance; Nurture
>
> **References:** Matthew 16:19; Hebrews 10:25

QUOTATION 522

Faith is the principal work of the Holy Spirit.... Prayer is the chief exercise of faith.

> **Citation:** John Calvin, *Institutes of the Christian Religion*
>
> **Topics:** Faith; Holy Spirit; Prayer; Regeneration; Spiritual Disciplines
>
> **References:** Matthew 17:20; John 16:13; 2 Corinthians 3:6; James 1:5–6

QUOTATION **523**

All the exhortations which can be given us to suffer for the name of Jesus Christ and in defense of the gospel will have no effect if we do not feel sure of the cause for which we fight.

Citation: John Calvin, in the sermon "Enduring Persecution for Christ"

Topics: Calling; Convictions; Meaning; Mission; Motivation; Motives; Suffering

References: Luke 17:5; John 6:29; Hebrews 6:11; 9:28; 11:1, 6

QUOTATION **524**

Every one of us is, even from his mother's womb, a master craftsman of idols.

Citation: John Calvin, *Commentary on the Acts of the Apostles*

Topics: Depravity; Human Condition; Human Nature; Idolatry; Irreverence; Original Sin; Sinful Nature

References: Genesis 11:1 – 9; Exodus 20:1 – 7; 32; Deuteronomy 6:1 – 25; Isaiah 44:9 – 20; 1 John 5:21

QUOTATION **525**

There is no worse screen to block out the Spirit than confidence in our own intelligence.

Citation: Unknown

Topics: Holy Spirit; Knowledge; Mind; Pride; Self-reliance

References: John 14:15 – 31; 16:5 – 16

QUOTATION **526**

There is not one blade of grass, there is no color in this world, that is not intended to make us rejoice.

Citation: Unknown

Topics: Awe; Creation; Creator; Joy; Praise; Worship

References: Genesis 1; Psalms 8; 19:1 – 6

QUOTATION **527**

There is no one so great or mighty that he can avoid the misery that will rise up against him when he resists and strives against God.

> **Citation:** Unknown
> **Topics:** Arrogance; God's Wrath; Idolatry; Misery; Pride; Rebellion; Sin
> **Reference:** Genesis 11:1 – 9

QUOTATION **528**

A dog barks when his master is attacked. I would be a coward if I saw that God's truth is attacked and yet would remain silent.

> **Citation:** John Calvin, in a letter to Margaret of Navarre
> **Topics:** Bible; Commitment; Complacency; Courage; Responsibility; Truth; Witness
> **References:** 2 Timothy 1:3 – 12; 3:10 – 4:8

TONY CAMPOLO
AMERICAN PASTOR, WRITER, AND ACTIVIST (1935 –)

QUOTATION **529**

Ours is an age in which spiritual blessings are being promised to those who buy material things. The spiritual is being absorbed by the physical. The fruit of the spirit, suggests the media, can be had without God and without spiritual disciplines.

> **Citation:** Tony Campolo, *Wake Up, America!*
> **Topics:** Blessings; Consumerism; Materialism; Money; Secularism; Spiritual Disciplines; Spiritual Growth; Worldliness
> **References:** Psalm 39:6; Ecclesiastes 2:26; Matthew 6:19; James 5:3

QUOTATION **530**

God created us in his image, but we have decided to return the favor and create a God who is in our image.

> **Citation:** Tony Campolo, in the *Christianity Today* article "U"

Topics: Arrogance; Culture; Humanism; Idolatry

References: Matthew 5:19; 7:15; 15:3; Luke 11:39

QUOTATION 531

Nothing is more dangerous than to live out the will of God in today's contemporary world. It changes your whole monetary lifestyle.... Let me put it quite simply: If Jesus had $40,000 and knew about the kids who are suffering and dying in Haiti, what kind of car would he buy?

Citation: Tony Campolo, in the *Christianity Today* article "U"

Topics: Christlikeness; Compassion; God's Will; Justice; Lifestyle; Materialism; Money; Poverty; Sacrifice; Self-denial; Social Impact; Stewardship

References: Proverbs 18:23; 19:17; Matthew 26:11; Galatians 2:10; James 1:27

QUOTATION 532

When you were born, you alone cried and everybody else was happy. The only question that matters is this—when you die, will *you* be happy when everybody else is crying?

Citation: Tony Campolo, quoting from a sermon preached by his pastor

Topics: Death; Eternal Death; Eternal Life; Heaven; Hell; Mortality; Immortality

Reference: Matthew 7:13–29

DOROTHY DAY
AMERICAN SOCIAL ACTIVIST (1897–1980)

QUOTATION 533

I have long since come to believe that people never mean half of what they say, and that it is best to disregard their talk and judge only their actions.

Citation: Dorothy Day, *The Long Loneliness*

Topics: Character; Holiness; Hypocrisy; Integrity; Lifestyle; Witness

References: Matthew 7:15–23; 25:31–46; James 2:14–26

QUOTATION 534

Tradition! We scarcely know the word anymore. We are afraid to be either proud of our ancestors or ashamed of them.

> **Citation:** Dorothy Day, *The Long Loneliness*
>
> **Topics:** Arrogance; Foolishness; Past; Pride; Tradition
>
> **Reference:** Hebrews 11

MAHATMA GANDHI
INDIAN POLITICAL AND SPIRITUAL LEADER AND ACTIVIST (1869 – 1948)

QUOTATION 535

No sacrifice is worth the name unless it is a joy. Sacrifice and a long face go ill together.

> **Citation:** Mahatma Gandhi, *Young India*
>
> **Topics:** Giving; Joy; Sacrifice; Self-denial
>
> **References:** 2 Corinthians 9:7; Philippians 1:12 – 30; James 1:2

QUOTATION 536

It is healthy to be reminded that the strongest might weaken and the wisest might err.

> **Citation:** Unknown
>
> **Topics:** Human Nature; Humility; Limitations; Perspective; Power; Strength; Weakness; Wisdom
>
> **References:** Psalms 20:7; 118; 1 Corinthians 10:12

QUOTATION 537

Wildlife is decreasing in the jungles, but it is increasing in the towns.

> **Citation:** Unknown
>
> **Topics:** Depravity; Human Condition; Last Days
>
> **References:** Romans 1:18 – 32; 2 Timothy 3:1 – 9

ALAN HIRSCH

AUSTRALIAN MISSIONAL LEADER, EDUCATOR, AND STRATEGIST (1959–)

QUOTATION 538

We have at our fingertips experiences and offerings available only to kings in previous eras. Offered "heaven now," we give up the ultimate quest in pursuit of that which can be immediately consumed, be it a service, product, or pseudo-religious experience. Consumerism has all the distinguishing traits of outright paganism—we need to see it for what it really is.

> **Citation:** Alan Hirsch, *The Forgotten Ways*
>
> **Topics:** Consumerism; Distractions; Materialism; Priorities; Temptation; Worldliness
>
> **References:** Luke 12:13–21; Ephesians 5:3; Colossians 3:5

QUOTATION 539

Mission is, and always was, the mother of good theology.

> **Citation:** Alan Hirsch, *The Forgotten Ways*
>
> **Topics:** Evangelism; Mission; Outreach; Theology
>
> **References:** Matthew 28:16–20; Luke 24:45–49; John 20:21

DAN KIMBALL

AMERICAN PASTOR AND WRITER (1960–)

QUOTATION 540

The early church was birthed into an environment of sorcerers, gods, goddesses, and many spiritual cults and religions. We are not facing anything new. We are not facing anything that the Holy Spirit of God ... cannot overcome.

> **Citation:** Dan Kimball, *The Emerging Church*
>
> **Topics:** Church; Culture; Evangelism; Holy Spirit; Power; Strength
>
> **References:** Acts 8:9–25; 13:4–12; 16:11–40; 17:16–34; 19

CORETTA SCOTT KING

AMERICAN ACTIVIST AND WIFE OF MARTIN LUTHER KING JR. (1927–2006)

QUOTATION **541**

Hate is too great a burden to bear. It injures the hater more than it injures the hated.

> **Citation:** Unknown
>
> **Topics:** Anger; Emotions; Hatred
>
> **References:** Genesis 4:1–12; Matthew 5:21–26

MARTIN LUTHER KING JR.

PASTOR AND CIVIL RIGHTS ACTIVIST (1929–68)

QUOTATION **542**

A great nation is a compassionate nation. No nation can be great if it does not have a concern for "the least of these."

> **Citation:** Martin Luther King Jr., *Where Do We Go from Here: Chaos or Community?*
>
> **Topics:** Benevolence; Brotherly Love; Compassion; Generosity; Giving; Justice; Kindness; Mercy; Poor People; Weakness
>
> **References:** Proverbs 19:17; 21:13; 29:14; Matthew 25:40, 45

QUOTATION **543**

Love is the only force capable of transforming an enemy into a friend.

> **Citation:** Martin Luther King Jr., *Strength to Love*
>
> **Topics:** Change; Compassion; Enemies; Forgiveness; Grace; Love; Mercy; Transformation; Witness
>
> **References:** Leviticus 19:18; Matthew 5:44; Romans 12:9–10; 1 John 4:7–8

QUOTATION **544**

The church must be reminded that it is not the master or the servant of the state, but rather the conscience of the state.

> **Citation:** Martin Luther King Jr., *Strength to Love*
>
> **Topics:** Accountability; Church; Conscience; Government; Justice; Politics; Responsibility
>
> **References:** Zechariah 2:8; Acts 20:28; Romans 13:5

QUOTATION **545**

The ultimate measure of a man is not where he stands in moments of comfort and convenience, but where he stands at times of challenge and controversy.

> **Citation:** Martin Luther King Jr., *Strength to Love*
>
> **Topics:** Character; Integrity; Overcoming; Persecution; Strength; Suffering; Tests; Trials
>
> **References:** Job 23:10; Isaiah 48:10; Jeremiah 12:5; James 1:2–4

QUOTATION **546**

Injustice anywhere is a threat to justice everywhere.

> **Citation:** Martin Luther King Jr., in his letter from the Birmingham, Alabama, jail
>
> **Topics:** Injustice; Justice
>
> **References:** Proverbs 13:23; 16:8

QUOTATION **547**

Some of us who have already begun to break the silence of the night have found that the calling to speak is often a vocation of agony, but we must speak. We must speak with all the humility that is appropriate to our limited vision, but we must speak.

> **Citation:** Martin Luther King Jr., in his sermon "A Time to Break Silence"
>
> **Topics:** Calling; Convictions; Fear; Justice; Preaching; Responsibility; Social Impact; Social Justice; Suffering; Vision
>
> **References:** Proverbs 31:8–9; Isaiah 6:8; Jeremiah 1:5; Luke 10:2

We must accept finite disappointment but never lose infinite hope.

Citation: Martin Luther King Jr., in a sermon

Topics: Disappointment; Discouragement; Hope; Overcoming; Perseverance; Trials

References: Romans 5:1–5; 1 Corinthians 13:13; James 1:2–4

QUOTATION **549**

Cowardice asks the question, "Is it safe?" Expedience asks: "Is it politic?" Vanity asks: "Is it popular?" But conscience asks the question: "Is it right?"

Citation: Martin Luther King, Jr., in a speech at Sacramento State College

Topics: Accountability; Conscience; Convictions; Courage; Fear; Social Impact; Social Justice

References: Acts 24:16; Romans 2:15; 1 Timothy 1:5; 1:9–11; 1 Peter 3:16

QUOTATION **550**

If it falls your lot to be a street sweeper, sweep streets like Michelangelo painted pictures, sweep streets like Beethoven composed music, sweep streets like Shakespeare wrote poetry. Sweep streets so well that all the hosts of heaven and earth will have to pause and say: Here lived a great street sweeper who swept his job well.

Citation: Martin Luther King Jr., speaking to students at Barratt Junior High School in Philadelphia on October 26, 1967, six months before he was assassinated

Topics: Calling; Commitment; Dedication; Ministry; Service; Vocation; Work

References: 1 Corinthians 10:31; Ephesians 6:7; Colossians 3:17–24

JOHN KNOX

SCOTTISH PREACHER AND REFORMER (1510–72)

QUOTATION **551**

If Satan fume and roar against you, whether it be against your bodies by persecution, or inwardly in your consciences by a spiritual battle, do not be discouraged, as though you were less acceptable in God's presence, or that Satan might at any time prevail against you.... I have good hope, and my prayer will likewise be, that you may be so strengthened, that the world and Satan himself may understand and perceive, that God is fighting your battle.

Citation: Unknown

Topics: Evil; Opposition; Power; Satan; Spiritual Warfare; Strength; Victory

References: 2 Samuel 22:40; Isaiah 40:31; Ephesians 3:16

MARTIN LUTHER
GERMAN THEOLOGIAN AND REFORMER (1483 – 1546)

QUOTATION 552

Thus it is with the church of Christ: it goes on in apparent weakness; and yet in its weakness, there is such mighty strength and power, that all the worldly wise and powerful must stand amazed thereat and fear.

Citation: Martin Luther, *The Table Talk of Martin Luther*

Topics: Church; Influence; Overcoming; Persecution; Perseverance; Strength; Weakness; Wisdom; World

References: 1 Corinthians 1:18 – 2:16; 2 Corinthians 12:1 – 10

QUOTATION 553

No man should be alone when he opposes Satan. The church and the ministry of the Word were instituted for this purpose, that hands may be joined together and one may help another. If the prayer of one doesn't help, the prayer of another will.

Citation: Martin Luther, *The Table Talk of Martin Luther*

Topics: Accountability; Church; Community; Division; Individualism; Prayer; Relationships; Satan; Spiritual Warfare; Unity

References: Proverbs 27:17; Ecclesiastes 4:9 – 10; Ephesians 4:12

QUOTATION **554**

The true Christian religion ... does not begin at the top, as all other religions do; it begins at the bottom. You must run directly to the manger and the mother's womb, embrace this Infant and Virgin's Child in your arms, and look at Him — born, being nursed, growing up, going about in human society, teaching, dying, rising again, ascending above all the heavens, and having authority over all things.

Citation: Martin Luther, *Lectures on Galatians*

Topics: Advent; Christmas; Hope; Humility; Jesus Christ; Submission; Victory

References: Isaiah 7:14; John 1:14; 1 Timothy 3:16

QUOTATION **555**

Nothing is more perilous than to be weary of the Word of God. Thinking he knows enough, a person begins little by little to despise the Word until he has lost Christ and the gospel altogether.

Citation: Martin Luther, *Galatians Commentary*

Topics: Bible; Bible Study; Complacency; Spiritual Growth

References: Matthew 4:4; 1 Peter 2:2 – 3

QUOTATION **556**

God's wonderful works which happen daily are lightly esteemed, not because they are of no import but because they happen so constantly and without interruption.

Citation: Martin Luther, *Day by Day We Magnify Thee*

Topics: Distractions; Focus; God's Sovereignty; Providence; Provision; Thanksgiving

References: Psalm 31:9; Matthew 14:15; John 2:9

QUOTATION **557**

God is not hostile to sinners, but only to unbelievers.

Citation: Martin Luther, *The Christian in Society*

Topics: Belief; Grace; Mercy; Unbelief

References: Matthew 13:58; Luke 22:67; John 3:36

QUOTATION **558**

Not only are we the freest of kings, we are also priests forever—which is far more excellent than being kings, for as priests we are worthy to appear before God to pray for others and to teach one another divine things.

> Citation: Martin Luther, *On Christian Liberty*
>
> Topics: Intercession; Ministry; Prayer; Service; Worth
>
> References: Exodus 19:6; Isaiah 61:6; 1 Peter 2:5; Revelation 1:6

QUOTATION **559**

Next to the Word of God, music deserves the highest praise.

> Citation: Martin Luther, Preface to Georg Rhau's *Symphoniae iucundae*
>
> Topics: Bible; Music; Praise; Worship
>
> References: Psalms 92; 95; 98; 1 Corinthians 14:26; Ephesians 5:19; Colossians 3:16

QUOTATION **560**

A free will desires nothing of its own. It only cares for the will of God, and so it remains free, cleaving and clinging to nothing.

> Citation: Martin Luther, in his exposition of the Lord's Prayer
>
> Topics: Freedom; Free Will; God's Will; Human Will; Submission
>
> References: Matthew 6:10; Acts 7:51; 2 Peter 2:10

QUOTATION **561**

Our office is a ministry of grace and salvation. It subjects us to great burdens and labors, dangers and temptations, with little reward or gratitude from the world. But Christ himself will be our reward if we labor faithfully.

> Citation: Martin Luther, in his catechism
>
> Topics: Eternal Life; Grace; Ministry; Outreach; Persecution; Rewards; Salvation; Suffering; Work; World
>
> References: Matthew 10:32; 16:26; 20:1–16; 25:34; Luke 12:8

QUOTATION **562**

Temptations, of course, cannot be avoided, but because we cannot prevent the birds from flying over our heads, there is no need that we should let them nest in our hair.

Citation: Unknown

Topics: Complacency; Lust; Mind; Purity; Self-discipline; Temptation

References: Genesis 39; Judges 16:1 – 22; Matthew 4:1 – 17; James 1:2 – 18

QUOTATION **563**

As it is the business of tailors to make clothes and of cobblers to mend shoes, so it is the business of Christians to pray.

Citation: Unknown

Topics: Devotional Life; Intercession; Prayer

References: Matthew 6:9 – 13; Ephesians 6:18

QUOTATION **564**

The Bible is alive, it speaks to me; it has feet, it runs after me; it has hands, it lays hold of me.

Citation: Unknown

Topics: Bible; Change; Holy Spirit; Illumination; Regeneration; Transformation

References: Jeremiah 23:29; Ephesians 6:17; Hebrews 4:12

QUOTATION **565**

Peace, if possible, but the truth at any rate.

Citation: Unknown

Topics: Peace; Relationships; Truth

References: Psalm 119:127; John 14:6; 18:37; Romans 12:18

QUOTATION **566**

I have often learned much more in one prayer than I have been able to glean from much reading and reflection.

Citation: Unknown

Topics: Bible Study; Insight; Prayer; Teachability; Wisdom

References: Luke 11:9; Romans 8:26–27; Ephesians 6:18

QUOTATION **567**

I have held many things in my hands, and I have lost them all; but whatever I have placed in God's hands, that I still possess.

Citation: Unknown

Topics: God's Will; Human Will; Materialism; Sacrifice; Self-denial; Stewardship; Submission; Trust

References: Matthew 6:20; Luke 21:1–4; Romans 6:13; James 4:7

QUOTATION **568**

I find it impossible to avoid offending guilty men, for there is no way of avoiding it but by our silence or their patience; and silent we cannot be because of God's command, and patient they cannot be because of their guilt.

Citation: Unknown

Topics: Courage; Evangelism; Guilt; Outreach; Witness

References: Luke 17:3; 1 Timothy 5:20; Titus 2:15

QUOTATION **569**

It is the highest grace of God when love continues to flourish in married life. The first love is ardent, is an intoxicating love, so that we are blinded and are drawn to marriage. After we have slept off our intoxication, sincere love remains in the married life of the godly; but the godless are sorry they ever married.

Citation: Unknown

Topics: Grace; Love; Marriage; Regrets; Spouses

References: Proverbs 18:22; 21:9; Hosea 2:19

QUOTATION **570**

The Christian is supposed to love his neighbor, and since his wife is his nearest neighbor, she should be his deepest love.

Citation: Unknown

Topics: Love; Marriage; Spouses

References: Matthew 22:39; Ephesians 5:25; 1 Peter 3:7

QUOTATION **571**

Human nature is like a drunk peasant. Lift him into the saddle on one side, over he topples on the other side.

Citation: Unknown

Topics: Foolishness; Human Condition; Human Nature; Weakness

References: Jeremiah 2:36; Ephesians 4:14; James 1:6

QUOTATION **572**

There's a lot to get used to in the first year of marriage. One wakes up in the morning and finds a pair of pigtails on the pillow that were not there before.

Citation: Unknown

Topics: Change; Marriage; Spouses

References: Genesis 2:24; Proverbs 18:22; Song of Songs 8:7

QUOTATION **573**

God creates out of nothing. Therefore, until a man is nothing, God can make nothing out of him.

Citation: Unknown

Topics: Conversion; Creation; Humility; Limitations; Sanctification; Submission; Transformation

References: Proverbs 22:4; Isaiah 57:15; Matthew 18:4; James 4:10

NELSON MANDELA
FORMER PRESIDENT OF SOUTH AFRICA AND ANTI-APARTHEID ACTIVIST (1918–)

QUOTATION 574

We must use time wisely and forever realize that the time is always ripe to do right.

Citation: Unknown

Topics: Calling; Discernment; Opportunity; Responsibility; Social Impact; Spiritual Perception

References: 1 Chronicles 12:32; Matthew 9:35–38; Luke 10:2

BRIAN D. MCLAREN
AMERICAN PASTOR, WRITER, AND ACTIVIST (1956–)

QUOTATION 575

Forgiveness without conviction is not forgiveness; it is irresponsible toleration.

Citation: Brian D. McLaren, *Generous Orthodoxy*

Topics: Accountability; Conviction of Sin; Forgiveness; Mercy; Tolerance

References: 2 Samuel 12:7–14; Matthew 18:15–20; Galatians 2:11–21

QUOTATION 576

[Passion] can easily degenerate into sentimental or cheesy or hotheaded or hardheaded or softheaded, and too often it has done so. But if I have a choice between the kind of trouble that comes from too much passion or the kind that comes from too little, my choice will be easy.

Citation: Brian D. McLaren, *Generous Orthodoxy*

Topics: Commitment; Convictions; Passion; Purpose

Reference: 2 Timothy 1:3–12

QUOTATION **577**

Think of the difference between a corpse and a living, breathing body, and you'll understand the difference between a bunch of words and words vitalized with God's breath.

Citation: Brian D. McLaren, *Generous Orthodoxy*

Topics: Bible; Inspiration of Scripture; Revelation; Truth; Wisdom

References: 2 Timothy 3:14–17; 2 Peter 1:12–21

QUOTATION **578**

If life is a machine, then sin is a bad gear that makes the machine malfunction.
If life is a kingdom, then sin is a terrorist movement in the kingdom.
If life is a family, then sin is a feud between family members.
If life is a body, then sin is an untreated disease that poisons the whole system.
If life is a river, then sin is mercury or arsenic that pollutes it.
If life is a garden, then sin is the army of slugs that eat your tomatoes.
If life is a computer, then sin is a virus that destroys your hard drive.

Citation: Brian D. McLaren, in his sermon "Sin 101: Why Sin Matters"

Topics: Consequences; Depravity; Evil; Human Condition; Life; Sin

References: Genesis 4:7; Psalm 38:3–5; Romans 3:10–20; Ephesians 4:22; Hebrews 3:13; James 1:15

JOHN NEWTON
ANGLICAN CLERGYMAN AND ABOLITIONIST (1725–1807)

QUOTATION **579**

If the Lord be with us, we have no cause of fear. His eye is upon us, his arm over us, his ear open to our prayer — his grace sufficient, his promise unchangeable.

Citation: John Newton, in a letter to the Rev. Mr. R****

Topics: Fear; God's Sovereignty; Grace; Guidance; Power; Promises; Worth

References: Joshua 1; Psalms 2; 11; 24; 30; 31; Jeremiah 1:4–8; Matthew 10:26–31

What will it profit a man if he gains his cause, and silences his adversary, if at the same time he loses that humble, tender frame of spirit in which the Lord delights?

Citation: John Newton, in a letter to a friend facing controversy

Topics: Gentleness; Humility; Pride; Teachability

References: 2 Timothy 2:24; Titus 3:2; James 3:17

QUOTATION **581**

A stranger to prayer is equally a stranger to God and to happiness.

Citation: John Newton, in his sermon "On Searching the Scriptures"

Topics: Devotional Life; Happiness; Prayer

References: Ephesians 6:18; Philippians 4:6; James 5:18

JOHN A. SHEDD
AMERICAN WRITER (1859 – 1928)

QUOTATION **582**

A ship in harbor is safe, but that is not what ships are built for.

Citation: John A. Shedd, *Salt from My Attic*

Topics: Calling; Courage; Fear; Lifestyle; Risk; Suffering; Trials; Vision

References: Matthew 28:16 – 20; Luke 24:45 – 49; John 20:21

LEONARD SWEET
AMERICAN THEOLOGIAN, WRITER, AND FUTURIST (1947 –)

QUOTATION **583**

The church is a counterflow to the undertow.

Citation: Leonard Sweet, *Soul Tsunami*

Topics: Church; Culture; Evangelism; Influence; Witness

References: 2 Timothy 3:10 – 4:8; 1 John 2:15 – 17

QUOTATION **584**

The simple life of faith can be lived only by passing through immense complexities. Simplicity is not the starting point, but the ending point.

Citation: Leonard Sweet, *Soul Tsunami*

Topics: Christian Life; Faith; Goals; Simplicity; Teachability; Trials

Reference: Hebrews 5:11 – 6:12

QUOTATION **585**

Forget felt-needs in favor of God-wants.

Citation: Leonard Sweet, *Soul Tsunami*

Topics: Obedience; Sacrifice; Self-denial; Pride

References: Matthew 8:18 – 22; 10:37 – 39; 16:21 – 28; Mark 8:31 – 9:1; Luke 14:25 – 35

QUOTATION **586**

This culture hasn't gotten more secular; if anything, it's more superstitious.

Citation: Unknown

Topics: Culture; Religion; Spirituality; Superstition; Worldliness

References: 1 Kings 20:23; Daniel 4:8; Acts 19:13 – 19

MOTHER TERESA
ALBANIAN ROMAN CATHOLIC NUN AND HUMANITARIAN (1910 – 97)

QUOTATION **587**

Do not think that love, in order to be genuine, has to be extraordinary. What we need is to love without getting tired.

Citation: Mother Teresa, *No Greater Love*

Topics: Brotherly Love; Calling; Influence; Lifestyle; Marriage; Mercy; Perseverance

References: Romans 12:9–21; 1 Corinthians 13; 1 John 3:11–24; 4:7–21

QUOTATION **588**

The hunger for love is much more difficult to remove than the hunger for bread.

Citation: Mother Teresa, *No Greater Love*

Topics: Benevolence; Compassion; Kindness; Love; Mercy; Social Impact; Social Justice

References: John 6:25–59; 1 Corinthians 13

QUOTATION **589**

I have found the paradox that if I love until it hurts, then there is no more hurt, but only more love.

Citation: Unknown

Topics: Compassion; Love; Pain; Sacrifice; Suffering

References: Matthew 22:39; John 13:34–35; 15:12; 1 Peter 1:22

DESMOND TUTU
SOUTH AFRICAN ANGLICAN ARCHBISHOP AND ACTIVIST (1931–)

QUOTATION **590**

There is nothing the government can do to me that will stop me from being involved in what I believe God wants me to do. I do not do it because I like doing it. I do it because I am under what I believe to be the influence of God's hand. I cannot help it. When I see injustice, I cannot keep quiet, for, as Jeremiah says, when I try to keep quiet, God's Word burns like a fire in my breast.

But what is it that they can ultimately do? The most awful thing that they can do is to kill me, and death is not the worst thing that could happen to a Christian.

Citation: Desmond Tutu, while under scrutiny by his apartheid government's Eloff Commission

Topics: Commitment; Convictions; Government; Injustice; Martyrdom; Persecution; Politics; Social Action; Suffering; Trials

References: Jeremiah 20:9; Matthew 8:18–22; 10:37–39; 16:21–28; Mark 8:31–9:1; Luke 14:25–35; Acts 7

QUOTATION 591

I have two lasting impressions: the horror of what we are able to do to each other and almost exhilaration at the nobility of the human spirit that so many demonstrate.

Citation: Desmond Tutu, when reflecting on genocide in South Africa

Topics: Depravity; Dignity; Human Condition; Human Nature; Worth

References: Psalm 8:3–9; Jeremiah 7:9–10; Romans 7:7–25; Galatians 5:16–25; Ephesians 4:17–5:21; Colossians 2:6–23

JIM WALLIS
AMERICAN WRITER AND POLITICAL ACTIVIST (1948–)

QUOTATION 592

The Bible doesn't mind prosperity; it just insists that it be shared.

Citation: Jim Wallis, *Faith Works*

Topics: Benevolence; Generosity; Giving; Materialism; Money; Prosperity; Stewardship; Tithing

References: Matthew 6:1–4; 19:16–29; Mark 12:41–44; Acts 2:42–47; 4:32–36; 2 Corinthians 8:1–15; 9:6–15; Philippians 4:10–20

QUOTATION 593

Hope unbelieved is always considered nonsense. But hope believed is history in the process of being changed.

Citation: Jim Wallis, *The Soul of Politics*

Topics: Belief; Change; Faith; Foolishness; Hope; Politics; Social Impact; Transformation; Trust; Vision

References: Psalms 25; 42; 71; 130; Romans 4:18; 8:18–27; Colossians 3:24–27

GEORGE WEIGEL

AMERICAN ROMAN CATHOLIC WRITER AND SOCIAL ACTIVIST (1951 –)

QUOTATION **594**

We are not congealed stardust, an accidental by-product of cosmic chemistry. We are not just something; we are someone.

> **Citation:** George Weigel, in an article in *Newsweek* magazine
> **Topics:** Creation; Creator; Meaning; Purpose; Science; Worth
> **References:** Genesis 1:26 – 27; 9:6; Psalm 8:3 – 5; John 3:16; Acts 17:29

WILLIAM WILBERFORCE

BRITISH POLITICIAN, PHILANTHROPIST, AND ABOLITIONIST (1759 – 1833)

QUOTATION **595**

The title of Christian is a reproach to us if we turn our selves away from him after whom we are named.... We should allow the name of Jesus to be engraved deeply on the heart, written there by the finger of God himself in everlasting characters. It is our sure and undoubted title to present peace and future glory.

> **Citation:** William Wilberforce, *A Practical View of the Prevailing Religious System of Professed Christians*
> **Topics:** Christian Life; Eternal Life; Future; Glory; Peace; Present
> **References:** Luke 24:47; John 14:13; Acts 3:16; Philippians 2:9 – 11

QUOTATION **596**

In the Scriptures, no national crime is condemned so frequently and few so strongly as oppression and cruelty, and the not using our best endeavors to deliver our fellow-creatures from them.

> **Citation:** William Wilberforce, in a diary entry
> **Topics:** Compassion; Good Deeds; Injustice; Kindness; Oppression; Persecution; Poverty
> **References:** Proverbs 14:31; Ezekiel 16:49; Amos 2:6 – 7

NIKOLAUS LUDWIG VON ZINZENDORF
GERMAN REFORMER AND BISHOP OF THE MORAVIAN CHURCH (1700–1760)

QUOTATION 597

I have but one passion: It is He, it is He alone. The world is the field and the field is the world; and henceforth that country shall be my home where I can be most used in winning souls for Christ.

Citation: Unknown

Topics: Calling; Evangelism; Jesus Christ; Missions; Purpose; Service

References: Matthew 5:13–16; 9:35–38; 28:16–20; Luke 8:16–18; 9:1–9; 15; 24:45–49; John 20:21

ULRICH ZWINGLI
SWISS THEOLOGIAN AND REFORMER (1484–1531)

QUOTATION 598

Not to fear is the armor!

Citation: Unknown

Topics: Courage; Fear; Trust

References: Deuteronomy 31:6; 2 Chronicles 32:7; Philippians 1:28

QUOTATION 599

Truth wears a happy face.

Citation: Unknown

Topics: Happiness; Joy; Truth

References: Proverbs 23:23; Jeremiah 15:16

PART 7: LOFTY WORDS FROM THEOLOGIANS AND THEORISTS

WILLIAM FRENCH ANDERSON

AMERICAN PHYSICIAN, GENETICIST, AND MOLECULAR BIOLOGIST (1936–)

QUOTATION **600**

Nothing about having a 176 IQ means you have good judgment.

> **Citation:** William French Anderson, after being convicted of child molestation charges
>
> **Topics:** Decisions; Depravity; Discernment; Human Will; Insight; Knowledge; Wisdom
>
> **References:** Proverbs 1:7; 3:13; 14:12; 16:25; 23:23; 1 Corinthians 1:18–31; 3:19

ST. ANSELM

ITALIAN PHILOSOPHER, THEOLOGIAN, AND ARCHBISHOP OF CANTERBURY (1033–1109)

QUOTATION **601**

To sin is to fail to render to God what God is entitled to.

> **Citation:** St. Anselm, *Why God Became Man*
>
> **Topics:** Disobedience; Duty; Fall of Humanity; Fear of God; Godlessness; Human Nature; Irreverence; Responsibility; Sin; Vices
>
> **References:** Genesis 3:1–19; Romans 6:1–14; Colossians 3:5

ST. THOMAS AQUINAS

ITALIAN ROMAN CATHOLIC PRIEST, PHILOSOPHER, AND THEOLOGIAN (c. 1225–74)

QUOTATION **602**

God plays. God creates playing. And man should play if he is to live as humanly as possible and to know reality, since it is created by God's playfulness.

> **Citation:** St. Thomas Aquinas, *Summa Theologica*

Topics: Creation; Experiencing God; Joy; Life; Play; Praise; Recreation; Sabbath

References: Ecclesiastes 8:15; 1 Timothy 4:4; 6:17

QUOTATION 603

No one can live without delight, and that is why a man deprived of spiritual joy goes over to carnal pleasures.

Citation: St. Thomas Aquinas, *Summa Theologica*

Topics: Delight; Fulfillment; Happiness; Human Nature; Joy; Lust; Passion; Pleasure; Sin; Worldliness

References: Psalm 37:4; Ecclesiastes 2:1; 8:15; Philippians 4:4

QUOTATION 604

As a matter of honor, one man owes it to another to manifest the truth.

Citation: St. Thomas Aquinas, *Summa Theologica*

Topics: Accountability; Encouragement; Honesty; Insight; Integrity; Relationships; Responsibility; Truth

References: 2 Samuel 12:7–14; Matthew 18:15–20; Colossians 3:16

QUOTATION 605

God destines us for an end beyond the grasp of reason.

Citation: St. Thomas Aquinas, *Summa Theologica*

Topics: Blessings; Eternal Life; Forgiveness; Freedom; Glory; Heaven; Hope; Mysteries; Resurrection

References: Luke 23:43; John 14:1–4; 1 Corinthians 15:35–58; 2 Corinthians 4:7–18; Revelation 21:1–7; 22:1–6

QUOTATION 606

To one who has faith, no explanation is necessary. To one without faith, no explanation is possible.

Citation: Unknown

Topics: Atheism; Belief; Doubt; Faith; Lostness; Mysteries; Perspective; Questions; Skepticism; Trust; Unbelief

References: Numbers 13:30–33; 14:5–9; Ephesians 3:14–21

KARL BARTH
SWISS THEOLOGIAN (1886–1968)

QUOTATION 607

To clasp hands in prayer is the beginning of an uprising against the disorder of the world.

Citation: Karl Barth, *Prayer*

Topics: Power; Prayer; Spiritual Warfare; World

References: Matthew 21:22; John 15:7; Acts 16:25–26; James 5:18

QUOTATION 608

Of all the sciences which stir the head and heart, theology is the fairest. It is closest to human reality, and gives us the clearest view of truth after which all science quests.

Citation: Karl Barth, in a series of lectures at the Free Protestant Theological Faculty in Paris

Topics: Doctrine; Heart; Illumination; Insight; Mind; Perspective; Religion; Revelation; Science; Theology; Truth

References: Galatians 1:6–9; 1 Timothy 4; Titus 2

RICHARD BAXTER
BRITISH PURITAN CHURCH LEADER
AND THEOLOGIAN (1615–91)

QUOTATION 609

Choose not that in which you may be most rich or honorable in the world; but that in which you may do most good, and best escape sinning.

Citation: Richard Baxter, *A Christian Directory*

Topics: Benevolence; Calling; Character; Decisions; Discernment; Giving; Good Deeds; Materialism; Service; Social Action; Work

References: Ecclesiastes 9:10; Ephesians 4:28

ALEXANDER GRAHAM BELL
SCOTTISH SCIENTIST AND INVENTOR (1847 – 1922)

QUOTATION **610**

When one door closes, another opens, but we often look so long and regretfully at the closed door that we do not see the one that has opened for us.

Citation: Unknown

Topics: Change; Contentment; Guidance; Opportunity

References: Proverbs 1:28; Luke 12:47; 1 Corinthians 16:9

NICHOLAS BERDYAEV
RUSSIAN RELIGIOUS AND POLITICAL PHILOSOPHER (1874 – 1948)

QUOTATION **611**

All beauty in the world is either a memory of Paradise or a prophecy of the transfigured world.

Citation: Nicholas Berdyaev, *The Divine and the Human*

Topics: Afterlife; Awe; Beauty; Creation; Future; Heaven; Resurrection; World

References: Genesis 1; Revelation 21; 22

QUOTATION **612**

In a certain sense, every single human soul has more meaning and value than the whole of history with its empires, its wars and revolutions, its blossoming and fading civilizations.

Citation: Nicholas Berdyaev, *The Fate of Man in the Modern World*

Topics: Government; Politics; Soul; Worth

References: Job 7:17; Psalms 8:3–9; 103:17; 1 John 3:1–3

RICHARD BLIESE
AMERICAN PROFESSOR AND PRESIDENT OF LUTHER SEMINARY (MINNEAPOLIS) (1956–)

QUOTATION 613

Meaningful worship and meaningful meals are critical to any attempts at renewal, and one doesn't work well without the other. Never trust a Christian fellowship where Christians regularly worship together but don't like to eat together, or where they eat together but neglect worship.

Citation: Richard H. Bliese, in a *Christian Century* article

Topics: Church; Community; Fellowship; Meals; Praise; Relationships; Renewal; Worship

References: Psalm 34:3; Acts 2:42–47; 1 Corinthians 11:20–22

PAUL BRAND
BRITISH SURGEON AND WRITER (1914–2003)

QUOTATION 614

So much of the sorrow in the world is due to the selfishness of one living organism that simply does not care when another suffers. In Christ's Body we suffer because we do not suffer enough.

Citation: Paul Brand, in the *Leadership* journal article "Putting Pain to Work"

Topics: Attitudes; Church; Community; Compassion; Empathy; Pain; Self-centeredness; Suffering; Unity

References: 1 Corinthians 10:24; 12:26; Philippians 2:4

EDGAR S. BRIGHTMAN
AMERICAN PHILOSOPHER AND THEOLOGIAN (1884 – 1953)

QUOTATION 615

Carelessness is the initial phase of sinning.

Citation: Unknown

Topics: Apathy; Carelessness; Complacency; Distractions; Sin; Temptation

References: Proverbs 6:6 – 11; Matthew 25:26 – 27; Ephesians 5:15 – 16; Hebrews 6:12

F. F. BRUCE
SCOTTISH BIBLE SCHOLAR (1910 – 90)

QUOTATION 616

Sanctification is glory begun. Glory is sanctification completed.

Citation: F. F. Bruce, *The Epistle to the Hebrews*

Topics: Glory; Goals; Holiness; Maturity; Sanctification

References: John 17:6 – 19; Philippians 1:3 – 11; 1 Thessalonians 4:1 – 12; 2 Thessalonians 2:13 – 17

EMIL BRUNNER
SWISS THEOLOGIAN (1889 – 1966)

QUOTATION 617

What oxygen is to the lungs, such is hope to the meaning of life.

Citation: Unknown

Topics: Hope; Life; Meaning; Purpose

References: Psalms 25; 42; 71; 130; Romans 4:18; 8:18 – 27; Colossians 3:24 – 27

JEAN DE LA BRUYÈRE
FRENCH ESSAYIST AND MORALIST (1645–96)

QUOTATION 618

The slave has but one master; the ambitious man has as many as there are persons whose aid may contribute to the advancement of his fortunes.

Citation: Unknown

Topics: Ambition; Bondage; Greed; Materialism; Money; Worldliness

References: Psalm 10:2; Proverbs 11:2; 16:18; 1 John 2:16

D. A. CARSON
AMERICAN THEOLOGIAN AND BIBLE SCHOLAR (1946–)

QUOTATION 619

We drift toward compromise and call it tolerance; we drift toward disobedience and call it freedom; we drift toward superstition and call it faith. We cherish the indiscipline of lost self-control and call it relaxation; we slouch toward prayerlessness and delude ourselves into thinking we have escaped legalism; we slide toward godlessness and convince ourselves we have been liberated.

Citation: D. A. Carson, *For the Love of God*

Topics: Apathy; Character; Complacency; Deceit; Freedom; Holiness; Integrity; Legalism; Self-control; Spiritual Disciplines; Spiritual Growth; Tolerance

Reference: 1 Thessalonians 5:1–11

QUOTATION 620

When he says he loves us, does not God ... mean something like the following: "Morally speaking, you are the people of the halitosis, the bulbous nose, the greasy hair, the disjointed knees, the abominable personality. Your sins have made you disgustingly ugly. But I love you anyway, not because you are attractive, but because it is my nature to love."

Citation: D. A. Carson, *The Difficult Doctrine of the Love of God*

Topics: God; God's Love; Grace; Mercy; Worth

References: John 3:16; Romans 8:31–39; Ephesians 1:4–8; 2:8; Titus 3:3–7

GEORGE WASHINGTON CARVER
AMERICAN BOTANICAL RESEARCHER AND AGRONOMY EDUCATOR (1864–1943)

QUOTATION 621

How far you go in life depends on your being tender with the young, compassionate with the aged, sympathetic with the striving, and tolerant of the weak and strong—because someday in life you will have been all of these.

Citation: Unknown

Topics: Attitudes; Compassion; Gentleness; Kindness; Love; Mercy; Tolerance

References: Matthew 7:12; Galatians 6:7–10

LEWIS CHAFER
AMERICAN THEOLOGIAN AND PREACHER (1871–1952)

QUOTATION 622

When led of the Spirit, the child of God must be as ready to wait as to go, as prepared to be silent as to speak.

Citation: Unknown

Topics: Direction; Guidance; Holy Spirit; Self-discipline; Spiritual Perception; Submission; Teachability; Waiting on God

References: John 14:15–31; 16:5–16; Romans 8:1–17; James 1:19

ERWIN CHARGAFF

AUSTRIAN BIOCHEMIST (1905–2002)

QUOTATION 623

A balance that does not tremble cannot weigh. A man who does not tremble cannot live.

Citation: Erwin Chargaff, *Heraclitean Fire*

Topics: Awe; Fear of God; Humility; Pride

References: Psalms 18:27; 25:9; 147:6; 149:4; Proverbs 3:34; Matthew 18:4; 23:12; Luke 14:10–11; 18:14; Philippians 2:12; James 4:1–12

ST. CYRIL

THEOLOGIAN OF THE EARLY CHURCH (C. 315–386)

QUOTATION 624

Just as a mustard seed contains a great number of branches in its tiny grain, so also this summary of the faith brings together in a few words the entire knowledge of the true religion which is contained in the Old and New [Testaments].

Citation: St. Cyril, *Catechesis*

Topics: Belief; Bible; Bible Study; Doctrine; Faith; Gospel; Theology

References: Genesis 12:1–3; 2 Corinthians 2:12–3:18; Hebrews 8

RENÉ DESCARTES

FRENCH PHILOSOPHER, MATHEMATICIAN, SCIENTIST, AND WRITER (1596–1650)

QUOTATION 625

If you would be a real seeker after truth, it is necessary that at least once in your life you doubt, as far as possible, all things.

Citation: René Descartes, *Principles of Philosophy*

Topics: Confusion; Discernment; Doubt; Faith; Mysteries; Truth; Wisdom

References: Matthew 14:31; Mark 4:40; Hebrews 5:14

QUOTATION **626**

It is not enough to have a good mind. The main thing is to use it well.

Citation: Unknown

Topics: Education; Knowledge; Mind; Morality; Responsibility; Wisdom

References: Romans 12:1–8; 2 Timothy 3:10–17

ALBERT EINSTEIN
GERMAN-BORN THEORETICAL PHYSICIST (1879 – 1955)

QUOTATION **627**

Great spirits have always encountered violent opposition from mediocre minds.

Citation: Unknown

Topics: Criticism; Enemies; Mind; Oppression; Violence

References: Matthew 5:10–12; 1 Corinthians 4:1–2; 2 Timothy 3:12

QUOTATION **628**

The real problem is in the hearts and minds of men. It is not a problem of physics but of ethics. It is easier to denature plutonium than to denounce the evil spirit of man.

Citation: Unknown

Topics: Depravity; Fall of Humanity; Human Condition; Lostness; Science; Sinful Nature

References: Jeremiah 17:9–10; Matthew 15:1–20; Romans 1:18–32; 3:9–26

QUOTATION **629**

There are only two ways to live your life. One is as if nothing is a miracle. The other is as if everything is.

Citation: Unknown

Topics: Awe; Beauty; Life; Perspective; Spiritual Perception; Thanksgiving; Wonder

References: Psalms 8; 19

JACQUES ELLUL

FRENCH PHILOSOPHER, SOCIOLOGIST, AND THEOLOGIAN (1912 – 94)

QUOTATION 630

God is … an easy temporary replacement until we find the real explanation, which will, of course, be scientific. …

For me, God is certainly not the God of the gaps.

Citation: Jacques Ellul, *What I Believe*

Topics: Doctrine; God; Science; Truth

References: 1 Chronicles 29:12; Job 26:12; Luke 1:37

QUOTATION 631

If I step outside this faith, the human adventure has no orientation of its own. It is not true that history as such has meaning. … Human history is in fact a tale told by an idiot.

Citation: Jacques Ellul, *What I Believe*

Topics: Foolishness; Goals; History; Humanism; Limitations; Idolatry; Meaning; Purpose

References: Matthew 13:39; Hebrews 6:8; 2 Peter 3:10

EPICTETUS

GREEK STOIC PHILOSOPHER (c. AD 55 – 135)

QUOTATION 632

Contentment comes not so much from great wealth as from few wants.

Citation: Unknown

Topics: Attitudes; Contentment; Coveting; Desires; Greed; Happiness; Lust; Money; Peace

References: Philippians 4:4–13; 1 Timothy 6:6–10

VIKTOR FRANKL
AUSTRIAN NEUROLOGIST AND PSYCHIATRIST (1905–97)

QUOTATION **633**

Freedom is only part of the story and half the truth.... That is why I recommend that the Statue of Liberty on the East Coast be supplemented by a Statue of Responsibility on the West Coast.

> **Citation:** Viktor Frankl, *Man's Search for Meaning*
>
> **Topics:** Freedom; Human Will; Individualism; Responsibility
>
> **References:** 1 Corinthians 6:12; 10:23–24; Galatians 5:13; 1 Peter 2:16

QUOTATION **634**

What is to give light must endure the burning.

> **Citation:** Unknown
>
> **Topics:** Growth; Pain; Regeneration; Sanctification; Suffering; Trials
>
> **References:** Matthew 5:10–12; 1 Corinthians 4:1–2; 2 Timothy 3:12

SIGMUND FREUD
AUSTRIAN NEUROLOGIST AND PSYCHIATRIST (1856–1939)

QUOTATION **635**

I have found little that is "good" about human beings on the whole. In my experience most of them are trash, no matter whether they publicly subscribe to this or that ethical doctrine or to none at all.

> **Citation:** Sigmund Freud, in a letter to a friend
>
> **Topics:** Depravity; Godlessness; Human Condition; Human Nature; Original Sin; Sinful Nature; Worth
>
> **References:** Genesis 1:26–31; John 3:16; Romans 4:1–8; Ephesians 2:1–10

JOHN KENNETH GALBRAITH

CANADIAN-AMERICAN ECONOMIST (1908–2006)

QUOTATION **636**

If you get a reputation for being honest, you have 95 percent of the competition already beat.

> **Citation:** Unknown
>
> **Topics:** Character; Honesty; Integrity; Reputation; Witness
>
> **References:** Matthew 5:13–16; 1 Thessalonians 2:1–16

CHARLES GORE

BRITISH THEOLOGIAN AND ANGLICAN BISHOP (1853–1932)

QUOTATION **637**

Inadequate conceptions of Christ's person go hand in hand with inadequate conceptions of what human nature wants.

> **Citation:** Charles Gore, *Our Lord's Human Example*
>
> **Topics:** Human Nature; Jesus Christ; Worldview
>
> **References:** John 1:1–18; 10:1–18; 14:1–14; 15:1–8

STANLEY GRENZ

AMERICAN THEOLOGIAN (1950–2005)

QUOTATION **638**

Finding ourselves means, among other things, finding the story in terms of which our lives make sense.

> **Citation:** Stanley Grenz, *Theology for the Community of God*
>
> **Topics:** Direction; Guidance; Meaning; Purpose; Truth; Vision
>
> **Reference:** Romans 1:18–25; 3:9–20; 5:1–11; 8:1–17

STANLEY HAUERWAS

AMERICAN THEOLOGIAN, ETHICIST, AND PROFESSOR OF LAW (1940–)

QUOTATION 639

It's hard to remember that Jesus did not come to make us safe, but rather to make us disciples, citizens of God's new age, a kingdom of surprise.

Citation: Unknown

Topics: Discipleship; Kingdom; Safety; Security; Wonder

References: Isaiah 65:17–18; Mark 1:15; 6:45–52; John 8:31–32; 2 Timothy 1:7; 3:12

GEORG WILHELM FRIEDRICH HEGEL

GERMAN PHILOSOPHER (1770–1831)

QUOTATION 640

Life has value only when it has something valuable as its object.

Citation: Georg Wilhelm Friedrich Hegel, *The Philosophy of History*

Topics: God; Life; Meaning; Purpose; Worship

References: Psalm 115:1–8; Mark 12:28–31; Ephesians 1:3–14; Philippians 3:7–21

ABRAHAM JOSHUA HESCHEL

JEWISH THEOLOGIAN AND WRITER (1907–72)

QUOTATION 641

Faith like Job's cannot be shaken, because it is the result of having been shaken.

Citation: Unknown

Topics: Faith; Perseverance; Sanctification; Tests; Trials

References: Job 23:8–12; Psalm 32:10; Isaiah 26:3–4

QUOTATION **642**

Racism is man's gravest threat to man — the maximum hatred for a minimum reason.

> Citation: Unknown
> Topics: Anger; Hatred; Human Nature; Racism
> References: Acts 10:34–38; 11:1–18; 15:1–21; Galatians 3:26–4:7

QUOTATION **643**

Wonder rather than doubt is the root of all knowledge.

> Citation: Unknown
> Topics: Awe; Doubt; Knowledge; Mysteries; Trust; Wonder
> Reference: Psalm 19

QUOTATION **644**

When I was young, I admired clever people. Now that I am old, I admire kind people.

> Citation: Unknown
> Topics: Compassion; Gentleness; Kindness; Wisdom
> References: Galatians 5:22; Colossians 3:12; 2 Peter 1:3–11

ELBERT HUBBARD
AMERICAN PHILOSOPHER AND WRITER (1856–1915)

QUOTATION **645**

We preserve our sanity only as we forget self in service.

> Citation: Elbert Hubbard, *The Notebook of Elbert Hubbard*
> Topics: Gentleness; Kindness; Service; Social Impact
> References: Matthew 20:28; John 13:1–17

QUOTATION **646**

Responsibility is the price of freedom.

> **Citation:** Unknown
>
> **Topics:** Freedom; Free Will; Responsibility
>
> **References:** Romans 14:1 – 15:13; 1 Corinthians 8

QUOTATION **647**

Genius may have its limitations, but stupidity is not thus handicapped.

> **Citation:** Unknown
>
> **Topics:** Foolishness; Knowledge; Mind
>
> **References:** Proverbs 10; 17; 26; 29

BARON FRIEDRICH VON HÜGEL
AUSTRIAN ROMAN CATHOLIC WRITER AND THEOLOGIAN (1852 – 1925)

QUOTATION **648**

The deeper we get into reality, the more numerous will be the questions we cannot answer.

> **Citation:** Baron Friedrich Von Hügel, *The Reality of God and Religion and Agnosticism*
>
> **Topics:** Limitations; Mind; Mysteries; Questions; Spiritual Perception; Truth
>
> **References:** Job 36:26; 37:5; 42:3; Psalm 139:6; Isaiah 40:13, 28; 55:8 – 9; Romans 11:33 – 34; 1 Corinthians 2:16

ALEXANDER VON HUMBOLDT

PRUSSIAN NATURALIST AND EXPLORER (1769 – 1859)

QUOTATION 649

First they ignore it, then they laugh at it, then they say they knew it all along.

Citation: Unknown

Topics: Change; Foolishness; Influence; Innovation; Leadership; Vision

Reference: Zechariah 4:10

JAMES DAVISON HUNTER

AMERICAN SOCIOLOGIST AND WRITER (1955 –)

QUOTATION 650

We Americans generally want to think of ourselves as good people. That, in many respects, is where the trouble begins.

Citation: Unknown

Topics: Arrogance; Depravity; Human Nature; Original Sin; Pride; Self-examination; Self-righteousness

References: Proverbs 11:2; Isaiah 2:17; Ezekiel 28:2; Romans 3:9 – 20

WILLIAM JAMES

AMERICAN PSYCHOLOGIST AND PHILOSOPHER (1842 – 1910)

QUOTATION 651

For him who confesses, shams are over, and realities have begun.

Citation: William James, *The Varieties of Religious Experience*

Topics: Change; Confession; Deceit; Honesty; Hypocrisy; Repentance; Transformation; Truth

References: Psalm 51:1 – 12; Proverbs 28:13; 1 John 1:8

CARL JUNG

SWISS PSYCHIATRIST (1875–1961)

QUOTATION 652

When goal goes, meaning goes; when meaning goes, purpose goes; when purpose goes, life is dead on our hands.

> **Citation:** Unknown
>
> **Topics:** Direction; Eternal Life; Future; Goals; Heaven; Meaning; Motivation; Purpose; Significance
>
> **References:** Jeremiah 29:11–14; Philippians 1:6; 2:12–13

SØREN KIERKEGAARD

DANISH PHILOSOPHER AND THEOLOGIAN (1813–55)

QUOTATION 653

What really counts in life is that at some time you have seen something, felt something, which is so great, so matchless, that everything else is nothing by comparison, that even if you forgot everything, you would never forget this.

> **Citation:** Søren Kierkegaard, *Journals and Papers*
>
> **Topics:** Awe; Beauty; Experiencing God; Illumination; Life; Passion; Praise; Worship
>
> **Reference:** 1 John 1:1–4

QUOTATION 654

God creates out of nothing. Wonderful, you say. Yes, to be sure, but he does what is still more wonderful: He makes saints out of sinners.

> **Citation:** Søren Kierkegaard, *Journals and Papers*
>
> **Topics:** Atonement; Creation; Creator; Redemption; Regeneration; Salvation; Sanctification; Transformation
>
> **References:** 1 Corinthians 1:30; Ephesians 5:26; 2 Timothy 2:21; 1 Peter 1:2

QUOTATION **655**

It is more blessed to give than to receive, but then it is also more blessed to be able to do without than to have to have.

Citation: Søren Kierkegaard, *Journals and Papers*

Topics: Benevolence; Blessings; Contentment; Giving; Greed; Materialism; Sacrifice; Self-denial

References: Acts 20:35; Philippians 4:11 – 13

QUOTATION **656**

When one preaches Christianity in such a way that the echo answers, "Away with that man, he does not deserve to live," know that this is the Christianity of the New Testament. Capital punishment is the penalty for preaching Christianity as it truly is.

Citation: Søren Kierkegaard, *Attack upon Christendom*

Topics: Evangelism; Gospel; Martyrdom; Opposition; Persecution; Preaching

References: Acts 7:54 – 60; 21:30 – 36; Ephesians 6:19 – 20; Philippians 1:27 – 30

QUOTATION **657**

There are, in the end, only two ways open to us: to honestly and honorably make an admission of how far we are from the Christianity of the New Testament, or to perform skillful tricks to conceal the true situation.

Citation: Søren Kierkegaard, in his essay "What Madness"

Topics: Christian Life; Confession; Deceit; Hypocrisy

References: Galatians 3:1 – 3; Revelation 2:2 – 5; 3:15 – 19

QUOTATION **658**

Christian truth itself has eyes to see with. In fact, it is all eye. That's very disquieting. Think of looking at a painting and discovering that the painting was looking at you. Precisely such is the case with Christian truth. It is looking back at me to see whether I do what it says I should do.

Citation: Unknown

Topics: Integrity; Obedience; Self-examination; Truth

References: John 8:31–32; 18:37; Hebrews 4:12

QUOTATION **659**

When you read God's Word, you must constantly be saying to yourself, "It is talking to me, and about me."

Citation: Unknown

Topics: Bible; Devotional Life; Obedience; Teachability

References: 1 Corinthians 10:11; Colossians 3:16; Hebrews 4:12

PETER KOESTENBAUM
AMERICAN PHILOSOPHER (1928–)

QUOTATION **660**

Unless the distant goals of meaning, greatness, and destiny are addressed, we can't make an intelligent decision about what to do tomorrow morning—much less set strategy for a company or for a human life.

Citation: Peter Koestenbaum, quoted in the *Fast Company* article "Do you Have the Will to Lead?"

Topics: Decisions; Goals; Lifestyle; Meaning; Planning; Purpose; Vision; Wisdom

References: Ecclesiastes 12:13–14; Philippians 2:12–13

QUOTATION **661**

Nothing is more practical than for people to deepen themselves. The more you understand the human condition, the more effective you are as a business-person. Human depth makes business sense.

Citation: Peter Koestenbaum, quoted in the *Fast Company* article "Do you Have the Will to Lead?"

Topics: Business; Discernment; Growth; Human Condition; Spiritual Disciplines; Teachability; Wisdom; Work

References: Ecclesiastes 12:13–14; Philippians 2:12–13

HANS KÜNG
SWISS THEOLOGIAN, PRIEST, AND WRITER (1928–)

QUOTATION 662

Doubt is the shadow cast by faith. One does not always notice it, but it is always there, though concealed. At any moment it may come into action. There is no mystery of the faith which is immune to doubt.

> **Citation:** Hans Küng, *That the World May Believe*
>
> **Topics:** Doubt; Faith; Mysteries; Tests; Trust
>
> **Reference:** Matthew 28:17

QUOTATION 663

A church which pitches its tents without constantly looking out for new horizons, which does not continually strike camp, is being untrue to its calling.... [We must] play down our longing for certainty, accept what is risky, and live by improvisation and experiment.

> **Citation:** Hans Küng, *The Church as the People of God*
>
> **Topics:** Calling; Church; Courage; Faith; Ministry; Risk; Teachability; Trust; Vision
>
> **Reference:** Numbers 13:30–33; 14:5–9

JOHN LOCKE
BRITISH PHILOSOPHER (1632–1704)

QUOTATION 664

I have always thought that the actions of men are the best interpreters of their thoughts.

> **Citation:** Unknown
>
> **Topics:** Character; Convictions; Integrity; Morality; Self-examination; Spiritual Perception; Thoughts
>
> **References:** Matthew 15:18–19; Luke 6:45; Romans 2:6–12; Colossians 1:21; Revelation 2:23

VLADIMIR LOSSKY
ORTHODOX THEOLOGIAN (1903–58)

QUOTATION 665

If in seeing God one can know what one sees, then one has not seen God in himself but something intelligible, something which is inferior to him. It is by *unknowing* that one may know him who is above every possible object of knowledge.

Citation: Vladimir Lossky, *The Mystical Theology of the Eastern Church*

Topics: Awe; Experiencing God; God; Illumination; Knowing God; Limitations; Mysteries

References: 1 Timothy 6:15–16; Revelation 19:12

MARTIN E. MARTY
AMERICAN RELIGIOUS SCHOLAR (1928–)

QUOTATION 666

The initial act of Jesus is to overcome the distance between Jerusalem and our town, to cut across the years from his own time to ours. He clears away all the debris and clutter of secondary themes and says, "For you."

Citation: Martin E. Marty, *The Lord's Supper*

Topics: Atonement; Cross; Incarnation; Jesus Christ; Lord's Supper; Redemption; Salvation

References: Luke 22:20; Galatians 2:20

ALISTER MCGRATH
AMERICAN THEOLOGIAN (1953 –)

QUOTATION 667

Paradoxically, what propels people toward atheism is above all a sense of revulsion against the excesses and failures of organized religion.

> **Citation:** Alister McGrath, in the *Christianity Today* article "The Twilight of Atheism"
>
> **Topics:** Atheism; Belief; Doubt; Hypocrisy; Religion
>
> **References:** Luke 6:42; 1 Thessalonians 4:9 – 12; 1 Peter 2:12

QUOTATION 668

Inattention to doctrine robs the church of her reason for existence and opens the way to enslavement and oppression by the world.

> **Citation:** Alister McGrath, in an article for *Journal of the Evangelical Theological Society*
>
> **Topics:** Bondage; Church; Doctrine; Guidance; Theology; Truth
>
> **References:** 1 Timothy 1:9 – 11; 4:16; 2 Timothy 4:3; Titus 1:9 – 11

DIANE MEDVED
AMERICAN PSYCHOLOGIST AND WRITER

QUOTATION 669

Divorce, as a cure, is far worse than the disease.

> **Citation:** Diane Medved, *The Case against Divorce*
>
> **Topics:** Divorce; Marriage; Spouses
>
> **References:** Matthew 5:31; Mark 10:11; Luke 16:18

JÜRGEN MOLTMANN

GERMAN THEOLOGIAN (1926–)

QUOTATION 670

It is through faith that man finds the path of true life, but it is only hope that keeps him on that path.

Citation: Jürgen Moltmann, *Theology of Hope*

Topics: Faith; Hope; Overcoming; Perseverance; Trust

References: Romans 4:18; Hebrews 6:18–20; 11:1

QUOTATION 671

God weeps with us so that we may someday laugh with him.

Citation: Unknown

Topics: Experiencing God; Joy; Pain; Suffering; Trials

References: Luke 6:21; John 11:35–44

RICHARD J. MOUW

AMERICAN PROFESSOR OF CHRISTIAN PHILOSOPHY AND PRESIDENT OF FULLER THEOLOGICAL SEMINARY (1940–)

QUOTATION 672

Theology is best understood as "a mystery discerning enterprise" rather than "a problem solving" one. To solve a problem is to make all of our puzzles go away, which is not the kind of resolution that we ought to expect as a matter of course in theological exploration. But we can hope to succeed in knowing "more precisely and clearly what the mystery is"—and this can be an important gain.

Citation: Richard J. Mouw, *He Shines in All That's Fair*

Topics: Discernment; Doctrine; Knowledge; Limitations; Mysteries; Theology; Truth; Understanding

References: Deuteronomy 29:29; Isaiah 55:8–9; 1 Timothy 3:16

LESSLIE NEWBIGIN
BRITISH THEOLOGIAN AND BISHOP (1909–98)

QUOTATION **673**

Tolerance with respect to what is not important is easy.

> **Citation:** Lesslie Newbigin, *Foolishness to the Greeks*
>
> **Topics:** Courage; Priorities; Tolerance; Worldliness
>
> **References:** Isaiah 42:17; Micah 4:5; Romans 14:1; 1 Corinthians 10:28

QUOTATION **674**

No belief system can be faulted by the fact that it rests on unproved assumptions; what can and must be faulted is the blindness of its proponents to the fact that this is so.

> **Citation:** Lesslie Newbigin, *Foolishness to the Greeks*
>
> **Topics:** Belief; Complacency; Faith; Perception; Religion; Spiritual Blindness; Truth; Worldview
>
> **References:** Isaiah 59:10; Matthew 6:23; 15:14; 2 Corinthians 4:4

QUOTATION **675**

Words without deeds are empty, but deeds without words are dumb.

> **Citation:** Lesslie Newbigin, *Mission in Christ's Way*
>
> **Topics:** Evangelism; Foolishness; Gentleness; Good Deeds; Kindness; Preaching; Testimony; Witness; Words
>
> **References:** Matthew 5:16; James 2:18; 1 Peter 2:12; 3:15

QUOTATION **676**

Mission is not a burden laid upon the church; it is a gift and a promise to the church that is faithful. The command arises from the gift. Jesus reigns and all authority has been given to him in earth and heaven. When we understand that, we shall not need to be told to let it be known. Rather, we shall not be able to keep silent.

> **Citation:** Lesslie Newbigin, *Mission in Christ's Way*

Topics: Church; Evangelism; Gospel; Great Commission; Ministry; Mission; Passion

References: Matthew 28:18–20; 1 Corinthians 15:10; Ephesians 1:18–19; 3:7; Colossians 1:28–29

REINHOLD NIEBUHR
AMERICAN THEOLOGIAN (1892–1971)

QUOTATION 677

Nothing worth doing is completed in one lifetime: therefore we must be saved by hope. Nothing true or beautiful makes complete sense in any context of history: therefore we must be saved by faith. Nothing we do, no matter how virtuous, can be accomplished alone: therefore we are saved by love.

Citation: Unknown

Topics: Faith; Hope; Love; Redemption; Salvation

References: Romans 15:4; Hebrews 6:18–20

QUOTATION 678

Most of the evil in this world does not come from evil people. It comes from people who consider themselves good.

Citation: Unknown

Topics: Deceit; Depravity; Evil; Human Condition; Hypocrisy; Self-examination; Self-righteousness; Sin

References: Psalm 36:2; Proverbs 20:9; Romans 3:23; 1 John 1:8

MARTIN NIEMÖLLER
GERMAN THEOLOGIAN AND PASTOR (1892–1984)

QUOTATION 679

More than fifty-five years ago my father told me, "The Bible does not belong on the shelf but in your hand, under your eye, and in your heart."

Citation: Unknown

Topics: Bible; Bible Study; Commitment; Guidance; Heart; Spiritual Disciplines; Wisdom

Reference: Psalm 119:11

FRIEDRICH NIETZSCHE
GERMAN PHILOSOPHER (1844–1900)

QUOTATION **680**

The most common lie is the lie one tells to oneself; lying to others is relatively the exception.

Citation: Friedrich Nietzsche, *The Anti-Christ*

Topics: Arrogance; Deceit; Honesty; Pride; Self-deception; Self-examination

References: Psalm 36:2; Isaiah 44:20; James 1:22; Revelation 3:17

JOHN OWEN
BRITISH THEOLOGIAN (1616–83)

QUOTATION **681**

However strong a castle may be, if a treacherous party resides inside (ready to betray at the first opportunity possible), the castle cannot be kept safe from the Enemy. Traitors occupy our own hearts, ready to side with every temptation and to surrender to them all.

Citation: John Owen, *The Temptation of Believers*

Topics: Depravity; Devil; Evil; Satan; Self-examination; Sinful Nature; Spiritual Warfare; Temptation

References: Proverbs 4:23; Matthew 26:41; Mark 14:38; Luke 22:40; Romans 7:18–24; James 1:13–18

QUOTATION **682**

Christ will try your love at the last day by your deportment in that church wherein you are.

Citation: John Owen, in his sermon "Gospel Charity"

Topics: Church; Community; Love; Relationships; Service

References: Proverbs 17:9; John 15:12; Romans 12:9–10

QUOTATION **683**

Temptation is like a knife that may either cut the meat or the throat of a man; it may be his food or his poison, his exercise or his destruction.

Citation: John Owen, in his sermon "Of Temptation: The Nature and Power of It"

Topics: Maturity; Spiritual Warfare; Temptation

References: Matthew 4:1–11; Luke 4:1–13

J. I. PACKER
BRITISH-CANADIAN THEOLOGIAN (1926–)

QUOTATION **684**

Opposition is a fact: the Christian who is not conscious of being opposed had better watch himself for he is in danger.

Citation: J. I. Packer, *Knowing God*

Topics: Enemies; Opposition; Persecution; Satan; Spiritual Warfare; Temptation

References: Hebrews 12:3; 1 Peter 4:12

QUOTATION **685**

The Almighty appeared on earth as a helpless human baby, needing to be fed and changed and taught to talk like any other child. The more you think about it, the more staggering it gets. Nothing in fiction is so fantastic as this truth of the Incarnation.

Citation: J. I. Packer, *Knowing God*

Topics: Incarnation; Jesus Christ; Mysteries

References: Isaiah 7:14; John 1:14; Philippians 2:7; 1 Timothy 3:16

QUOTATION **686**

If you want to judge how well a person understands Christianity, find out how much he makes of the thought of being God's child and having God as his Father. If this is not the thought that prompts and controls his worship and prayers and his whole outlook on life, it means that he does not understand Christianity very well at all.

> **Citation:** J. I. Packer, *Knowing God*
>
> **Topics:** Children of God; Devotion; God as Father; Identity; Worship
>
> **References:** John 1:12–13; Romans 8:17; Philippians 2:15; 1 John 3:1–10; 5:1–2

QUOTATION **687**

Meditation is ... often a matter of arguing with oneself, reasoning oneself out of moods of doubt and unbelief into a clear apprehension of God's power and grace.

> **Citation:** J. I. Packer, *Knowing God*
>
> **Topics:** Experiencing God; Meditation; Prayer; Solitude; Spiritual Disciplines; Thoughts
>
> **References:** Joshua 1:8; Psalms 1:2; 119:15; John 20:19–31; 2 Timothy 2:7; 1 Peter 5:6–7

QUOTATION **688**

[We should] choose the leisure activities that bring us closest to God, to people, to beauty, and to all that ennobles.

> **Citation:** J. I. Packer, *God's Plans for You*
>
> **Topics:** Beauty; Choices; Entertainment; Lifestyle; Recreation; Rest
>
> **References:** Psalm 23:2–3; Isaiah 40:30–31; Mark 6:31; 1 Corinthians 10:23–24; Philippians 4:8

QUOTATION **689**

If we are not constantly growing downward into humility, we shall be steadily swelling up and running to seed under the influence of pride.

> **Citation:** J. I. Packer, in the *Christianity Today* article "Rediscovering Holiness"

Topics: Arrogance; Bondage; Humility; Pride

References: Proverbs 11:2; 29:23; Micah 6:8; Matthew 18:4

QUOTATION **690**

When the fathomless wells of rage and hatred in the normal human heart are tapped, the results are fearful.... Only restraining and renewing grace enables anyone to keep the sixth commandment.

Citation: J. I. Packer, in the *Christianity Today* article "Lord, I Want to Be a Christian"

Topics: Anger; Grace; Hatred; Human Condition; Murder; Sin; Sinful Nature

References: Exodus 20:13; Isaiah 64:6; Romans 7:11

QUOTATION **691**

It is impossible at the same time to give the impression both that I am a great Christian and that Jesus Christ is a great Master. So the Christian will practice curling up small, as it were, so that in and through him or her the Savior may show himself great. That is what I mean by growing downward.

Citation: J. I. Packer, in the *Christianity Today* article "Rediscovering Holiness"

Topics: Humility; Maturity; Spiritual Growth; Submission

References: Proverbs 16:19; Ephesians 4:15; Hebrews 6:1; James 4:10

QUOTATION **692**

It needs to be said loud and clear that in the kingdom of God there ain't no comfort zone and never will be.

Citation: J. I. Packer, in the *Christianity Today* forum "We Can Overcome"

Topics: Christian Life; Kingdom; Oppression; Suffering; Trials

References: Psalm 66:8 – 20; Romans 5:4; 1 Peter 2:19 – 21; 3:13 – 22

QUOTATION **693**

Along with much bad thinking ... goes split living.

Citation: J. I. Packer, in the *Christianity Today* article "Your Father Loves You"

Topics: Double-mindedness; Hypocrisy; Lifestyle; Truth; Wisdom

References: 2 Kings 17:33; Luke 16:13; James 4:8

THOMAS PAINE

BRITISH PHILOSOPHER (1737 – 1809)

QUOTATION **694**

A long habit of not thinking a thing wrong gives it a superficial appearance of being right.... Time makes more converts than reason.

Citation: Thomas Paine, *Common Sense*

Topics: Correction; Deceit; Discernment; Immorality; Morality; Reason

References: John 7:24; 2 Timothy 4:2

WOLFHART PANNENBERG

GERMAN THEOLOGIAN (1928 –)

QUOTATION **695**

The evidence for Jesus' resurrection is so strong that nobody would question it except for two things: First, it is a very unusual event. And second, if you believe it happened, you have to change the way you live.

Citation: Wolfhart Pannenberg, in a *Prism* magazine interview

Topics: Change; Discipleship; Jesus Christ; Repentance; Resurrection; Transformation

References: Matthew 28:1 – 15; Mark 16:1 – 8; Luke 24:1 – 12; John 20

BLAISE PASCAL

FRENCH MATHEMATICIAN, PHYSICIST, AND RELIGIOUS PHILOSOPHER (1623–62)

QUOTATION **696**

The knowledge of God without that of our wretchedness creates pride. The knowledge of our wretchedness without that of God creates despair. The knowledge of Jesus Christ is the middle way, because in him we find both God and our wretchedness.

> **Citation:** Blaise Pascal, *Pensées*
>
> **Topics:** Depravity; Despair; Human Condition; Jesus Christ; Knowledge; Misery
>
> **References:** Jeremiah 9:24; 17:3; John 8:31–32

QUOTATION **697**

Men never do evil so completely and cheerfully as when they do it from religious conviction.

> **Citation:** Blaise Pascal, *Pensées*
>
> **Topics:** Convictions; Evil; Human Condition; Hypocrisy; Religion; Sin
>
> **References:** Proverbs 26:23; Ezekiel 33:31; Titus 1:16

QUOTATION **698**

It is dangerous to show man too clearly how much he resembles the beast, without at the same time showing him his greatness. It is also dangerous to allow him too clear a vision of his greatness without his baseness. It is even more dangerous to leave him in ignorance of both.

> **Citation:** Blaise Pascal, *Pensées*
>
> **Topics:** Depravity; Human Condition; Sinful Nature; Worth
>
> **References:** Psalm 8; Romans 1:18–32

QUOTATION **699**

All the good maxims have been written. It only remains to put them into practice.

Citation: Unknown

Topics: Commitment; Dedication; Lifestyle; Obedience

References: Proverbs 3:13; Ezekiel 33:31; Luke 8:21

QUOTATION **700**

The history of the church should more accurately be called the history of truth.

Citation: Unknown

Topics: Christian Life; Church; Truth; Wisdom

References: Revelation 6:9; 20:4

M. SCOTT PECK
AMERICAN PSYCHIATRIST AND WRITER (1936–2005)

QUOTATION **701**

Since love is work, the essence of non-love is laziness.

Citation: M. Scott Peck, *The Road Less Traveled*

Topics: Complacency; Laziness; Love

References: Proverbs 13:4; Ecclesiastes 10:18

QUOTATION **702**

Often the most loving thing we can do when a friend is in pain is to share the pain—to be there even when we have nothing to offer except our presence and even when being there is painful to ourselves.

Citation: M. Scott Peck, *The Different Drum*

Topics: Encouragement; Fellowship; Presence; Relationships; Sacrifice

References: Proverbs 17:17; 27:10, 17; Ecclesiastes 4:9–10

JAROSLAV PELIKAN

THEOLOGIAN, PROFESSOR, AND WRITER (1923–2006)

QUOTATION 703

Tradition is the living faith of the dead; traditionalism is the dead faith of the living.

> **Citation:** Jaroslav Pelikan, in a *U.S. News & World Report* interview
>
> **Topics:** Change; Faith; Idolatry; Past; Tradition
>
> **References:** Mark 7:8; Colossians 2:8; Titus 1:14

QUOTATION 704

If Christ is risen, nothing else matters. And if Christ is not risen—nothing else matters.

> **Citation:** Jaroslav Pelikan, before dying
>
> **Topics:** Hope; Jesus Christ; Life; Meaning; Perspective; Resurrection
>
> **References:** Romans 5:12–21; 6:1–14; 1 Corinthians 15

JOHN PIPER

AMERICAN THEOLOGIAN, WRITER, AND PASTOR (1946–)

QUOTATION 705

Christian fasting, at its root, is the hunger of a homesickness for God.

> **Citation:** John Piper, *A Hunger for God*
>
> **Topics:** Desires; Experiencing God; Fasting; Heaven; Self-discipline; Spiritual Disciplines
>
> **References:** Psalm 84:2; Mark 2:18–20; Luke 6:21

QUOTATION 706

Missions is not the ultimate goal of the church. Worship is. Missions exists because worship doesn't.

> **Citation:** John Piper, *Let the Nations Be Glad!*

Topics: Church; Evangelism; Missions; Motivation; Purpose; Worship

References: Matthew 5:13–16; 9:35–38; 28:16–20; Luke 9:1–9; 15; 24:45–49; John 20:21

QUOTATION 707

In missions we simply aim to bring the nations into the white-hot employment of God's glory.

Citation: John Piper, *Let the Nations Be Glad!*

Topics: Evangelism; Goals; Missions; Motivation; Purpose; Worship

References: Matthew 5:13–16; 9:35–38; 28:16–20; Luke 8:16–18; 9:1–9; 15; 24:45–49; John 20:21

QUOTATION 708

The cost of food in the kingdom is hunger for the bread of heaven, instead of the white bread of the world. Do you want it? Are you hungry? Or are you satisfied with yourself and your television and your computer and your job and your family?

Citation: John Piper, in his sermon "The Present Power of a Future Possession"

Topics: Desires; Distractions; Kingdom; Priorities

Reference: Psalm 63:1–8

MARY PIPHER
AMERICAN CLINICAL PSYCHOLOGIST AND WRITER (1947–)

QUOTATION 709

Girls … are caught in the crossfire of our culture's mixed sexual messages. Sex is considered both a sacred act between two people united by God and the best way to sell suntan lotion.

Citation: Mary Pipher, *Reviving Ophelia*

Topics: Conscience; Culture; Lust; Purity; Sex; Temptation

References: Matthew 5:27–30; 1 Corinthians 6:12–20

CORNELIUS PLANTINGA JR.

AMERICAN THEOLOGIAN, WRITER, AND PRESIDENT OF CALVIN THEOLOGICAL SEMINARY (1947–)

QUOTATION **710**

Even when sin is depressingly familiar, it is never normal.

> **Citation:** Cornelius Plantinga Jr., *Not the Way It's Supposed to Be*
>
> **Topics:** Depravity; Human Condition; Sin
>
> **Reference:** Romans 1:18–32

QUOTATION **711**

Sin is both the overstepping of a line and the failure to reach it—both transgression and shortcoming.

> **Citation:** Cornelius Plantinga Jr., *Not the Way It's Supposed to Be*
>
> **Topics:** Depravity; Human Condition; Sin
>
> **Reference:** Romans 3:21–31

QUOTATION **712**

Everything sin touches begins to die, but we do not focus on that. We see only the vitality of the parasite, glowing with stolen life.

> **Citation:** Cornelius Plantinga Jr., *Not the Way It's Supposed to Be*
>
> **Topics:** Consequences; Deceit; Depravity; Evil; Human Condition; Sin; Spiritual Warfare
>
> **References:** Genesis 3; Romans 2:1–16; 5:12–21; 6:23

QUOTATION **713**

To do its worst, evil needs to look its best. Evil has to spend a lot on makeup.... Vices have to masquerade as virtues—lust as love, thinly veiled sadism as military discipline, envy as righteous indignation, domestic tyranny as parental concern.

> **Citation:** Cornelius Plantinga Jr., *Not the Way It's Supposed to Be*

Topics: Deceit; Depravity; Evil; Human Condition; Satan; Sin; Spiritual Warfare; Vices; Virtues

References: Genesis 3; Matthew 4:1 – 11; Luke 4:1 – 13; James 1:13 – 18

QUOTATION **714**

Wisdom is, broadly speaking, the knowledge of God's world and the knack of fitting oneself into it.

Citation: Cornelius Plantinga Jr., *Not the Way It's Supposed to Be*

Topics: Direction; Knowledge; Life; Purpose; Wisdom

References: Proverbs 1:1 – 7; James 3:13 – 18

QUOTATION **715**

Intelligence and education are only raw materials for good judgment.

Citation: Cornelius Plantinga Jr., *Not the Way It's Supposed to Be*

Topics: Decisions; Discernment; Knowledge; Wisdom

References: Proverbs 1:7; 3:13; 4:7; 14:12; 16:25; 23:23; 1 Corinthians 1:18 – 31; 3:19

KARL POPPER
AUSTRIAN-BRITISH PHILOSOPHER (1902 – 94)

QUOTATION **716**

It might be well for all of us to remember that, while differing widely in the various little bits we know, in our infinite ignorance we are all equal.

Citation: Karl Popper, *Conjectures and Refutations: The Growth of Scientific Knowledge*

Topics: Foolishness; Limitations; Perspective

References: Isaiah 55:8 – 9; Matthew 24:36; Luke 12:35 – 40; 1 Thessalonians 5:1 – 11

VIRGINIA SATIR
AMERICAN WRITER AND PSYCHOTHERAPIST (1916–88)

QUOTATION 717

Most people prefer the certainty of misery to the misery of uncertainty.

Citation: Unknown

Topics: Habits; Misery; Obedience; Risk; Uncertainties

References: Exodus 16:3; Numbers 13:30–33; 14:5–9

ALBERT SCHWEITZER
ALSATIAN THEOLOGIAN, PHILOSOPHER, AND PHYSICIAN (1875–1965)

QUOTATION 718

Truth has no special time of its own. Its hour is now—always.

Citation: Albert Schweitzer, *Out of My Life and Thought*

Topics: Courage; Time; Truth

References: 2 Samuel 7:28; Proverbs 23:23; Ephesians 6:14

QUOTATION 719

If your soul has no Sunday, it becomes an orphan.

Citation: Unknown

Topics: Priorities; Recreation; Rest; Sabbath; Worship

References: Exodus 20:8–11; Deuteronomy 5:12–15; Matthew 11:29; Hebrews 4:11; 10:25; 13:15

QUOTATION 720

One thing I know: The only ones among you who will be really happy are those who will have sought and found how to serve.

Citation: Unknown

Topics: Calling; Joy; Purpose; Self-denial; Service; Spiritual Gifts
References: John 13:1–17; Philippians 2:1–11

SENECA
ROMAN STOIC PHILOSOPHER AND STATESMAN (c. 4 BC–AD 65)

QUOTATION 721

We should give as we would receive: cheerfully, quickly, and without hesitation; for there is no grace in a benefit that sticks to the fingers.

Citation: Seneca, *Seneca's Morals*

Topics: Benevolence; Generosity; Giving; Grace; Greed; Money; Stewardship

References: Matthew 6:3; 10:8; Romans 12:8; 2 Corinthians 9:7

LEWIS B. SMEDES
AMERICAN WRITER AND THEOLOGIAN (1921–2002)

QUOTATION 722

The secret of grace is that it can be all right at the center even when it is all wrong on the edges.

Citation: Lewis B. Smedes, *How Can It Be All Right When Everything Is All Wrong?*

Topics: Grace; Hope; Joy; Peace; Perseverance; Perspective

References: Acts 15:11; Romans 5:15; Titus 2:11

QUOTATION 723

Healthy anger drives us to do something to change what makes us angry; anger can energize us to make things better. Hate does not want to change things for the better; it wants to make things worse.

Citation: Lewis B. Smedes, *Forgive and Forget*

Topics: Anger; Change; Hatred; Maturity; Spiritual Growth; Transformation

Reference: Ephesians 4:26–27

If we do not keep our promises, what once was a human community turns into a combat zone of competitive self-maximizers.

> **Citation:** Lewis B. Smedes, in his sermon "The Power of Promises"
> **Topics:** Character; Community; Integrity; Promises; Self-centeredness; Trust
> **Reference:** Numbers 23:19

R. C. SPROUL
AMERICAN THEOLOGIAN AND PASTOR (1939–)

QUOTATION **725**

Most of our ethical theories we develop to excuse ourselves.

> **Citation:** R. C. Sproul, in his sermon "The Insanity of Luther"
> **Topics:** Deceit; Depravity; Ethics; Excuses; Morality
> **References:** Romans 7:11; Titus 3:3; 1 John 1:8

QUOTATION **726**

Even if I am a model of personal righteousness, that does not excuse my participation in social evil. The man who is faithful to his wife while he exercises bigotry toward his neighbor is no better than the adulterer who crusades for social justice.

> **Citation:** Unknown
> **Topics:** Holiness; Injustice; Integrity; Priorities; Social Action; Social Justice; Values
> **References:** Leviticus 19:4; Psalm 72:4; Proverbs 17:15

HELMUT THIELICKE
GERMAN THEOLOGIAN (1908–86)

QUOTATION **727**

In us men truth and love are seldom combined.

> **Citation:** Helmut Thielicke, *A Little Exercise for Young Theologians*

Topics: Gentleness; Human Nature; Kindness; Love; Mercy; Truth

References: 1 Corinthians 13; Ephesians 4:15; Colossians 4:6

QUOTATION **728**

Jesus Christ can only be regarded rightly if we are ready to meet him on the plane where he is active, that is, within the Christian church.

Citation: Helmut Thielicke, *A Little Exercise for Young Theologians*

Topics: Church; Experiencing God; Jesus Christ; Ministry; Teachability

References: Matthew 16:13–20; 28:16–20; Mark 8:27–29; Luke 9:18–20; Hebrews 10:25

PAUL TILLICH

GERMAN-AMERICAN THEOLOGIAN AND EXISTENTIALIST PHILOSOPHER (1886–1965)

QUOTATION **729**

The courage to be is the courage to accept oneself as accepted in spite of being unacceptable.

Citation: Paul Tillich, *Writings on Religion*

Topics: Atonement; Courage; Justification; Mercy; Redemption

References: Romans 5:1–11; 8:1–4, 28–39; 12:1–2; 1 Timothy 1:3–17

QUOTATION **730**

Doubt is not the opposite of faith; it is one element of faith.

Citation: Unknown

Topics: Belief; Confusion; Doubt; Faith; Trials

Reference: Mark 9:14–32

QUOTATION **731**

Boredom is rage spread thin.

Citation: Unknown

Topics: Anger; Boredom; Complacency; Hatred

References: Proverbs 29:8; Matthew 5:21–26; 1 Thessalonians 5:12–15; 2 Thessalonians 3:6–15

QUOTATION **732**

The first duty of love is to listen.

Citation: Unknown

Topics: Community; Compassion; Fellowship; Listening; Love; Relationships

References: 1 Corinthians 13; James 1:19–21

PAUL TOURNIER
SWISS PSYCHIATRIST (1898–1986)

QUOTATION **733**

Christianity is not one ideology over against other ideologies. It is a life inspired by the Holy Spirit. Its victories are nothing but victories over itself, not over others. It propagates itself through humility and self-examination, not through triumphs.

Citation: Paul Tournier, *The Whole Person in a Broken World*

Topics: Compassion; Gentleness; Holy Spirit; Humility; Self-examination

References: Proverbs 22:4; Matthew 18:4; Romans 12:1–3; Galatians 5:22–23

QUOTATION **734**

A diffuse and vague guilt feeling kills the personality, whereas the conviction of sin gives life to the personality. The former depends on people, on public opinion, while the latter depends on God.

Citation: Paul Tournier, *Escape from Loneliness*

Topics: Conscience; Conviction of Sin; Guilt; Wholeness

References: Job 11:15; Psalms 32:3; 51:3; 2 Peter 3:14

QUOTATION 735

Nothing makes us so lonely as our secrets.

> Citation: Paul Tournier, *Secrets*
>
> Topics: Confession; Deceit; Honesty; Loneliness; Pride
>
> References: John 8:31–32; Romans 6:1–14

ELTON TRUEBLOOD
AMERICAN QUAKER THEOLOGIAN AND WRITER (1900–1994)

QUOTATION 736

We have not advanced very far in our spiritual lives if we have not encountered the basic paradox of freedom, to the effect that we are most free when we are bound.

> Citation: Elton Trueblood, *The New Man for Our Time*
>
> Topics: Commitment; Freedom; Obedience; Paradoxes
>
> References: Isaiah 1:18–20; John 7:17; 8:31–32; 1 Corinthians 6:12

DAVID F. WELLS
AMERICAN PROFESSOR, THEOLOGIAN, AND WRITER (1939–)

QUOTATION 737

Petitionary prayer ... is rebellion — rebellion against the world in its fallenness, the absolute and undying refusal to accept as normal what is pervasively abnormal.

> Citation: David F. Wells, in the *Christianity Today* article "Prayer: Rebelling against the Status Quo"
>
> Topics: Intercession; Prayer; Spiritual Warfare; Trust; World
>
> References: Matthew 6:5–15; 7:7–12; Luke 11:1–13; 18:1–8

CORNELL WEST
AMERICAN PROFESSOR AND SCHOLAR (1956–)

QUOTATION 738

The categories of optimism and pessimism don't exist for me. I'm a blues man. A blues man is a prisoner of hope, and hope is a qualitatively different category than optimism. Optimism is a secular construct, a calculation of probability.

> **Citation:** Cornell West, in a *Rolling Stone* interview
>
> **Topics:** Hope; Optimism; Peace; Trust
>
> **References:** Psalms 25; 42; 71; 130; Romans 4:18; 8:18–27; Colossians 3:24–27

DALLAS WILLARD
AMERICAN PHILOSOPHER AND WRITER (1935–)

QUOTATION 739

The really good news for humanity is that Jesus is now taking students in the master class of life.

> **Citation:** Dallas Willard, *The Divine Conspiracy*
>
> **Topics:** Discipleship; Jesus Christ; Kingdom; Teachability
>
> **References:** Matthew 4:18–22; Mark 1:14–20; Luke 5:1–11; John 1:36–51

QUOTATION 740

"Spiritual" is not just something we *ought* to be. It is something we *are* and cannot escape, regardless of how we may think or feel about it.

> **Citation:** Dallas Willard, *The Divine Conspiracy*
>
> **Topics:** Human Condition; Spirituality
>
> **References:** John 3:1–21; Romans 8:1–17

QUOTATION 741

"The Lord is my shepherd" is written on many more tombstones than lives.

Citation: Dallas Willard, *The Divine Conspiracy*

Topics: Commitment; Discipleship; Hypocrisy; Lifestyle

Reference: Psalm 23

QUOTATION 742

There is nothing that can be done with anger that cannot be done better without it.

Citation: Dallas Willard, *The Divine Conspiracy*

Topics: Anger; Forgiveness; Kindness

References: Proverbs 29:8; Matthew 5:21–26

QUOTATION 743

Nondiscipleship is the elephant in the church.

Citation: Dallas Willard, *The Divine Conspiracy*

Topics: Church; Commitment; Discipleship

References: Matthew 4:18–22; 28:16–20; Mark 1:14–20; Luke 5:1–11; John 1:36–51

RANDY ALCORN
AMERICAN WRITER (1954–)

QUOTATION 744

Those who know their unworthiness seize grace as a hungry man seizes bread, while the self-righteous resent grace.

Citation: Randy Alcorn, *Edge of Eternity*

Topics: Grace; Justification by Works; Pride; Righteousness; Self-righteousness

Reference: Ephesians 2:8–10

MAYA ANGELOU
AMERICAN WRITER AND POET (1928–)

QUOTATION 745

There's a world of difference between truth and facts. Facts can obscure truth.

Citation: Maya Angelou, in response to criticism about her autobiographies not being factual

Topics: Knowledge; Science; Trust; Truth; Wisdom

Reference: 1 Peter 1:3–9

JO-ANN BADLEY
AMERICAN PROFESSOR

QUOTATION 746

Unlike Israel's exile, our process of secularization is not clearly marked by a hostile takeover. We are losing the land by way of a thousand little changes.

Citation: Jo-Ann Badley, quoted in *Stories of Emergence*

Topics: Apathy; Culture; Spiritual Warfare; Temptation; Tolerance; Worldliness

Reference: 1 John 2:15–17

ST. JOSEMARÍA ESCRIVÁ DE BALAGUER
SPANISH ROMAN CATHOLIC PRIEST AND FOUNDER OF OPUS DEI (1902 – 75)

QUOTATION **747**

Don't say, "That person bothers me." Think: "That person sanctifies me."

Citation: St. Josemaría Escrivá, *The Way*

Topics: Enemies; Relationships; Sanctification; Suffering; Teachability; Trials

References: John 17:6 – 19; Philippians 1:3 – 11; 1 Thessalonians 4:1 – 12; 2 Thessalonians 2:13 – 17

WILLIAM BARCLAY
SCOTTISH WRITER AND PREACHER (1907 – 78)

QUOTATION **748**

In the church we are more than in touch with the whole wide world; we are more than in touch with almost twenty centuries of history; we are in touch with eternity.

Citation: William Barclay, *In the Hands of God*

Topics: Church; Eternity; Experiencing God; Past; Power; Tradition

References: Matthew 16:13 – 20; Romans 8:28 – 39; 1 John 4:4

QUOTATION **749**

It has always been fairly safe to talk about God; it is when we start to talk about men that the trouble starts.

Citation: William Barclay, *Ethics in a Permissive Society*

Topics: Consequences; Enemies; Human Nature

References: Matthew 10:32; 16:26; 25:34; Luke 12:8

QUOTATION 750

A man may well be condemned, not for doing something, but for doing nothing.

Citation: William Barclay, *Ethics in a Permissive Society*

Topics: Apathy; Commitment; Complacency; Condemnation; Punishment; Responsibility; Service

References: Matthew 7:24–27; 25; Luke 19:12–17; James 2:14–26

QUOTATION 751

More people have been brought into the church by the kindness of real Christian love than by all the theological arguments in the world, and more people have been driven from the church by the hardness and ugliness of so-called Christianity than by all the doubts in the world.

Citation: William Barclay, *New Testament Words*

Topics: Compassion; Evangelism; Gentleness; Holiness; Hypocrisy; Integrity; Kindness; Love; Mercy; Testimony; Witness

References: Romans 12:9–10; 1 Corinthians 13:1; Jude 19

QUOTATION 752

A saint is someone whose life makes it easier to believe in God.

Citation: William Barclay, *The Letters of James and Peter*

Topics: Character; Example; Godliness; Holiness; Influence; Lifestyle; Testimony; Witness

References: Psalm 52:9; Ephesians 1:18–19; Colossians 1:10–12

QUOTATION 753

The best way to prepare for the coming of Christ is never to forget the presence of Christ.

Citation: Unknown

Topics: Focus; Jesus Christ; Perspective; Second Coming

References: Matthew 28:20; Luke 12:40; Revelation 16:15

QUOTATION **754**

Endurance is not just the ability to bear a hard thing, but to turn it into glory.

Citation: Unknown

Topics: Commitment; Endurance; Glory; Overcoming; Perseverance; Suffering; Trials

References: Ecclesiastes 9:11; Romans 5:1–5; 1 Corinthians 9:19–27; 2 Corinthians 4:7–18; Hebrews 12:1–2; James 1:2–4

BRUCE BARTON
AMERICAN WRITER AND POLITICIAN (1886–1967)

QUOTATION **755**

Sometimes when I consider what tremendous consequences come from little things ... I am tempted to think there are no little things.

Citation: Unknown

Topics: Character; Consequences; Decisions; Integrity

References: Matthew 5:27–30; 25:31–46

QUOTATION **756**

When you're through changing, you're through.

Citation: Unknown

Topics: Change; Sanctification; Spiritual Growth; Teachability; Transformation

References: John 17:6–19; Romans 12:1–2; Philippians 1:3–11; 1 Thessalonians 4:1–12; 2 Thessalonians 2:13–17

DON BASHAM
AMERICAN PREACHER AND WRITER (1926–89)

QUOTATION 757

Sometimes I think the whole Christian world is made up of just two groups: those who speak their faith and accomplish significant things for God; and those who criticize and malign the first group.

Citation: Don Basham, in his *New Wine* article "On the Tip of My Tongue"

Topics: Courage; Criticism; Discouragement; Gossip; Speech; Testimony

References: 2 Thessalonians 3:11–13; 1 Timothy 5:13; 1 Peter 4:15

ROB BELL
AMERICAN PREACHER AND WRITER (1970–)

QUOTATION 758

The moment God is figured out with nice, neat lines and definitions, we are no longer dealing with God.

Citation: Rob Bell, *Velvet Elvis*

Topics: God's Sovereignty; Idolatry; Limitations; Mysteries

References: Exodus 32:1–14; Job 42:1–6; Isaiah 46

QUOTATION 759

God is always present. We're the ones who show up.

Citation: Rob Bell, *Velvet Elvis*

Topics: God's Sovereignty; Limitations; Presence of God

References: Genesis 1:1–2; Exodus 3:1–15; Joshua 1:1–9; Isaiah 6:1–13; Matthew 1:22–23

QUOTATION **760**

Missions ... is less about the transportation of God from one place to another and more about the identification of a God who is already there.

Citation: Rob Bell, *Velvet Elvis*

Topics: Evangelism; God's Sovereignty; Missions; Presence of God

References: Matthew 5:13–16; 28:16–20; Mark 6:6–13; Luke 8:16–18; 24:45–49; John 20:21

QUOTATION **761**

Somewhere in you is the you whom you were made to be. We need you to be you.

Citation: Rob Bell, *Velvet Elvis*

Topics: Calling; Identity; Individualism; Purpose; Self-worth

References: Psalm 139; Jeremiah 1:4–19; Romans 12:3–8; 1 Corinthians 12:1–11; Ephesians 4:1–16

SAUL BELLOW
AMERICAN WRITER (1915–2005)

QUOTATION **762**

A man is only as good as what he loves.

Citation: Saul Bellow, *Seize the Day*

Topics: Character; Holiness; Integrity; Love; Passion; Righteousness

References: 1 Corinthians 13:13; Galatians 5:6; 1 John 4:16

JOHN BLANCHARD
AMERICAN PREACHER AND WRITER (1932–)

QUOTATION **763**

Christ's statements are either cosmic or comic.

Citation: Unknown

Topics: Atheism; Belief; Jesus Christ; Unbelief; Worldview

References: John 6:25 – 59; 8:12 – 30, 48 – 59; 9:35 – 41; 10:7 – 21, 25 – 38; 11:25 – 26

ERMA LOUISE BOMBECK

AMERICAN HUMORIST (1927 – 96)

QUOTATION **764**

People shop for a bathing suit with more care than they do a husband or wife. The rules are the same. Look for something you'll feel comfortable wearing. Allow for room to grow.

Citation: Unknown

Topics: Decisions; Growth; Marriage; Spouses

References: 1 Corinthians 7; Ephesians 5:21 – 33; Colossians 3:18 – 19; 1 Peter 3:1 – 7

QUOTATION **765**

When I stand before God at the end of my life, I would hope that I would not have a single bit of talent left and could say, "I used everything you gave me."

Citation: Unknown

Topics: Calling; Final Judgment; Good Deeds; Ministry; Responsibility; Spiritual Gifts

References: Matthew 25:14 – 30; Luke 19:12 – 17

GREGORY A. BOYD

AMERICAN PREACHER, THEOLOGIAN, AND WRITER (1957 –)

QUOTATION **766**

The kingdom of God advances by people lovingly placing themselves under others, in service to others, at cost to themselves.

Citation: Gregory A. Boyd, *The Myth of a Christian Nation*

Topics: Compassion; Cost; Kingdom; Sacrifice; Self-denial; Service; Submission

References: Romans 13:1–7; Philippians 2:1–11

RAY BRADBURY

AMERICAN SCIENCE FICTION WRITER (1920–)

QUOTATION 767

You've got to jump off cliffs and build your wings on the way down.

Citation: Unknown

Topics: Calling; Courage; Overcoming; Risk; Trust

References: Romans 4:18–25; Philippians 3:12–16; Hebrews 11; 12:1–13

ANN BRADSTREET

AMERICAN WRITER AND POET (1612–72)

QUOTATION 768

Authority without wisdom is like a heavy axe without an edge—fitter to bruise than polish.

Citation: Unknown

Topics: Authority; Teachability; Wisdom

References: Proverbs 11:2; James 3:13–18

PHILLIPS BROOKS

AMERICAN PREACHER AND WRITER (1835–93)

QUOTATION 769

Pray the largest prayers. You cannot think a prayer so large that God, in answering it, will not wish you had made it larger. Pray not for crutches but for wings!

Citation: Phillips Brooks, *The More Abundant Life*

Topics: Courage; God's Sovereignty; Prayer; Provision; Trust

References: Matthew 7:7; Luke 18:1 – 8; Ephesians 6:18; James 5:13

QUOTATION **770**

Do not pray for easy lives; pray to be stronger people! Do not pray for tasks equal to your powers; pray for powers equal to your tasks.

Citation: Unknown

Topics: Calling; Guidance; Limitations; Power; Prayer; Provision; Strength

References: Matthew 6:5 – 15; 7:7 – 12; Luke 11:1 – 13; 18:1 – 8

QUOTATION **771**

A man who lives right, and is right, has more power in his silence than another has by his words.

Citation: Unknown

Topics: Character; Godliness; Holiness; Hypocrisy; Influence; Integrity; Morality; Speech; Testimony; Words

References: Matthew 5:13 – 16; 1 Peter 2:11 – 12

FREDERICK BUECHNER
AMERICAN WRITER AND PREACHER (1926 –)

QUOTATION **772**

If there is a terror about darkness because we cannot see, there is also a terror about light because we can see. There is a terror about light because much of what we see in the light about ourselves and our world we would rather not see, would rather not have be seen.

Citation: Frederick Buechner, *The Hungering Dark*

Topics: Accountability; Deceit; Illumination; Revelation; Self-examination; Truth

References: 2 Samuel 12:7 – 14; Romans 2:1 – 11; 3:10 – 18, 23; 7:7 – 25

QUOTATION **773**

The trouble with steeling yourself against the harshness of reality is that the same steel that secures your life against being destroyed secures your life also against being opened up and transformed by the holy power that life itself comes from.

Citation: Frederick Buechner, *The Sacred Journey*

Topics: Confession; Pride; Spiritual Growth; Submission; Teachability; Vulnerability

References: Psalm 95:8; Hebrews 3:7 – 19

QUOTATION **774**

Faith. Hope. Love … our going-away presents from beyond time to carry with us through time to lighten our step as we go.

Citation: Frederick Buechner, *The Sacred Journey*

Topics: Eternal and Temporary; Faith; Hope; Love

Reference: 1 Corinthians 13

QUOTATION **775**

I believe that to love ourselves means to extend to those various selves that we have been along the way the same degree of compassion and concern that we would extend to anyone else.

Citation: Frederick Buechner, *Telling Secrets*

Topics: Compassion; Forgiveness; Grace; Self-examination; Self-worth

Reference: Ephesians 4:20 – 32; Colossians 3:12 – 17

QUOTATION **776**

Go where your best prayers take you.

Citation: Frederick Buechner, *Telling Secrets*

Topics: Direction; Discernment; Guidance; Prayer

References: Matthew 6:5 – 15; 7:7 – 12; Luke 11:1 – 13; 18:1 – 8

QUOTATION **777**

The gospel is bad news before it is Good News.

> **Citation:** Frederick Buechner, *Telling the Truth*
> **Topics:** Christian Life; Gospel; Repentance; Transformation; Truth
> **Reference:** Romans 3:9–20; 5:1–2, 6–8

QUOTATION **778**

Of the Seven Deadly Sins, anger is possibly the most fun. To lick your wounds, to smack your lips over grievances long past, to roll over your tongue the prospect of bitter conversations still to come, to savor to the last toothsome morsel both the pain you are given and the pain you are giving back—in many ways it is a feast fit for a king. The chief drawback is that what you are wolfing down is yourself. The skeleton at the feast is you.

> **Citation:** Frederick Buechner, *Wishful Thinking: A Theological ABC*
> **Topics:** Anger; Enemies; Hatred; Sin; Vices
> **References:** Genesis 4:1–8; Matthew 5:21–26; Ephesians 4:26

QUOTATION **779**

The place God calls you to is the place where your deep gladness and the world's deep hunger meet.

> **Citation:** Frederick Buechner, *Wishful Thinking: A Theological ABC*
> **Topics:** Calling; Direction; Meaning; Purpose; Spiritual Gifts; Vocation
> **References:** Psalms 22; 139; Jeremiah 1:4–19; Romans 12:3–8;
> 1 Corinthians 12:1–11; Ephesians 4:1–16

QUOTATION **780**

Of all powers, love is the most powerful and the most powerless. It is the most powerful because it alone can conquer that final and most impregnable stronghold which is the human heart. It is the most powerless because it can do nothing except by consent.

> **Citation:** Frederick Buechner, *Wishful Thinking: A Theological ABC*

Topics: Love; Power; Weakness

References: Proverbs 15:17; Galatians 5:22

QUOTATION **781**

The suffering that Buddha's eyes close out is the suffering of the world that Christ's eyes close in and hallow.

Citation: Frederick Buechner, *Now and Then*

Topics: Jesus Christ; Pain; Suffering; World

References: Matthew 27:32 – 56; Mark 15:22 – 32; Luke 19:10; 23:33 – 43; John 1:1 – 18; 19:17 – 24

QUOTATION **782**

Maybe what is good about religion is playing that the Kingdom will come, until—in the joy of your playing, the hope and rhythm and comradeship and poignance and mystery of it—you start to see that the playing is itself the first-fruits of the Kingdom's coming and of God's presence within us and among us.

Citation: Frederick Buechner, *Now and Then*

Topics: Kingdom; Lifestyle; Presence of God; Religion

References: Matthew 6:5 – 15; Luke 11:2 – 4

JOHN BUNYAN
BRITISH WRITER AND PREACHER (1628 – 88)

QUOTATION **783**

Even old truths are new if they come to us with the smell of heaven upon them.

Citation: Unknown

Topics: Bible; Eternal and Temporary; Heaven; Insight; Preaching; Teaching; Truth; Wisdom

Reference: Psalm 119:18

THOMAS CARLYLE
SCOTTISH WRITER (1795 – 1881)

QUOTATION 784

One example is worth a thousand arguments.

> **Citation:** Unknown
> **Topics:** Character; Conflict; Example; Honesty; Influence; Testimony
> **References:** 2 Timothy 1:13; 1 Peter 5:1–4

QUOTATION 785

A person who is gifted sees the essential point and leaves the rest as surplus.

> **Citation:** Unknown
> **Topics:** Distractions; Focus; Insight; Perspective; Understanding
> **Reference:** Ecclesiastes 12:13–14

OSWALD CHAMBERS
SCOTTISH PREACHER AND WRITER (1874 – 1917)

QUOTATION 786

There are no such things as prominent service and obscure service; it is all the same with God.

> **Citation:** Oswald Chambers, *So Send I You*
> **Topics:** Humility; Servanthood; Service
> **References:** Matthew 6:1–4; 20:25–28; 1 Corinthians 15:58; Colossians 3:23–24

QUOTATION 787

When you meet a man or woman who puts Jesus Christ first, knit that one to your soul.

> **Citation:** Oswald Chambers, *So Send I You*
> **Topics:** Friendship; Jesus Christ; Priorities; Relationships
> **References:** Romans 12:10; Ephesians 3:14–21; Philippians 3:10–11

QUOTATION 788

It is easy to say we believe in God as long as we remain in the little world we choose to live in; but get out into the great world of facts, the noisy world where people are absolutely indifferent to you, where your message is nothing more than a crazy tale belonging to a bygone age, can you believe God there?

Citation: Oswald Chambers, *God's Workmanship*

Topics: Belief; Distractions; Faith; Focus; Perseverance; Temptation; Tests; World

References: Matthew 13:22; Luke 21:34; Ephesians 2:2

QUOTATION 789

If you are a saint, God will continually upset your program, and if you are wedded to your program, you will become that most obnoxious creature under heaven—an irritable saint.

Citation: Oswald Chambers, *Run Today's Race*

Topics: Attitudes; Pride; Sanctification; Spiritual Growth; Teachability

References: Ephesians 5:26; 2 Timothy 2:21; 1 Peter 1:2

QUOTATION 790

If you are going to be used by God, he will take you through a multitude of experiences that are not meant for you at all; they are meant to make you useful in his hands.

Citation: Oswald Chambers, *My Utmost for His Highest*

Topics: Character; Maturity; Ministry; Sanctification; Tests; Transformation; Trials

References: 2 Corinthians 1:3–7; 1 Thessalonians 2:9–13

QUOTATION 791

It is the most natural thing in the world to be scared, and the clearest evidence that God's grace is at work in our hearts is when we do not get into panics.... The remarkable thing about fearing God is that when you fear God you fear nothing else, whereas if you do not fear God you fear everything else.

Citation: Unknown

Topics: Courage; Fear; Fear of God; Grace; Panic; Peace; Worry

References: Deuteronomy 6:13; Luke 12:4–7; 2 Corinthians 5:11; 1 Peter 1:17–18; 3:14–15

QUOTATION **792**

Every time we pray, our horizon is altered, our attitude to things is altered — not sometimes but every time — and the amazing thing is that we don't pray more.

Citation: Unknown

Topics: Commitment; Maturity; Perspective; Prayer; Spiritual Growth; Vision

References: 1 Chronicles 16:11; John 16:24; Ephesians 6:18; 1 Thessalonians 5:17

QUOTATION **793**

God never gives us discernment in order that we may criticize, but that we may intercede.

Citation: Unknown

Topics: Criticism; Discernment; Intercession; Judging Others; Prayer; Spiritual Perception

References: 1 Kings 3:9; Isaiah 11:3; Hebrews 5:14

MARIE D'AGOULT
FRENCH WRITER (1805–76)

QUOTATION **794**

When one has smashed everything around oneself, one has also smashed oneself.

Citation: Marie d'Agoult, after leaving her children to be with composer Franz Liszt

Topics: Community; Consequences; Family; Self-centeredness; Sexual Immorality; Temptation

References: Romans 6:23; 1 Corinthians 6:12–20; Galatians 6:7–8; 1 Thessalonians 4:1–12; Hebrews 13:4; 2 Peter 2:19

ROBERTSON DAVIES

CANADIAN NOVELIST, PLAYWRIGHT, AND PROFESSOR (1913–95)

QUOTATION **795**

The world is full of people whose notion of a satisfactory future is, in fact, a return to an idealized past.

> **Citation:** Robertson Davies, *A Voice from the Attic*
>
> **Topics:** Future; Growth; Leadership; Past; Perspective
>
> **References:** Exodus 16:1–3; Numbers 14:1–4

ANNIE DILLARD

AMERICAN WRITER (1945–)

QUOTATION **796**

Nothing could more surely convince me of God's unending mercy than the continued existence on earth of the church.

> **Citation:** Annie Dillard, *Holy the Firm*
>
> **Topics:** Church; Forgiveness; Grace; Mercy
>
> **References:** Psalms 103:17; 108:4; Malachi 3:17; Matthew 16:18–19

QUOTATION **797**

You can't test courage cautiously.

> **Citation:** Annie Dillard, *An American Childhood*
>
> **Topics:** Boldness; Commitment; Courage; Danger; Fear; God's Sovereignty; Risk; Trust
>
> **References:** Numbers 13:30–33; 14:5–9; Philippians 1:20

ISAK DINESEN (PEN NAME OF KAREN VON BLIXEN-FINECKE)
DANISH WRITER (1885 – 1962)

QUOTATION 798

God made the world round so we would never be able to see too far down the road.

Citation: Unknown

Topics: Guidance; Limitations; Mysteries; Perspective; Trust

Reference: Proverbs 3:5 – 6

JAMES DOBSON
AMERICAN WRITER AND FOUNDER OF FOCUS ON THE FAMILY (1936 –)

QUOTATION 799

I put my family first, and the Lord did the rest. What I thought was the end turned out to be the beginning.

Citation: Unknown

Topics: Children; Family; Marriage; Parenting; Priorities; Spouses

References: Deuteronomy 6:7; 31:13; Proverbs 22:6; Acts 10:2; Ephesians 5:21 – 33

QUOTATION 800

Nothing brings husbands, wives, and children together more effectively than a face-to-face encounter with the Creator of families.

Citation: Unknown

Topics: Children; Creator; Experiencing God; Family; Marriage; Parenting; Spouses

References: Deuteronomy 4:9; Job 1:5; Proverbs 22:6; John 4:53

QUOTATION **801**

Even if marriages are made in heaven, man has to be responsible for the maintenance.

Citation: Unknown

Topics: Marriage; Priorities; Responsibility; Spouses

References: Genesis 2:24; Matthew 5:32; Mark 10:9; Ephesians 5:21–33

FYODOR DOSTOYEVSKY
RUSSIAN WRITER (1821–81)

QUOTATION **802**

The awful thing is that beauty is mysterious as well as terrible. God and the Devil are fighting there and the battlefield is the heart of man.

Citation: Fyodor Dostoyevsky, *The Brothers Karamazov*

Topics: Beauty; Devil; God; Heaven; Hell; Spiritual Warfare; Temptation

References: Ecclesiastes 3:11; 1 John 2:15–17

QUOTATION **803**

We have never truly breathed air nor seen light until we have breathed in the God-inspired Bible and see the world in the Bible's light.

Citation: Unknown

Topics: Bible; Illumination; Revelation; Wisdom

References: Psalms 19:8; 119:130; Proverbs 6:23; 2 Peter 1:19

GEORGE NORMAN DOUGLAS
BRITISH WRITER (1868–1952)

QUOTATION **804**

You can tell the ideals of a nation by its advertisements.

Citation: Norman Douglas, *South Wind*

MAXIE DUNNAM

AMERICAN PREACHER AND FORMER PRESIDENT OF ASBURY THEOLOGICAL SEMINARY (1934–)

QUOTATION **805**

We must be careful what we bury in our heart. To bury something does not mean it is dead. It may simply mean we have buried something alive that will devour and destroy us from within.

Citation: Maxie Dunnam, *Let Me Say That Again*

Topics: Evil; Heart; Purity; Self-examination; Spiritual Warfare; Temptation

References: Proverbs 4:23; 6:18; Jeremiah 4:14; Matthew 9:4; 15:18–19

JONATHAN EDWARDS

COLONIAL AMERICAN CONGREGATIONAL PREACHER (1703–58)

QUOTATION **806**

The enjoyment of [God] is the only happiness with which our souls can be satisfied.... Fathers and mothers, husbands, wives, or children, or the company of earthly friends are but shadows, but enjoyment of God is the substance. These are but scattered beams, but God is the sun. These are but streams, but God is the fountain. These are but drops, but God is the ocean.

Citation: Jonathan Edwards, *The Christian Pilgrim*

Topics: Community; Experiencing God; Family; Fulfillment; Joy; Knowing God; Purpose; Relationships; Satisfaction

References: Psalms 43:4; 62:1; 103:5; Ecclesiastes 2:26; Matthew 5:6

QUOTATION **807**

Self-denial destroys the very root and foundation of sorrow, and is nothing else but the lancing of a grievous and painful sore that effects a cure and brings abundance of health as a recompense for the pain of the operation.

Citation: Jonathan Edwards, in his sermon "Pleasantness of Religion"

Topics: Pride; Sacrifice; Self-denial; Sorrow

References: Matthew 16:24; Mark 8:34; Luke 9:23

QUOTATION **808**

There is a difference between having an opinion that God is holy and gracious, and having a sense of the loveliness and beauty of that holiness and grace. There is a difference between having a rational judgment that honey is sweet, and having a sense of its sweetness.

Citation: Jonathan Edwards, in his sermon "A Divine and Supernatural Light"

Topics: Awe; Beauty; Experiencing God; Intimacy; Passion; Worship

References: Psalm 34:8; John 1:16–18

QUOTATION **809**

If we will feed Christ with the food of our houses, even outward food, Christ will reward us with the food of his house, which is spiritual food.

Citation: Jonathan Edwards, in his sermon "Much in Deeds of Charity"

Topics: Compassion; Eternal Life; Good Deeds; Kindness; Poor People; Social Impact

References: Isaiah 58:6–12; Matthew 25:31–46

QUOTATION **810**

I go out to preach with two propositions in mind. First, every person ought to give his life to Christ. Second, whether or not anyone else gives him his life, I will give him mine.

Citation: Unknown

Topics: Devotion; Evangelism; Preaching; Surrender

References: Mark 12:30; Romans 10:1; Philippians 3:7–11

GEORGE ELIOT (PEN NAME OF MARY ANN EVANS)
BRITISH WRITER (1819–80)

QUOTATION 811

There is no despair so absolute as that which comes with the first moments of our first great sorrow, when we have not yet known what it is to have suffered and be healed, to have despaired and recovered hope.

> Citation: George Eliot, *Adam Bede*
>
> Topics: Depression; Despair; Healing; Hope; Sorrow; Suffering
>
> References: Numbers 7:12; Job 3:1; Psalm 31:22

QUOTATION 812

Oh, the inexpressible comfort of feeling safe with a person; having neither to weigh thoughts nor measure words, but to pour them all out, just as they are, chaff and grain together, knowing that a faithful hand will take and sift them, keep what is worth keeping, and then, with the breath of kindness, blow the rest away.

> Citation: Unknown
>
> Topics: Friendship; Honesty; Kindness; Relationships; Vulnerability
>
> References: Psalm 55:13; Proverbs 17:17; 18:24; Ecclesiastes 4:9

TED ENGSTROM
AMERICAN WRITER AND HEAD OF WORLD VISION INTERNATIONAL (1916–2006)

QUOTATION 813

We terribly overestimate what we can do in one year and underestimate what we can do in five.

> Citation: Unknown
>
> Topics: Calling; Goals; Limitations; Ministry; Power; Vision
>
> References: Psalm 90:12; 1 Corinthians 7:29–31; Ephesians 5:15–16

ANTOINE DE SAINT EXUPÉRY
FRENCH WRITER AND AVIATOR (1900 – 1944)

QUOTATION 814

A single event can awaken within us a stranger totally unknown to us. To live is to be slowly born.

Citation: Unknown

Topics: Change; Growth; Maturity; Rebirth; Revival; Self-examination; Transformation

References: Job 17:9; Psalm 84:7; John 3:3 – 8; 2 Corinthians 5:17

F. SCOTT FITZGERALD
AMERICAN WRITER (1896 – 1940)

QUOTATION 815

Never confuse a single defeat with a final defeat.

Citation: Unknown

Topics: Commitment; Courage; Difficulties; Failure; Overcoming; Perseverance; Perspective; Strength; Victory

References: Romans 8:35 – 39; 1 Corinthians 15:55 – 58

JOHN GARDNER
AMERICAN WRITER AND TEACHER (1933 – 82)

QUOTATION 816

We would not put up with a debauched king, but in a democracy all of us are kings, and we praise debauchery as pluralism.

Citation: John Gardner, *On Moral Fiction*

Topics: Depravity; Evil; Pluralism; Self-centeredness; Sin; Tolerance; Vices; Worldliness

References: Genesis 6:5; Mark 7:21; 2 Timothy 3:1–2; 2 Peter 2:12

RUTH BELL GRAHAM

AMERICAN PHILANTHROPIST, WRITER, AND POET (1920–2007)

QUOTATION **817**

Worship and worry cannot live in the same heart; they are mutually exclusive.

> **Citation:** Ruth Bell Graham, in the *Today's Christian Woman* article "Heart to Heart"
>
> **Topics:** Anxiety; Fear; God's Sovereignty; Trust; Worry; Worship
>
> **References:** Matthew 6:25, 31–32; 13:22; Philippians 4:6; 1 Peter 5:7

FATHER ANDREW GREELEY

IRISH-AMERICAN ROMAN CATHOLIC PRIEST AND WRITER (1928–)

QUOTATION **818**

Much of the history of Christianity has been devoted to domesticating Jesus — to reducing that elusive, enigmatic, paradoxical person to dimensions we can comprehend, understand, and convert to our own purposes. So far it hasn't worked.

> **Citation:** Andrew Greeley, in the *Chicago Sun-Times* article "There's No Solving the Mystery of Christ"
>
> **Topics:** Christian Life; Idolatry; Jesus Christ; Mysteries; Spiritual Perception
>
> **References:** Job 36:26; Psalm 145:3; Colossians 1:15–17; 2:2; 1 Timothy 3:16

ALEXANDER GROSSE
BRITISH PREACHER (c. 1595 – 1654)

QUOTATION 819

When Christ reveals himself there is satisfaction in the slenderest portion, and without Christ there is emptiness in the greatest fullness.

Citation: Unknown

Topics: Contentment; Despair; Emptiness; Hope; Jesus Christ; Joy; Meaning; Peace; Purpose; Satisfaction

Reference: Philippians 4:11 – 13

OS GUINNESS
BRITISH-AMERICAN WRITER AND SOCIAL CRITIC (1941 –)

QUOTATION 820

The main problem with American Christians is not that they aren't where they should be, but that they are not what they should be right where they are as doctors, housewives, lawyers, computer salesmen, or nurses.

Citation: Os Guinness, in a *Radix* magazine article

Topics: Calling; Influence; Lifestyle; Ministry; Social Impact; Stewardship; Vocation

References: Isaiah 43:10; Matthew 5:13 – 16; 25:14 – 30; John 15:27

ERNEST HEMINGWAY
AMERICAN WRITER (1899 – 1961)

QUOTATION 821

What is moral is what you feel good after, and what is immoral is what you feel bad after.

Citation: Ernest Hemingway, *Death in the Afternoon*

Topics: Conscience; Emotions; Feelings; Immorality; Morality; Postmodernism; Sinful Nature

References: Isaiah 51:7; Romans 2:15; 7:18–24

QUOTATION **822**

You can wipe out your opponents, but if you do it unjustly, you become eligible for being wiped out yourself.

Citation: Unknown

Topics: Enemies; Final Judgment; Hatred; Hypocrisy

References: Exodus 20:13; 21:24; Leviticus 24:20; Matthew 5:38–48; Luke 6:27–42

HOWARD HENDRICKS
AMERICAN PREACHER AND PROFESSOR (1924–)

QUOTATION **823**

My greatest fear for you is not that you will fail but that you will succeed in doing the wrong thing.

Citation: Unknown

Topics: Calling; Distractions; Failure; Spiritual Gifts; Success

References: Luke 10:38–42; 2 Timothy 3:1–9

OLIVER WENDELL HOLMES
AMERICAN WRITER, POET, AND PHYSICIAN (1809–94)

QUOTATION **824**

I find the great thing in this world is not so much where we stand, as in what direction we are moving: To reach the port of heaven, we must sail sometimes with the wind and sometimes against it—but we must sail, and not drift, nor lie at anchor.

Citation: Oliver Wendell Holmes, *The Autocrat of the Breakfast Table*

Topics: Calling; Courage; Culture; Discipleship; Focus; Growth; Influence; Lifestyle

References: Luke 13:24; 1 Corinthians 9:25; Colossians 1:29

PAUL JOHNSON
BRITISH ROMAN CATHOLIC WRITER (1928 –)

QUOTATION 825

The most extraordinary thing about the twentieth century was the failure of God to die. The collapse of mass religious belief, especially among the educated and prosperous, had been widely and confidently predicted. It did not take place. Somehow, God survived—flourished even.

Citation: Paul Johnson, *The Quest for God*

Topics: Atheism; Belief; Culture; Faith; God; God's Sovereignty; Humanism; Postmodernism; Religion; Science; Skepticism

Reference: Matthew 16:13 – 20

GARRISON KEILLOR
AMERICAN RADIO PERSONALITY AND WRITER (1942 –)

QUOTATION 826

There's no such thing as a successful marriage. There are marriages that give up, and marriages that keep on trying; that's the only difference.

Citation: Garrison Keillor, *Wobegon Boy*

Topics: Commitment; Marriage; Perseverance; Spouses; Trials

References: Genesis 2:22 – 25; Ephesians 5:21 – 33

QUOTATION 827

If you can't go to church and at least for a moment be given transcendence, if you can't pass briefly from this life into the next, then I can't see why anyone should go. Just a brief moment of transcendence causes you to come out of church a changed person.

Citation: Garrison Keillor, in a *Door* magazine interview

Topics: Awe; Church; Experiencing God; Mysteries; Power; Transformation; Worship

Reference: Isaiah 6:1 – 13

QUOTATION 828

You can become a Christian by going to church just about as easily as you can become an automobile by sleeping in a garage.

Citation: Unknown

Topics: Church; Conversion; Sanctification; Spiritual Disciplines

References: Matthew 18:3; Acts 3:19; James 5:20

HELEN KELLER
AMERICAN WRITER, ACTIVIST, AND LECTURER (1880 – 1968)

QUOTATION 829

Everything has its wonders, even darkness and silence, and I learn, whatever state I may be in, therein to be content.

Citation: Helen Keller, *The Story of My Life*

Topics: Contentment; Peace; Perspective; Teachability; Thanksgiving

References: Deuteronomy 31:6; Psalm 118; Philippians 4:10 – 20; Hebrews 13:5 – 6

QUOTATION **830**

We could never learn to be brave and patient, if there were only joy in the world.

Citation: Helen Keller, *The Miracle of Change*

Topics: Courage; Growth; Joy; Patience; Suffering; Tests; Trials

References: Job 23:10; 2 Corinthians 4:17; James 1:2–4; 1 Peter 1:7

QUOTATION **831**

Walking with a friend in the dark is better than walking alone in the light.

Citation: Unknown

Topics: Community; Encouragement; Friendship; Relationships; Togetherness

Reference: Ecclesiastes 4:7–12

JEAN KERR
AMERICAN WRITER AND PLAYWRIGHT (1922–2003)

QUOTATION **832**

Hope is the feeling you have that the feeling you have isn't permanent.

Citation: Jean Kerr, *Finishing Touches*

Topics: Eternal and Temporary; Hope; Overcoming; Peace; Perseverance; Perspective; Trust

References: Psalm 25; 42; 71; 130; Romans 4:18; 8:18–27; Colossians 3:24–27

RUDYARD KIPLING
BRITISH WRITER AND POET (1865–1936)

QUOTATION **833**

Of all the liars in the world, sometimes the worst are your own fears.

Citation: Unknown

Topics: Courage; Deceit; Fear; Trust

References: Numbers 13:30–33; 14:5–9; Joshua 1:1–9; 2 Timothy 1:6–12

ANNE LAMOTT
AMERICAN WRITER (1954 –)

QUOTATION **834**

Not forgiving is like drinking rat poison and then waiting for the rat to die.

Citation: Anne Lamott, *Traveling Mercies*

Topics: Bitterness; Conflict; Enemies; Foolishness; Forgiveness; Grace; Grudges; Hatred; Mercy

References: Matthew 5:38 – 42; 18:15 – 35; Luke 6:27 – 36; 2 Corinthians 2:5 – 11

QUOTATION **835**

Forgiveness means it finally becomes unimportant that you hit back.

Citation: Anne Lamott, *Plan B: Further Thoughts on Faith*

Topics: Anger; Conflict; Enemies; Forgiveness; Hatred; Kindness; Mercy; Revenge; Violence

References: Matthew 5:38 – 42; 18:15 – 35; Luke 6:27 – 36; 2 Corinthians 2:5 – 11

QUOTATION **836**

Grace means you're in a different universe from where you had been stuck, when you had absolutely no way to get there on your own.

Citation: Anne Lamott, *Plan B: Further Thoughts on Faith*

Topics: Atonement; Cross; Grace; Jesus Christ; Justification by Works; Mercy; Redemption; Salvation

References: Romans 3:9 – 26; 5:1 – 11; Ephesians 2:1 – 10

QUOTATION **837**

One secret of life is that the reason life works at all is that not everyone in your tribe is nuts on the same day. Another secret is that laughter is carbonated holiness.

Citation: Anne Lamott, *Plan B: Further Thoughts on Faith*

Topics: Community; Happiness; Holiness; Joy; Laughter; Relationships

References: Ecclesiastes 4:7–12; Acts 2:42–47; Philippians 4:4–7

QUOTATION **838**

You don't always have to chop with the sword of truth. You can point with it, too.

Citation: Anne Lamott, *Bird by Bird*

Topics: Accountability; Bible; Gentleness; Kindness; Influence; Mercy; Truth

References: 2 Samuel 12:7–14; Matthew 18:15–20; Galatians 2:11–16; 6:1–5; Ephesians 6:17; Philippians 4:2–9; Colossians 3:16

ANN LANDERS
AMERICAN ADVICE COLUMNIST (1918–2002)

QUOTATION **839**

Most of us would be willing to pay as we go if we could just finish paying for where we've been.

Citation: Unknown

Topics: Debt; Forgiveness; Repentance

References: Job 15:31–32; Ecclesiastes 2:26; Romans 6:23

LEWIS H. LAPHAM
AMERICAN WRITER (1935–)

QUOTATION **840**

Except in times of war or illness, moral awakening is as hard to come by as a winning number in the New Jersey lottery.

Citation: Lewis H. Lapham, *Money and Class in America*

Topics: Complacency; Morality; Regeneration; Revival

References: 2 Chronicles 31:1; Psalm 80:7; Habakkuk 3:2

BRUCE LARSON

AMERICAN WRITER AND PREACHER (1925–)

QUOTATION **841**

Quite often the absence of immediate success is the mark of a genuine call.

> **Citation:** Bruce Larson, *My Creator, My Friend*
>
> **Topics:** Calling; Failure; Motivation; Purpose; Success; Vocation
>
> **Reference:** Exodus 5:1–21

KALLE LASN

ESTONIAN-CANADIAN WRITER (1942–)

QUOTATION **842**

Quiet feels foreign now, but quiet may be just what we need. Quiet may be to a healthy mind what clean air and water and a chemical-free diet are to a healthy body.

> **Citation:** Kalle Lasn, *Culture Jam*
>
> **Topics:** Quietness; Sabbath; Silence; Solitude; Spiritual Disciplines
>
> **References:** 1 Kings 19:1–18; Mark 1:35

QUOTATION **843**

Our mental environment is a common-property resource like the air or the water. We need to protect ourselves from unwanted incursions into it, much the same way we lobbied for non-smoking areas ten years ago.

> **Citation:** Unknown
>
> **Topics:** Distractions; Focus; Mind; Purity; Thoughts
>
> **References:** Matthew 5:27–30; Romans 12:1–2; Philippians 4:8

MADELEINE L'ENGLE
AMERICAN WRITER (1918–2007)

QUOTATION **844**

I have a point of view. You have a point of view. God has view.

> **Citation:** Madeleine L'Engle, *A Wrinkle in Time*
>
> **Topics:** Bible; God's Sovereignty; Limitations; Perspective; Scripture; Truth; Vision
>
> **References:** Job 31:4; Psalm 33:13; Proverbs 3:5

QUOTATION **845**

Humility is throwing oneself away in complete concentration on something or someone else.

> **Citation:** Madeleine L'Engle, *A Circle of Quiet*
>
> **Topics:** Focus; Humility; Sacrifice; Self-denial; Service; Submission
>
> **References:** Mark 8:34–36; Romans 14:19–21; 15:1; Philippians 2:1–11

ST. THÉRÈSE OF LISIEUX
FRENCH ROMAN CATHOLIC NUN AND WRITER (1873–97)

QUOTATION **846**

Prayer and sacrifice can touch souls better than words.

> **Citation:** St. Thérèse, *The Prayers of St. Thérèse of Lisieux*
>
> **Topics:** Influence; Ministry; Prayer; Sacrifice; Self-denial; Words
>
> **References:** Matthew 5:16; John 15:9–17; 1 John 3:11–24

MARTYN LLOYD-JONES
WELSH PREACHER (1899–1981)

QUOTATION **847**

Religion is man searching for God; Christianity is God seeking man.

> **Citation:** Martyn Lloyd-Jones, *The Puritans: Their Origins and Their Successors*
>
> **Topics:** Christian Life; Experiencing God; God; Incarnation; Limitations; Religion
>
> **References:** Luke 19:10; John 1:1–18; Romans 3:9–26; Ephesians 2:8–10; Titus 3:3–7

QUOTATION **848**

Faith is the refusal to panic.

> **Citation:** Martyn Lloyd-Jones, *Spiritual Depression: Its Causes and Cure*
>
> **Topics:** Courage; Faith; Fear; Panic; Trust
>
> **References:** 1 Samuel 17:20–32; Daniel 6:1–23; Habakkuk 3:16–19; 2 Corinthians 5:7; Hebrews 11

MAX LUCADO
AMERICAN PREACHER AND WRITER (1955–)

QUOTATION **849**

Resentment is when you let your hurt become hate. Resentment is when you allow what is eating you to eat you up. Resentment is when you poke, stoke, feed, and fan the fire, stirring the flames and reliving the pain. Resentment is the deliberate decision to nurse the offense until it becomes a black, furry, growling grudge.

> **Citation:** Max Lucado, *The Applause of Heaven*
>
> **Topics:** Anger; Enemies; Forgiveness; Grudges; Hatred; Resentment
>
> **References:** Ephesians 4:26–27; James 2:12–13; 1 John 4:20–21

QUOTATION **850**

Fear doesn't want you to make the journey to the mountain. If he can rattle you enough, fear will persuade you to take your eyes off the peaks and settle for a dull existence in the flatlands.

> **Citation:** Max Lucado, in an article in *The Christian Reader*
>
> **Topics:** Courage; Distractions; Fear
>
> **References:** Numbers 14:3; Deuteronomy 20:8; Isaiah 30:17

ERWIN LUTZER
AMERICAN PASTOR, TEACHER, AND WRITER (1941 –)

QUOTATION **851**

There is more grace in God's heart than there is sin in your past.

> **Citation:** Unknown
>
> **Topics:** Forgiveness; Grace; Guilt; Past; Redemption; Salvation; Sin
>
> **References:** Mark 3:28; Acts 10:43; Romans 4:7; Ephesians 1:7; 1 John 2:12

JOHN MACARTHUR JR.
AMERICAN PREACHER AND WRITER (1939 –)

QUOTATION **852**

We don't want to be personally or institutionally offensive, but we cannot buffer the offense of the cross.

> **Citation:** John MacArthur Jr., in the *Leadership* journal interview "Our Sufficiency for Outreach"
>
> **Topics:** Cross; Evangelism; Witness
>
> **References:** Matthew 13:57; 1 Corinthians 1:18 – 25; Galatians 5:11

Some people get so caught up in their own holiness that they look at the Trinity for a possible vacancy.

Citation: Unknown

Topics: Arrogance; Holiness; Idolatry; Pride; Self-centeredness

References: Proverbs 25:6; Isaiah 14:13; Mark 10:37

GEORGE MACDONALD
SCOTTISH WRITER AND PREACHER (1824 – 1905)

QUOTATION **854**

We are often unable to tell people what they need to know because they want to know something else.

Citation: George MacDonald, *Lilith*

Topics: Evangelism; Foolishness; Knowledge

References: Isaiah 6:9 – 10; Mark 4:1 – 20; Luke 8:4 – 15; John 6:60 – 71; Romans 1:18 – 32; 2 Timothy 4:1 – 5

QUOTATION **855**

The Son of God suffered unto death, not that men might not suffer, but that their sufferings might be like his.

Citation: Unknown

Topics: Atonement; Christlikeness; Cross; Hope; Jesus Christ; Salvation; Suffering; Trials

References: Romans 5:3 – 5; 8:17; Philippians 1:29; 3:10; 1 Peter 4:13

BRENNAN MANNING

AMERICAN WRITER AND SPEAKER (1934–)

QUOTATION **856**

I believe that the real difference in the American church is not between conservatives and liberals, fundamentalists and charismatics, nor between Republicans and Democrats. The real difference is between the aware and the unaware.

> **Citation:** Brennan Manning, in a *Christianity Today* interview with Dick Staub
>
> **Topics:** Church; Discernment; Illumination; Listening; Self-discipline; Spiritual Perception
>
> **References:** 1 Thessalonians 5:6; 1 Peter 5:8

QUOTATION **857**

To ascertain where you really are with the Lord, recall what saddened you the past month. Was it the realization that you do not love Jesus enough? That you did not seek his face in prayer often enough? That you did not care for his people enough? Or did you get depressed over a lack of respect, criticism from an authority figure, your finances, a lack of friends, fears about the future, or your bulging waistline?

> **Citation:** Brennan Manning, in a *Christianity Today* interview with Dick Staub
>
> **Topics:** Discipleship; Focus; Perspective; Priorities; Self-examination
>
> **Reference:** 1 John 2:15–17

QUOTATION **858**

The splendor of a human heart that trusts and is loved unconditionally gives God more pleasure than Westminster Cathedral, the Sistine Chapel, Beethoven's Ninth Symphony, Van Gogh's *Sunflowers*, the sight of ten thousand butterflies in flight, or the scent of a million orchids in bloom. Trust is our gift back to God, and he finds it so enchanting that Jesus died for love of it.

> **Citation:** Brennan Manning, in a *Christianity Today* interview with Dick Staub
>
> **Topics:** Trust; Unconditional Love; Worship; Worth
>
> **References:** Genesis 15:6; Romans 4:16–24; Hebrews 11:6

PETER MARSHALL

SCOTTISH-AMERICAN PREACHER, WRITER, AND CHAPLAIN OF THE U.S. SENATE (1902–49)

QUOTATION **859**

Give us clear vision that we may know where to stand and what to stand for, because unless we stand for something, we shall fall for anything.

> **Citation:** Peter Marshall, *Mr. Jones, Meet the Master*
>
> **Topics:** Commitment; Convictions; Decisions; Discernment; Ethics; Goals; Guidance; Leadership; Spiritual Perception; Vision
>
> **References:** Psalm 5:8; Isaiah 30:21; 42:16; John 16:13

QUOTATION **860**

If God does not enter your kitchen, there is something wrong with your kitchen. If you can't take God into your recreation, there is something wrong with your play. We all believe in the God of the heroic. What we need most these days is the God of the humdrum, the commonplace, the everyday.

> **Citation:** Unknown
>
> **Topics:** Experiencing God; Family; Lifestyle; Presence of God; Recreation
>
> **References:** Proverbs 15:3; Jeremiah 23:24; Acts 17:27

QUOTATION **861**

It is a fact of Christian experience that life is a series of troughs and peaks. In his efforts to get permanent possession of a soul, God relies on the troughs more than the peaks. And some of his special favorites have gone through longer and deeper troughs than anyone else.

> **Citation:** Unknown
>
> **Topics:** Sanctification; Spiritual Formation; Spiritual Growth; Suffering; Tests; Trials
>
> **References:** Romans 8:17, 28–31; 1 Peter 2:20; 5:10

QUOTATION **862**

Lord, when we are wrong, make us willing to change. And when we are right, make us easy to live with.

Citation: Unknown

Topics: Change; Humility; Pride; Repentance; Submission; Teachability; Transformation

References: Proverbs 22:4; 29:23; Matthew 18:4

FREDERICA MATHEWES-GREEN
EASTERN ORTHODOX WRITER (1952–)

QUOTATION **863**

The main evidence that we are growing in Christ is not exhilarating prayer experiences, but steadily increasing, humble love for other people.

Citation: Frederica Mathewes-Green, *First Fruits of Prayer*

Topics: Christlikeness; Compassion; Humility; Love; Maturity; Sanctification; Spiritual Formation; Spiritual Growth

References: Matthew 22:39; John 13:34–35; 15:12–13; Romans 12:10; Philippians 2:1–11; 1 Peter 1:22; 1 John 3:16

QUOTATION **864**

Consider yourself the chief of sinners, not the chief of the sinned-against.

Citation: Frederica Mathewes-Green, quoted in *Stories of Emergence*

Topics: Honesty; Perspective; Self-examination; Sin

References: Matthew 18:21–35; Ephesians 4:26–32; 1 Timothy 1:15–16

ANDRÉ MAUROIS
FRENCH WRITER (1885 – 1967)

QUOTATION **865**

A happy marriage is a long conversation which always seems too short.

Citation: Unknown

Topics: Commitment; Marriage; Relationships; Spouses

References: Ruth 4:13 – 15; Proverbs 12:4; Ecclesiastes 9:9; Ephesians 5:21 – 33

ROBERT MURRAY M'CHEYNE
SCOTTISH PREACHER (1813 – 43)

QUOTATION **866**

For every look at self, take ten looks at Christ.

Citation: Unknown

Topics: Christian Life; Christlikeness; Self-centeredness; Self-examination

References: 1 Corinthians 2:1 – 5; Philippians 1:20 – 30; Hebrews 12:2

ERWIN RAPHAEL MCMANUS
AMERICAN PREACHER AND WRITER (1958 –)

QUOTATION **867**

The church is not called to survive humanity but to serve humanity.

Citation: Erwin Raphael McManus, *An Unstoppable Force*

Topics: Calling; Church; Influence; Ministry; Outreach; Servanthood; Service; Social Impact

References: Matthew 5:13 – 16; 9:35 – 38; 20:25 – 28; Luke 8:16 – 18; 24:45 – 49; John 20:21

No empire is more powerful than ethos.

Citation: Erwin Raphael McManus, *An Unstoppable Force*

Topics: Character; Ethics; Holiness; Influence; Kindness; Power; Righteousness

References: Romans 8:28–39; 1 John 4:4–6

J. ROBERTSON MCQUILKIN
AMERICAN WRITER, PREACHER, AND PRESIDENT OF COLUMBIA INTERNATIONAL UNIVERSITY (1927–)

QUOTATION **869**

We may not be able to prove from Scripture with absolute certainty that no soul since Pentecost has ever been saved by extraordinary means without the knowledge of Christ. But neither can we prove from Scripture that a single soul has been so saved. If there is an alternative, God has not told us of it.

Citation: J. Robertson McQuilkin, *The Great Omission*

Topics: Cross; Evangelism; Gospel; Grace; Jesus Christ; Justification by Works; Missions; Pluralism; Salvation

References: Matthew 7:13–14; John 3:16–21; 11:25–26; 14:5–14; Acts 4:12

HENRIETTA MEARS
AMERICAN WRITER AND EDUCATOR (1890–1963)

QUOTATION **870**

When God gives a command or a vision of truth, it is never a question of what he will do but of what we will do. To be successful in God's work is to fall in line with his will and to do it his way. All that is pleasing to him is a success.

Citation: Unknown

Topics: Discipleship; God's Will; Human Will; Obedience; Submission; Success; Truth

References: Deuteronomy 26:16; Joshua 1:8; 1 Samuel 15:22; Matthew 7:21

QUOTATION 871

The man who keeps busy helping the man below him won't have time to envy the man above him.

Citation: Unknown

Topics: Benevolence; Brotherly Love; Envy; Humility; Pride; Servanthood

References: Deuteronomy 15:7; Ecclesiastes 3:10; Matthew 5:42

QUOTATION 872

God never put anyone in a place too small to grow.

Citation: Unknown

Topics: Christian Life; Humility; Maturity; Ministry; Spiritual Growth

References: Psalm 92:12–13; Isaiah 54:2; Matthew 16:18; Mark 4:30–32; Luke 13:19; 2 Corinthians 9:10; 1 Peter 2:2; 2 Peter 3:18

ST. ANGELA MERICI
ITALIAN RELIGIOUS LEADER AND SAINT (1474–1540)

QUOTATION 873

Consider that the Devil doesn't sleep, but seeks our ruin in a thousand ways.

Citation: Unknown

Topics: Devil; Evil; Satan; Spiritual Warfare; Temptation

References: Matthew 4:1–11; Luke 4:1–13; James 4:7; 1 Peter 5:8

CALVIN MILLER
AMERICAN PROFESSOR, WRITER, AND POET (1936–)

QUOTATION 874

Unbridled lust: a cannibal committing suicide by nibbling on himself.

Citation: Calvin Miller, *A Requiem for Love*

Topics: Consequences; Death; Evil; Lust; Purity; Self-centeredness; Sex; Sin; Temptation

References: Proverbs 6:25–26; Matthew 5:28; James 1:15; 1 Peter 2:11

QUOTATION **875**

God … does not lavish his children with a jolly discipleship so that they may swim in spiritual ecstasy between conversion and death. God is a giver, but he does not give happiness. He gives redemption, meaning, security, love, victory, and the indwelling of the Holy Spirit. And happiness is our response to his gifts.

Citation: Calvin Miller, *The Taste of Joy*

Topics: Discipleship; Grace; Happiness; Joy; Redemption; Thanksgiving; Victory

References: Matthew 16:24; Luke 14:33; 1 Peter 2:21

QUOTATION **876**

Only once must we be born without our own consent. Only once must we die without our own permission.

Citation: Unknown

Topics: Conversion; Death; Decisions; Eternal Death; Eternal Life; Heaven; Hell; Self-denial

References: John 5:24; Romans 5:12–14; Colossians 2:13

DONALD MILLER
AMERICAN WRITER (1971–)

QUOTATION **877**

When one of my friends becomes a Christian … I see in their eyes the trueness of the story.

Citation: Donald Miller, *Blue Like Jazz*

Topics: Conversion; Evangelism; Gospel; Regeneration; Truth

Reference: John 4:39–54

QUOTATION **878**

Passion is tricky ... because it can point to nothing as easily as it points to something.

Citation: Donald Miller, *Blue Like Jazz*

Topics: Deceit; Emotions; Enthusiasm; Passion; Purpose; Zeal

References: Proverbs 19:2; Romans 10:2

QUOTATION **879**

The most difficult story I have ever contended with is this: Life is a story about me.

Citation: Donald Miller, *Blue Like Jazz*

Topics: Arrogance; Egotism; Individualism; Pride; Self-centeredness

References: Mark 8:34–36; Romans 14:19–21; 15:1; Philippians 2:1–11

ELISA MORGAN
AMERICAN FOUNDER OF MOPS INTERNATIONAL (1955–)

QUOTATION **880**

God, who sees us in our worst moments, does not measure us by them.

Citation: Elisa Morgan, *Mom to Mom*

Topics: Depravity; Forgiveness; God; Grace; Human Condition; Mercy; Sin; Sinful Nature

References: Psalm 147:4; Acts 15:8; Hebrews 4:13

ROBERT F. MORNEAU
AMERICAN ROMAN CATHOLIC BISHOP AND WRITER (1938–)

QUOTATION **881**

What is humility? It is that habitual quality whereby we live in the truth of things: the truth that we are creatures and not the Creator; the truth that our life is a composite of good and evil, light and darkness; the truth that in our littleness we have been given extravagant dignity.

Humility is saying a radical *yes* to the human condition.

> **Citation:** Robert F. Morneau, *Humility: 31 Reflections on Christian Virtue*
>
> **Topics:** Human Condition; Humility; Limitations; Pride; Self-examination; Self-image; Worth
>
> **References:** Philippians 2:1–11; Hebrews 2:9

ANDREW MURRAY
SOUTH AFRICAN PASTOR (1828–1917)

QUOTATION **882**

Prayer is the one hand with which we grasp the invisible; fasting, the other, with which we let loose and cast away the visible.

> **Citation:** Andrew Murray, *With Christ in the School of Prayer*
>
> **Topics:** Devotional Life; Fasting; Intercession; Prayer; Spiritual Disciplines
>
> **References:** Matthew 6:5–18; 7:7–12; Luke 11:1–13; 18:1–8

QUOTATION **883**

This is the fixed, eternal law of the kingdom: if you ask and receive not, it must be because there is something amiss or wanting in the prayer.

> **Citation:** Andrew Murray, *With Christ in the School of Prayer*
>
> **Topics:** Intercession; Kingdom; Motives; Prayer; Self-examination; Unanswered Prayer
>
> **References:** Matthew 6:5–15; 7:7–12; Luke 11:1–13; 18:1–8; James 4:1–12

QUOTATION **884**

God has no more precious gift to a church or an age than a man who lives as an embodiment of His will, and inspires those around him with the faith of what grace can do.

> **Citation:** Unknown

Topics: Character; Godliness; God's Will; Human Will; Influence; Integrity; Obedience; Passion; Submission

References: Romans 1:16–17; 2 Timothy 1:13

QUOTATION **885**

Beware in your prayer, above everything, of limiting God—not only by unbelief, but by fancying that you know what he can do.

Citation: Andrew Murray, *The Ministry of Intercession*

Topics: Devotional Life; God's Sovereignty; Mysteries; Prayer; Trust; Unbelief

References: Genesis 17:17; Zechariah 7:13; Matthew 7:7

VLADIMIR NABOKOV
RUSSIAN-AMERICAN WRITER (1899–1977)

QUOTATION **886**

Life is a great surprise. I do not see why death should not be an even greater one.

Citation: Unknown

Topics: Death; Eternal Life; Final Judgment; Heaven; Hell; Life; Mysteries

References: John 14:1–4; 1 Corinthians 15; Hebrews 9:27; Revelation 21:1–7

FLORENCE NIGHTINGALE
BRITISH WRITER AND PIONEER OF MODERN NURSING (1820–1910)

QUOTATION **887**

If I could give you information about my own life, it would be to show how a woman of very ordinary ability has been led by God in strange and unaccustomed paths to do in his service what he has done in her. And if I could tell you all, you would see how God has done all, and I nothing. I have worked hard, very hard, that is all; and I have never refused God anything.

Citation: Florence Nightingale, in a letter to Dr. Lemuel Moss

Topics: Direction; Discipleship; Guidance; Providence; Service; Surrender

References: Mark 10:43–44; Luke 10:36–37; 1 Corinthians 15:10; Galatians 6:9–10

ELIZABETH O'CONNOR
AMERICAN WRITER AND MINISTER (1928–1998)

QUOTATION **888**

Because our gifts carry us out into the world and make us participants in life, the uncovering of them is one of the most important tasks confronting any one of us.

Citation: Elizabeth O'Connor, *The Eighth Day of Creation*

Topics: Calling; Purpose; Spiritual Gifts; Vocation; Work

References: Romans 12:3–8; 1 Corinthians 12:1–11; Ephesians 4:1–16

QUOTATION **889**

While it is a crucial mistake to assume that churches can be on an outward journey without being on an inward one, it is equally disastrous to assume that one can make the journey inward without taking the journey outward.

Citation: Elizabeth O'Connor, *Journey Inward, Journey Outward*

Topics: Discipleship; Maturity; Servanthood; Spiritual Growth

References: Ephesians 4:15; 1 Thessalonians 3:12; 2 Peter 1:5–6; 3:18

EUGENE O'NEILL
AMERICAN PLAYWRIGHT (1888–1953)

QUOTATION **890**

Man is born broken. He lives by mending. The grace of God is glue.

Citation: Eugene O'Neill, *The Great God Brown*

Topics: Brokenness; Grace; Human Condition; Human Nature; Weakness

References: Romans 3:9–26; 5:1–11; 2 Corinthians 4:7–18; 12:7–10

WILLIAM EDWIN ORCHARD
BRITISH PREACHER AND WRITER (1877 – 1955)

QUOTATION 891

It may take a crucified church to bring a crucified Christ before the eyes of the world.

> **Citation:** W. E. Orchard, *The Temple*
>
> **Topics:** Church; Cross; Martyrdom; Missions; Outreach; Persecution; Sacrifice; Self-denial; Suffering; Witness
>
> **References:** Matthew 10:38; 16:24; Mark 10:21

JOHN ORTBERG
AMERICAN PREACHER AND WRITER (1957 –)

QUOTATION 892

The problem with spending your life climbing up the ladder is that you will go right past Jesus, for he's coming down.

> **Citation:** John Ortberg, *When the Game Is Over, It All Goes Back in the Box*
>
> **Topics:** Ambition; Career; Humility; Jesus Christ; Pride; Priorities; Success
>
> **References:** Matthew 20:28; John 13:1 – 17; Philippians 2:1 – 11

QUOTATION 893

There is an immense difference between *training* to do something and *trying* to do something.… Spiritual transformation is not a matter of trying harder, but of training wisely.… Following Jesus simply means learning from him how to arrange my life around activities that enable me to live in the fruit of the Spirit.

> **Citation:** John Ortberg, *The Life You've Always Wanted*
>
> **Topics:** Discipleship; Fruit of the Spirit; Sanctification; Spiritual Formation
>
> **References:** Matthew 11:28 – 30; Galatians 5:22 – 23; 1 Timothy 4:7

QUOTATION **894**

If we cannot be transformed, we will settle for being informed or conformed.

Citation: John Ortberg, *The Life You've Always Wanted*

Topics: Conformity; Knowledge; Spiritual Growth; Transformation

References: Matthew 7:13 – 14; Romans 12:1 – 2

QUOTATION **895**

The ministry of bearing with one another is learning to hear God speak through difficult people.

Citation: John Ortberg, *The Life You've Always Wanted*

Topics: Community; Enemies; Listening; Perseverance; Teachability

References: Romans 15:1 – 7; Ephesians 4:1 – 6; Colossians 3:12 – 17

GEORGE ORWELL
BRITISH WRITER (1903 – 50)

QUOTATION **896**

When men stop worshiping God, they promptly start worshiping man, with disastrous results.

Citation: George Orwell, in an article for *The Observer*

Topics: Humanism; Idolatry; Pride; Worship

References: Deuteronomy 11:16; Romans 1:21 – 23

VIRGINIA STEM OWENS
AMERICAN WRITER (1941 –)

QUOTATION **897**

Thanksgiving is not a result of perception; thanksgiving is the access to perception.

Citation: Virginia Stem Owens, *And the Trees Clap Their Hands*

Topics: Discernment; Illumination; Insight; Spiritual Perception; Thanksgiving

References: Psalms 100; 107; 118; 136

QUOTATION **898**

I am always suspicious when the word *Christian* is employed as an adjective instead of a noun. It is in such cases usually being used either to sell something or as an excuse for second-rate work, as though piety could make up for poor quality.

Citation: Virginia Stem Owens, in the *Reformed Journal* article "On Eating Words"

Topics: Christian Life; Excuses; Identity; Piety

References: Acts 11:26; 26:28; 1 Peter 4:16

NORMAN VINCENT PEALE
AMERICAN PREACHER AND WRITER (1898 – 1993)

QUOTATION **899**

The trouble with most of us is that we would rather be ruined by praise than saved by criticism.

Citation: Unknown

Topics: Accountability; Criticism; Praise; Pride; Rebuke; Teachability

References: 2 Samuel 12:7 – 14; Matthew 18:15 – 20; 1 Corinthians 5:1 – 11; Colossians 3:16

EUGENE PETERSON
AMERICAN PASTOR, SCHOLAR, WRITER, AND POET (1932 –)

QUOTATION **900**

Those people who pray know what most around them either don't know or choose to ignore: centering life in the insatiable demands of the ego is the sure path to doom…. They know that life confined to the self is a prison, a joy-killing, neurosis-producing, disease-fomenting prison.

Citation: Eugene Peterson, *Where Your Treasure Is*

Topics: Bondage; Egotism; Freedom; Individualism; Joy; Prayer; Self-centeredness; Spiritual Disciplines

References: 2 Corinthians 3:17–18; Colossians 3:1–4; 4:2–4

QUOTATION 901

Two commands direct us from the small-minded world of self-help to the large world of God's help. First, "Come, behold the works of the Lord."… The second command is "Be still, and know that I am God."

Citation: Eugene Peterson, *Where Your Treasure Is*

Topics: Experiencing God; Limitations; Provision; Solitude; Submission

Reference: Psalm 46

QUOTATION 902

Prayer is political action. Prayer is social energy. Prayer is public good. Far more of our nation's life is shaped by prayer than is formed by legislation. That we have not collapsed into anarchy is due more to prayer than to the police.

Citation: Eugene Peterson, *Where Your Treasure Is*

Topics: Culture; Influence; Intercession; Politics; Prayer; Social Impact

References: Genesis 18:32; Deuteronomy 9:25; Proverbs 11:11

QUOTATION 903

Feeling sorry for yourself has been developed into an art form. The whining and sniveling that wiser generations ridiculed with satire is given best-seller status among us.

Citation: Eugene Peterson, *Where Your Treasure Is*

Topics: Complaining; Contentment; Grumbling; Self-centeredness; Self-pity

References: John 6:43; Philippians 2:14

QUOTATION 904

Neither the adventure of goodness nor the pursuit of righteousness gets headlines.

Citation: Eugene Peterson, *Run with the Horses*

Topics: Adventure; Christian Life; Godliness; Righteousness

References: Genesis 6:12; Psalm 12:1; Isaiah 59:14; 2 Timothy 3:1–2

QUOTATION **905**

The greatest errors in the spiritual life are not committed by the novices but by the adepts.

Citation: Eugene Peterson, *Working the Angles*

Topics: Devotional Life; Failure; Pride; Self-righteousness

References: Matthew 7:27; 23; Mark 12:38–39; Luke 20:45–46

QUOTATION **906**

The Hebrew evening/morning sequence conditions us to the rhythms of grace. We go to sleep, and God begins his work.... We wake into a world we didn't make, into a salvation we didn't earn.

Citation: Eugene Peterson, *Working the Angles*

Topics: Atonement; God's Sovereignty; Grace; Limitations; Mercy; Salvation

References: Psalms 37:39; 127:1–2; Luke 3:6; Ephesians 2:8; Titus 2:11

QUOTATION **907**

I can be active and pray; I can work and pray; but I cannot be busy and pray.

Citation: Eugene Peterson, *The Contemplative Pastor*

Topics: Busyness; Devotional Life; Distractions; Double-mindedness; Prayer; Spiritual Disciplines; Work

References: Psalm 141:4; Ecclesiastes 3:10; James 1:11

QUOTATION **908**

In a world where nearly everything can be weighed, explained, quantified, subjected to psychological analysis and scientific control, I persist in making the center of my life a God whom no eye hath seen, nor ear heard, whose will no one can probe. That's a risk.

Citation: Eugene Peterson, in the *Christianity Today* article "Living the Message"

Topics: Christian Life; Courage; Faith; Risk; Trust

References: Romans 10:17; 1 Corinthians 2:9; Galatians 5:6; Hebrews 11:1; 1 John 5:4

QUOTATION **909**

Apparently a broken will mends the same way a broken arm or leg does, stronger at the line of fracture.

Citation: Unknown

Topics: Brokenness; Healing; Human Will; Pride; Self-centeredness; Surrender

References: Deuteronomy 1:43; Psalm 51:17; Isaiah 28:12

QUOTATION **910**

Life is not something we manage to hammer together; it is an unfathomable gift.

Citation: Unknown

Topics: Grace; Life; Thanksgiving

References: Matthew 16:26; John 1:4; 1 John 5:12

QUOTATION **911**

In prayer, we are aware that God is in action and that when the circumstances are ready, when others are in the right place, and when our hearts are prepared, he will call us into the action. Waiting in prayer is a disciplined refusal to act before God acts.

Citation: Unknown

Topics: God's Will; Ministry; Patience; Prayer; Self-discipline; Waiting on God

References: Psalm 40:1; Romans 12:12; James 5:7

QUOTATION **912**

If I want potatoes for dinner tomorrow, it will do me little good to plant them in my garden tonight. There are long stretches of darkness and invisibility and silence that separate planting and reaping. During the stretches of waiting, there is cultivating and weeding and nurturing and planting still other seeds.

Citation: Unknown

Topics: Fruitfulness; Patience; Sowing and Reaping; Waiting on God
References: Psalm 126:5; Galatians 6:9; James 5:7

WILLIAM LYON PHELPS
AMERICAN WRITER (1865 – 1943)

QUOTATION 913

You can learn more about human nature by reading the Bible than by living in New York.

Citation: William Lyon Phelps, *Human Nature in the Bible*
Topics: Bible; Bible Study; God's Will; Human Nature
References: Isaiah 2:3; Romans 15:4; Hebrews 4:12

REBECCA MANLEY PIPPERT
AMERICAN WRITER

QUOTATION 914

Being an extrovert isn't essential to evangelism — obedience and love are.

Citation: Unknown
Topics: Evangelism; Gentleness; Kindness; Love; Obedience; Witness
References: Matthew 28:18 – 20; Acts 1:8

NEIL POSTMAN
AMERICAN PROFESSOR, WRITER, AND CULTURAL CRITIC (1931 – 2003)

QUOTATION 915

I believe I am not mistaken in saying that Christianity is a demanding and serious religion. When it is delivered as easy and amusing, it is another kind of religion altogether.

Citation: Neil Postman, *Amusing Ourselves to Death*

Topics: Christian Life; Cost; Discipleship; Sanctification; Trials

References: Matthew 16:24; Luke 14:33; John 8:31–32; Philippians 3:7–16

CHERI REGISTER
AMERICAN WRITER (1945–)

QUOTATION **916**

Lived fully, the experience of illness can free you from the curse of perfectionism that makes happiness conditional on having everything just right.

Citation: Cheri Register, *Living with Chronic Illness*

Topics: Control; Disease; Happiness; Perfection; Sickness

References: Psalm 126:5; James 5:11; 1 Peter 1:6–7

HADDON ROBINSON
AMERICAN PREACHER, WRITER, AND PROFESSOR (1931–)

QUOTATION **917**

A kind of arithmetic has been spawned in the counting rooms of hell. This kind of arithmetic is always interested in reaching the masses but somehow never gets down to a man or a woman. This kind of arithmetic always talks about winning the world for God but doesn't think much about winning a neighborhood for God. That arithmetic makes it valiant to cross oceans and never really crosses streets.

Citation: Haddon Robinson, in his sermon "A Case Study of a Mugging"

Topics: Complacency; Distractions; Evangelism; Focus; Missions; Satan; Witness

References: Proverbs 11:30; Matthew 4:19; Jude 23

ADRIAN ROGERS

AMERICAN PASTOR AND PRESIDENT OF THE SOUTHERN BAPTIST CONVENTION (1931–2005)

QUOTATION 918

An atheist can't find God for the same reason a thief can't find a policeman.

> **Citation:** Unknown
>
> **Topics:** Atheism; God; Hiding; Rebellion; Seekers; Unbelief
>
> **References:** Psalm 10:4; Romans 3:11; Hebrews 11:6

RONALD ROLHEISER

AMERICAN ROMAN CATHOLIC PRIEST AND PRESIDENT OF THE OBLATE SCHOOL OF THEOLOGY

QUOTATION 919

We want to be saints, but we also want to feel every sensation experienced by sinners; we want to be innocent and pure, but we also want to be experienced and taste all of life; we want to serve the poor and have a simple lifestyle, but we also want all the comforts of the rich; we want to have the depth afforded by solitude, but we also do not want to miss anything; we want to pray, but we also want to watch television, read, talk to friends, and go out.

> **Citation:** Ronald Rolheiser, *The Holy Longing*
>
> **Topics:** Choices; Distractions; Double-mindedness; Priorities; Spiritual Disciplines; Temptation; Values; Wholehearted Devotion
>
> **References:** Matthew 6:24; Luke 16:13; 1 Corinthians 10:21; Galatians 6:7–8; 1 Thessalonians 4:1–12; James 4:8

QUOTATION 920

All boredom and contempt is an infallible sign that we have fallen out of a healthy fear of God.

> **Citation:** Ronald Rolheiser, *The Shattered Lantern*

Topics: Awe; Boredom; Fear of God; Irreverence; Worship

References: Romans 12:1–2; 1 Corinthians 15:58; Ephesians 6:7; 2 Timothy 1:7

LELAND RYKEN
AMERICAN PROFESSOR AND WRITER (1942–)

QUOTATION 921

We worship our work, work at our play, and play at our worship.

Citation: Leland Ryken, quoted in a *Critique* magazine article

Topics: Idolatry; Priorities; Recreation; Work; Worship

References: Exodus 20:1–11; Matthew 4:10; Acts 14:15

DOROTHY SAYERS
BRITISH WRITER (1893–1957)

QUOTATION 922

It is not true at all that dogma is "hopelessly irrelevant" to the life and thought of the average man. What is true is that ministers of the Christian religion often assert that it is, present it for consideration as though it were, and, in fact, by their faulty exposition of it make it so. The central dogma of the Incarnation is that by which relevance stands or falls.

Citation: Dorothy Sayers, *Creed or Chaos?*

Topics: Doctrine; Incarnation; Knowledge; Teachability; Theology; Truth

References: John 1:1–18; 1 Corinthians 15:1–11; 1 Timothy 1:3–11; 2 Timothy 2:3–18; 4:1–5

QUOTATION 923

I believe it a grave mistake to present Christianity as something charming and popular with no offense in it.

Citation: Dorothy Sayers, *The Whimsical Christian*

Topics: Christian Life; Cost; Discipleship; Tests; Trials

References: Matthew 8:18–22; 10:37–39; 16:21–28; Mark 8:31–9:1; Luke 9:22–27; 9:57–62; 14:25–35; John 6:66–69

QUOTATION **924**

In the world it is called Tolerance, but in hell it is called Despair.

Citation: Dorothy Sayers, *The Whimsical Christian*

Topics: Despair; Hell; Postmodernism; Tolerance; World

References: Matthew 7:13–14; Romans 1:18–32; 2 Timothy 3:1–9

QUOTATION **925**

It is curious that people who are filled with horrified indignation whenever a cat kills a sparrow can hear the story of the killing of God told Sunday after Sunday and not experience any shock at all.

Citation: Dorothy Sayers, *The Man Born to Be King*

Topics: Atonement; Cross; Crucifixion; Foolishness; Perspective

References: Matthew 27:32–56; Mark 15:22–32; Luke 23:33–43; John 19:17–24; Philippians 2:5–11

QUOTATION **926**

[Christ] did not stop the crucifixion; he rose from the dead.

Citation: Dorothy Sayers, *The Greatest Drama Ever Staged*

Topics: Atonement; Cross; Crucifixion; Jesus Christ; Overcoming; Resurrection; Salvation; Suffering; Victory

References: Matthew 27:32–56; 28:1–10; Mark 15:22–32; 16:1–8; Luke 23:33–43; 24:1–12; John 19:17–24; 20:1–9; Philippians 2:5–11

GEORGE BERNARD SHAW
IRISH PLAYWRIGHT (1856 – 1950)

QUOTATION **927**

The science to which I pinned my faith is bankrupt. Its counsels, which should have established the millennium, led instead directly to the suicide of Europe. I believed them once. In their name I helped to destroy the faith of millions of worshipers in the temples of a thousand creeds. And now they look at me and witness the great tragedy of an atheist who has lost his faith.

> **Citation:** George Bernard Shaw, *Too Good to Be True*
>
> **Topics:** Atheism; Deceit; Faith; Knowledge; Religion; Science; Technology
>
> **References:** Isaiah 2:22; 31:1; Jeremiah 17:5; 1 John 2:22

HANNAH WHITALL SMITH
AMERICAN PREACHER AND WRITER FOR THE HOLINESS MOVEMENT (1832 – 1911)

QUOTATION **928**

Perfect obedience would be perfect happiness if only we had perfect confidence in the power we are obeying.

> **Citation:** Hannah Whitall Smith, *The Christian's Secret of a Happy Life*
>
> **Topics:** Authority; Discipleship; Obedience; Power
>
> **References:** Matthew 5:48; 2 Corinthians 13:11; Ephesians 4:13

QUOTATION **929**

The mother eagle teaches her little ones to fly by making their nest so uncomfortable that they are forced to leave it and commit themselves to the unknown world of air outside. And just so does our God to us.

> **Citation:** Unknown
>
> **Topics:** Difficulties; Maturity; Spiritual Growth; Tests; Trials
>
> **References:** Matthew 10:1 – 10; 28:16 – 20; Luke 24:45 – 49; John 17:6 – 19; 20:21; Acts 8:1 – 3

ALEKSANDR SOLZHENITSYN
RUSSIAN WRITER (1918–2008)

QUOTATION 930

Gradually it was disclosed to me that the line dividing good and evil passes not through states, nor between classes, nor between political parties either—but right through every human heart.

Citation: Aleksandr Solzhenitsyn, *Gulag II*

Topics: Depravity; Evil; Flesh; Human Nature; Sin

References: Psalm 58:2; Proverbs 20:9; Jeremiah 17:9–10; Matthew 7:21; 12:34; 15:18–19

CHARLES HADDON SPURGEON
BRITISH PREACHER AND TEACHER (1834–92)

QUOTATION 931

When you speak of heaven, let your face light up. When you speak of hell, well, then your everyday face will do.

Citation: Charles Haddon Spurgeon, *Lectures to My Students*

Topics: Eternal Perspective; Heaven; Hell

References: Psalm 16:11; Matthew 5:12; Luke 6:23; 13:28; Acts 7:55; 1 Corinthians 2:9

QUOTATION 932

Get your friends to tell you your faults, or better still, welcome an enemy who will watch you keenly and sting you savagely. What a blessing such an irritating critic will be to a wise man, what an intolerable nuisance to a fool!

Citation: Charles Haddon Spurgeon, *Lectures to My Students*

Topics: Accountability; Community; Correction; Criticism; Relationships

References: 2 Samuel 12:7–14; Ecclesiastes 4:7–12; Matthew 18:15–20; 1 Corinthians 5:1–11; Galatians 6:1–5; Philippians 4:2–9

QUOTATION **933**

Nobody ever outgrows Scripture; the book widens and deepens with our years.

Citation: Charles Haddon Spurgeon, in his sermon "The Talking Book"

Topics: Bible; Experiencing God; Teachability

References: Psalms 19:7–14; 119; 2 Timothy 3:14–17; 2 Peter 1:12–21

QUOTATION **934**

The greatest works are done by the ones. The hundreds do not often do much — the companies never. It is the units, the single individuals, that are the power and the might.

Citation: Unknown

Topics: Accomplishment; Calling; Individualism; Work

References: Isaiah 40:31; Micah 3:8; Zechariah 4:6; Acts 1:8; 19:11–12

QUOTATION **935**

Success can go to my head, and will unless I remember that it is God who accomplishes the work, and that he will be able to make out with other means whenever he cuts me down to size.

Citation: Unknown

Topics: Arrogance; God's Sovereignty; Humility; Limitations; Work

References: 1 Corinthians 3:10–23; 15:10; Philippians 1:4–6; 2:12–13

QUOTATION **936**

Many men owe the grandeur of their lives to their tremendous difficulties.

Citation: Unknown

Topics: Affliction; Growth; Suffering; Tests; Trials

References: Job 23:10; Isaiah 48:10; Jeremiah 1:18–19; 2 Corinthians 4:17; 11:16–33; Revelation 7:14

TIM STAFFORD
AMERICAN WRITER (1950–)

QUOTATION 937

I would rather be cheated a hundred times than develop a heart of stone.

Citation: Unknown

Topics: Generosity; Giving; Poverty; Teachability

References: Proverbs 17:9; Romans 15:1; 1 Peter 4:8

JOHN STEINBECK
AMERICAN WRITER (1902–68)

QUOTATION 938

A sad soul can kill you quicker, far quicker than a germ.

Citation: John Steinbeck, *Travels with Charley*

Topics: Death; Depression; Despair; Emotions; Sadness; Soul

References: Nehemiah 8:10; Proverbs 15:13, 15; John 15:11

ROBERT LOUIS STEVENSON
SCOTTISH NOVELIST AND POET (1850–94)

QUOTATION 939

Sooner or later, we sit down to a banquet of consequences.

Citation: Unknown

Topics: Consequences; Eternal Death; Eternal Life; Final Judgment; Sin; Sowing and Reaping

References: Matthew 7:13–29; Romans 1:18–32; Galatians 6:7–10

JOHN R. W. STOTT

BRITISH ANGLICAN CLERGYMAN AND WRITER (1921 –)

QUOTATION **940**

The essence of sin is man substituting himself for God, while the essence of salvation is God substituting himself for man.

Citation: John R. W. Stott, *The Cross of Christ*

Topics: Atonement; Cross; Human Condition; Idolatry; Jesus Christ; Redemption; Salvation; Substitution

References: Genesis 3:1 – 19; John 6:25 – 59; Romans 1:18 – 32; 5:6 – 8; 2 Corinthians 5:21; Ephesians 2:1 – 10; Hebrews 9; 10:1 – 18

QUOTATION **941**

In the Bible we do not see man groping for God; we see God reaching after man.

Citation: John R. W. Stott, *Basic Christianity*

Topics: Experiencing God; God; Grace; Redemption; Revelation

References: Genesis 12:1 – 3; Luke 19:10; John 1:1 – 18; 1 Timothy 1:12 – 20

QUOTATION **942**

God is not interesting. He is deeply upsetting.

Citation: John R. W. Stott, *Basic Christianity*

Topics: Experiencing God; Fear of God; God; Knowing God; Mysteries

Reference: Genesis 22:1 – 19; Job 42:1 – 6; Psalm 8:1 – 2

HARRIET BEECHER STOWE
AMERICAN WRITER (1811 – 96)

QUOTATION 943

I would not attack the faith of a heathen without being sure I had a better one to put in its place.

Citation: Harriet Beecher Stowe, in a personal letter on how to treat those critical of the Christian faith

Topics: Atheism; Belief; Evangelism; Outreach

References: Ephesians 4:17 – 32; 5:1 – 20

QUOTATION 944

Common sense is seeing things as they are, and doing things as they ought to be.

Citation: Unknown

Topics: Character; Discernment; Integrity; Morality; Perception; Wisdom

References: Proverbs 1; 2; 9; 24

CHUCK SWINDOLL
AMERICAN WRITER AND PREACHER (1934 –)

QUOTATION 945

God's never missed the runway through all the centuries of fearful fog.

Citation: Chuck Swindoll, *Growing Strong in the Seasons of Life*

Topics: Fear; God's Sovereignty; Trust

References: Psalm 37:5; Proverbs 3:5; Isaiah 50:10

QUOTATION 946

The longer I live the more convinced I become that life is 10 percent what happens to us and 90 percent how we respond to it.

Citation: Charles R. Swindoll, *Strengthening Your Grip*

Topics: Attitudes; Faith and Circumstances; Life; Overcoming

Reference: Philippians 4:11–13

QUOTATION **947**

Being unselfish in attitude strikes at the very core of our being. It means we are willing to forgo our own comfort, our own preferences, our own schedule, our own desires for another's benefit. And that brings us back to Christ.

Citation: Charles Swindoll, *Laugh Again*

Topics: God's Will; Human Will; Sacrifice; Self-denial; Selflessness

References: Matthew 20:25–28; Romans 12:10; 1 Corinthians 10:33; 13:1–8; 2 Corinthians 8:9; Philippians 2:3–8

JONI EARECKSON TADA

AMERICAN WRITER, ARTIST, AND FOUNDER OF JONI AND FRIENDS (1949–)

QUOTATION **948**

Just think: Every promise God has ever made finds its fulfillment in Jesus. God doesn't just give us grace; he gives us Jesus, the Lord of grace. If it's peace, it's only found in Jesus, the Prince of Peace. Even life itself is found in the Resurrection and the Life. Christianity isn't all that complicated … it's Jesus.

Citation: Joni Eareckson Tada, *Lamp unto My Feet*

Topics: Christian Life; Grace; Jesus Christ; Peace; Promises; Resurrection; Wisdom

References: John 1:3; 11:25–26; Ephesians 2:20; Hebrews 1:1–2

QUOTATION **949**

Always, love is a choice. You come up against scores of opportunities every day to love or not to love. You encounter hundreds of small chances to please your friends, delight your Lord, and encourage your family. That's why love and obedience are intimately linked—you can't have one without the other.

Citation: Joni Eareckson Tada, *Diamonds in the Dust*

Topics: Choices; Decisions; Love; Obedience

References: John 15:12–13; Ephesians 6:6; Philippians 2:12; 1 Timothy 6:18

QUOTATION **950**

We ask less of this life because we know full well that more is coming in the next. The art of living with suffering is just the art of readjusting our expectations in the here and the now.

Citation: Unknown

Topics: Contentment; Disabilities; Eternal Life; Heaven; Hope; Life; Pain; Perseverance; Perspective; Promises; Suffering

References: Proverbs 15:16; 1 Timothy 6:6; Hebrews 13:5

BARBARA BROWN TAYLOR
AMERICAN WRITER AND PROFESSOR (1951 –)

QUOTATION **951**

When we repay evil with evil, evil is all there is, in bigger and more toxic piles. The only way to reverse the process is to behave in totally unexpected ways.

Citation: Barbara Brown Taylor, *God in Pain*

Topics: Enemies, Evil; Forgiveness; Kindness; Love

Reference: Matthew 5:21–26; 5:38–48; 18:15–35

QUOTATION **952**

I do not mean to make an idol of health, but it does seem to me that at least some of us have made an idol of exhaustion. The only time we know we have done enough is when we are running on empty and when the ones we love most are the ones we see the least.

Citation: Barbara Brown Taylor, while explaining why she took a "year of Jubilee" in 2000 — not accepting any out-of-town speaking engagements and working only forty hours a week in ministry (quoted in the *Christian Century* article "Divine Subtraction")

Topics: Busyness; Family; Idolatry; Lifestyle; Priorities; Recreation; Rest; Sabbath; Work

References: Exodus 23:12; 31:12–17; Isaiah 44:9–11; 46

WILLIAM TEMPLE
ARCHBISHOP OF CANTERBURY (1881–1944)

QUOTATION 953

The only thing of my very own which I contribute to redemption is the sin from which I need to be redeemed.

Citation: William Temple, *Nature, Man, and God*

Topics: Grace; Redemption; Salvation; Sin; Sinful Nature

References: Romans 3:9–26; 5; 6; 7:7–25

QUOTATION 954

Worship is the submission of all of our nature to God. It is the quickening of conscience by his holiness, nourishment of mind by his truth, purifying of imagination by his beauty, opening of the heart to his love, and submission of will to his purpose. And all this gathered up in adoration is the greatest of human expressions of which we are capable.

Citation: William Temple, *Writings in St. John*

Topics: Conscience; God; God's Will; Holiness; Human Will; Submission; Surrender; Truth; Wisdom; Worship

References: Isaiah 6:1–7; Matthew 22:37; Mark 12:30; Luke 10:27; Romans 12:1–2; Revelation 4:8–11; 5:8–14

QUOTATION 955

The sermons for which we are most grateful are those which help us to believe vitally what we knew quite well before the sermon started.

Citation: William Temple, *Writings in St. John*

Topics: Convictions; Emotions; Knowledge; Preaching

Reference: Acts 2:14–41

The church is the only society that exists for the benefit of those who are not its members.

Citation: Unknown

Topics: Christian Life; Church; Evangelism; Outreach; Service; Social Impact

Reference: Matthew 5:13–16

CORRIE TEN BOOM
DUTCH HOLOCAUST SURVIVOR AND WRITER (1892–1983)

QUOTATION **957**

If Jesus were born one thousand times in Bethlehem and not in me, then I would still be lost.

Citation: Corrie ten Boom, *Each New Day*

Topics: Abiding in Christ; Advent; Christmas; Incarnation; Receiving Christ; Regeneration

References: Matthew 10:40; John 1:12–13; 3:1–8; 15:4

QUOTATION **958**

Forgiveness is an act of the will, and the will can function regardless of the temperature of the heart.

Citation: Corrie ten Boom, *Tramp for the Lord*

Topics: Anger; Forgiveness; Human Will

References: Matthew 18:15–35; 2 Corinthians 2:5–11

QUOTATION **959**

Never be afraid to trust an unknown future to a known God.

Citation: Unknown

Topics: Faith; Fear; Future; Trust; Worry

References: Genesis 12:1–9; 1 Peter 1:3–9

QUOTATION **960**

The measure of a life … is not its duration, but its donation.

> Citation: Unknown
> Topics: Life; Meaning; Purpose; Sacrifice; Servanthood
> Reference: Philippians 1:12–30

QUOTATION **961**

Worry is a cycle of inefficient thoughts whirling around a center of fear.

> Citation: Unknown
> Topics: Fear; Trust; Worry
> References: Matthew 6:25–34; Luke 12:22–34

STUDS TERKEL
AMERICAN WRITER AND BROADCASTER (1912–)

QUOTATION **962**

I think most of us are looking for a calling, not a job. Most of us, like the assembly line worker, have jobs that are too small for our spirit. Jobs are not big enough for people.

> Citation: Studs Terkel, *Working*
> Topics: Calling; Career; Employees; Limitations; Vocation; Work
> References: Exodus 20:9; Colossians 3:23–24; 2 Thessalonians 3:8; James 5:4

HENRY DAVID THOREAU
AMERICAN WRITER, NATURALIST, AND PHILOSOPHER (1817–62)

QUOTATION **963**

It is not when I am going to meet him, but when I am just turning away and leaving him alone, that I discover that God is.

> Citation: Henry David Thoreau, *Letters to a Spiritual Seeker*

Topics: Experiencing God; Presence of God

References: Jeremiah 29:13; Hosea 10:12; Acts 17:27

JAMES THURBER

AMERICAN HUMORIST AND CARTOONIST (1894 – 1961)

QUOTATION **964**

All human beings should try to learn, before they die, what they are running from, and to, and why.

> **Citation:** Unknown
>
> **Topics:** Death; Meaning; Motives; Running from God; Seekers; Self-examination; Spiritual Perception
>
> **References:** Psalm 39:4; Lamentations 3:40; Luke 9:25; 2 Corinthians 13:5; Hebrews 9:27

QUOTATION **965**

There are two kinds of light — the glow that illuminates and the glare that obscures.

> **Citation:** Unknown
>
> **Topics:** Character; Evangelism; Lifestyle; Outreach; Testimony; Witness
>
> **References:** Matthew 5:13 – 16; Philippians 2:12 – 18

J. R. R. TOLKIEN

BRITISH WRITER AND PROFESSOR (1892 – 1973)

QUOTATION **966**

No man can estimate what is really happening at the present. All we do know, and that to a large extent by direct experience, is that evil labors with vast power and perpetual success — in vain: preparing always only the soil for unexpected good to sprout in.

> **Citation:** J. R. R. Tolkien, in a letter to his son Christopher

Topics: Evil; God's Sovereignty; Spiritual Warfare; Triumph of Good

References: Genesis 50:20; Psalm 37:1 – 11; Romans 5:3 – 5; 8:28; 1 Peter 4:12 – 19

LEO TOLSTOY
RUSSIAN WRITER (1828 – 1910)

QUOTATION 967

One can move a man either by influencing his animal being or by influencing his spiritual essence.

Citation: Leo Tolstoy, in his essay "Why Do Men Stupefy Themselves?"

Topics: Human Nature; Motivation; Spirituality

References: Job 32:8; Psalm 51:10; Ecclesiastes 12:7; Galatians 5:16 – 25

RICHARD TRENCH
IRISH ANGLICAN ARCHBISHOP AND POET (1807 – 86)

QUOTATION 968

Prayer is not overcoming God's reluctance ... it is laying hold of his highest willingness.

Citation: Richard Trench, *Notes on the Parables of Our Lord*

Topics: Prayer; Trust

References: 1 Kings 18:36 – 38; 2 Kings 19:14 – 19; Matthew 7:7 – 12; Luke 18:1 – 8

MARK TWAIN
AMERICAN WRITER (1835 – 1910)

QUOTATION 969

One of the most striking differences between a cat and a lie is a cat only has nine lives.

Citation: Mark Twain, *Pudd'nhead Wilson*

Topics: Deceit; Gossip; Lying

References: Proverbs 11:13; 16:28; 18:8; 26:20, 22; 2 Corinthians 12:20; 1 Peter 2:1

QUOTATION 970

Why is it that we rejoice at a birth and grieve at a funeral? It is because we are not the person involved.

Citation: Mark Twain, *Pudd'nhead Wilson*

Topics: Death; Funerals; Pain; Suffering

References: Ecclesiastes 3:1–8; Luke 23:43; Philippians 1:23

QUOTATION 971

We may not pay [Satan] reverence, for that would be indiscreet, but we can at least respect his talents. A person who has, for untold centuries, maintained the imposing position of spiritual head of four-fifths of the human race, and political head of the whole of it, must be granted the possession of executive abilities of the loftiest order.

Citation: Mark Twain, in his essay "Concerning the Jews"

Topics: Evil; Satan; Spiritual Warfare

References: Luke 4:6; John 16:11; Acts 26:18

QUOTATION 972

Heaven goes by favor. If it went by merit, you would stay out and your dog would go in.

Citation: Mark Twain, in his essay "Etiquette for the Afterlife"

Topics: Cross; Faith; Good Deeds; Grace; Heaven; Justification by Works; Mercy; Salvation

References: Romans 3:21–31; 5:1–11; 6; 7; Ephesians 2:1–10

QUOTATION 973

Always do right; it will gratify some people and astonish the rest.

Citation: Mark Twain, in his address "To the Young People's Society, Greenpoint Presbyterian Church, Brooklyn"

Topics: Character; Good Deeds; Integrity

References: Matthew 5:16; James 2:18; 1 Peter 2:12

QUOTATION 974

Most people are bothered by those Scripture passages which they cannot understand. But for me, the passages in Scripture which trouble me most are those which I do understand.

Citation: Unknown

Topics: Bible; Final Judgment; Teachability

References: Exodus 20:1–17; Jeremiah 5:14; Romans 1:16–17; 3:9–20; Hebrews 4:12; 1 John 2:15–17; Revelation 20:11–15

QUOTATION 975

Forgiveness is the fragrance that the flower leaves on the heel of the one who crushed it.

Citation: Unknown

Topics: Enemies; Forgiveness; Relationships

References: Mark 11:25; Luke 17:4; Colossians 3:13

QUOTATION 976

Often, the less there is to justify a traditional custom, the harder it is to get rid of it.

Citation: Unknown

Topics: Idolatry; Legalism; Tradition

References: Matthew 9:14–17; 23; Mark 2:18–22; Luke 5:33–39; Philippians 3:1–6

QUOTATION 977

I am an old man and have known a great many troubles, but most of them have never happened.

Citation: Unknown

Topics: Faith; Trust; Worry

References: Matthew 6:25 – 34; Luke 12:22 – 34

JOHN UPDIKE
AMERICAN WRITER (1932 –)

QUOTATION 978

All church services have this wonderful element: People with other things to do get up on a Sunday morning, put on good clothes and assemble out of nothing but faith—some vague yen toward something larger. Simply as a human gathering I find it moving, reassuring, and even inspiring. A church is a little like a novel in that both are saying there's something very important about being human.

Citation: John Updike, in a *U.S. News & World Report* article

Topics: Church; Community; Faith; Presence of God; Worship

References: Job 32:8; Ecclesiastes 12:7; Hebrews 10:25

QUOTATION 979

The fact that … we still live well cannot ease the pain of feeling that we no longer live nobly.

Citation: Unknown

Topics: Character; Lifestyle; Righteousness

References: Proverbs 28:20; Ecclesiastes 2:26; Matthew 6:19; James 5:3

ST. JEAN-BAPTISTE MARIE VIANNEY
FRENCH ROMAN CATHOLIC PRIEST AND SAINT (1786 – 1859)

QUOTATION 980

God does not require of us the martyrdom of the body; he requires only the martyrdom of the heart and the will.

Citation: Unknown

Topics: Consecration; Death to Self; God's Will; Human Will; Surrender; Martyrdom

References: Matthew 16:21–28; Mark 8:31–9:1; Luke 9:22–27; Acts 2:38; Galatians 2:20

KURT VONNEGUT
AMERICAN WRITER (1922–2007)

QUOTATION **981**

True terror is to wake up one morning and discover that your high school class is running the country.

> **Citation:** Kurt Vonnegut, quoted in an article for the *Denver Post*
>
> **Topics:** Aging; Fear; Maturity; Politics; Teens
>
> **Reference:** Psalm 20:7

RICK WARREN
AMERICAN PREACHER AND WRITER (1954–)

QUOTATION **982**

You can be sincere, but you can be sincerely wrong. The fact is, it takes more than sincerity to make it in life. It takes truth.

> **Citation:** Rick Warren, in his sermon "Myths That Make Us Miserable"
>
> **Topics:** Bible; Doctrine; Sincerity; Truth
>
> **References:** Psalm 101:7; Proverbs 21:6; 23:23; John 14:6

RICHARD WHATELY

BRITISH THEOLOGICAL WRITER AND
ARCHBISHOP OF DUBLIN (1787 – 1863)

QUOTATION 983

If my faith be false, I ought to change it; whereas if it be true, I am bound to propagate it.

Citation: Unknown

Topics: Evangelism; Faith; Integrity; Truth

References: Matthew 5:13 – 16; 9:35 – 38; 28:16 – 20; Mark 6:6 – 13; Luke 8:16 – 18; 24:45 – 49; John 20:21

E. B. WHITE

AMERICAN WRITER (1899 – 1985)

QUOTATION 984

To perceive Christmas through its wrapping becomes more difficult each year.

Citation: Unknown

Topics: Advent; Christmas; Distractions; Focus; Meaning

References: Matthew 1:18 – 25; Luke 2:1 – 20; John 1:1 – 18

WARREN WIERSBE

AMERICAN PREACHER AND WRITER (1929 –)

QUOTATION 985

Submission is not subjugation. Subjugation turns a person into a thing, destroys individuality, and removes all liberty. Submission makes a person become more of what God wants him to be; it brings out individuality; it gives him the freedom to accomplish all that God has for his life and ministry.

Citation: Warren Wiersbe, in the *Leadership* journal article "Principles Are the Bottom Line"

Topics: Obedience; Purpose; Submission; Surrender

References: Romans 13:1–7; Ephesians 5:21–24; Colossians 3:18–19; 1 Timothy 2:11; 1 Peter 3:1–7; 5:3

OSCAR WILDE
IRISH WRITER (1854–1900)

QUOTATION **986**

In this world there are only two tragedies. One is not getting what one wants, and the other is getting it.

Citation: Oscar Wilde, in his play *Lady Windermere's Fan*

Topics: Contentment; Desires; Perspective; Self-centeredness

Reference: Romans 1:18–32

GARY WILLS
AMERICAN WRITER (1934–)

QUOTATION **987**

Journalists miss the point when they keep asking, after each new church scandal, if a preacher's fall has shaken the believers' faith. Sin rather confirms than challenges a faith that proclaims human corruption. The drama of salvation is played out against the constant backdrop of original sin.

Citation: Gary Wills, *Under God*

Topics: Church Discipline; Depravity; Immorality; Leadership; Original Sin; Salvation; Sin

References: Psalm 53:3; Proverbs 20:9; Isaiah 53:6; Romans 3:23; 1 John 1:8

N. T. WRIGHT
BRITISH WRITER AND BISHOP OF DURHAM (1948–)

QUOTATION **988**

The way to Christian growth is often to allow oneself to be puzzled and startled by new apparent complexity.... Is it, after all, Jesus we want to discover and follow, or would we prefer an idol of our own making?

> **Citation:** N. T. Wright, *The Challenge of Jesus*
>
> **Topics:** Decisions; Discipleship; Growth; Idolatry; Jesus Christ; Maturity
>
> **References:** Exodus 20:3; 1 Timothy 3:16; Hebrews 6:1; 1 Peter 2:2; 2 Peter 3:18; 1 John 5:21

QUOTATION **989**

We have seen in our century what happens when people dream wild dreams of world domination, and use the normal methods of force and power to implement them. We have not yet seen what might happen if those who worship the Servant King, now enthroned as Lord of the world, were to take him seriously enough to take up our cross and follow him.

> **Citation:** N. T. Wright, *Following Jesus*
>
> **Topics:** Christian Life; Cross; Discipleship; Kingdom; Service; Submission
>
> **References:** Matthew 16:21–28; Mark 8:31–9:1; Luke 9:22–27

QUOTATION **990**

We are not to be surprised if living as Christians brings us to the place where we find we are at the end of our own resources, and that we are called to rely on the God who raises the dead.

> **Citation:** N. T. Wright, *Following Jesus*
>
> **Topics:** Discipleship; God; Grace; Mercy; Resurrection; Submission
>
> **References:** 1 Corinthians 2:1–5; 2 Corinthians 4:7; Philippians 3:7–11

QUOTATION **991**

We live in an age that is dying for power, and that is in fact dying *of* power.

> **Citation:** N. T. Wright, *Following Jesus*
> **Topics:** Arrogance; Death; Power; Pride
> **Reference:** Genesis 11:1–9

QUOTATION **992**

Writing the history of Jesus is far more complicated than simply documenting the life of a figure from the past. It is more like writing the biography of a friend who is still very much alive and still liable to surprise us.

> **Citation:** N. T. Wright, *Simply Christian*
> **Topics:** Experiencing God; Gospels; History; Jesus Christ
> **References:** Luke 1:1–4; John 20:30–31

QUOTATION **993**

Christian prayer is simple, in the sense that a small child can pray the prayer Jesus taught. But it's hard in the demands it makes as we go on with it.

> **Citation:** N. T. Wright, *Simply Christian*
> **Topics:** Discipleship; Prayer; Spiritual Growth
> **References:** Matthew 6:5–15; 7:7–12; Luke 11:1–13; 18:1–8

MICHAEL YACONELLI
AMERICAN WRITER AND SATIRIST (1942–2003)

QUOTATION **994**

Accepting the reality of our broken, flawed lives is the beginning of spirituality not because the spiritual life will remove our flaws but because we let go of seeking perfection and, instead, seek God, the one who is present in the tangledness of our lives.

> **Citation:** Michael Yaconelli, *Messy Spirituality*

Topics: Brokenness; Human Condition; Limitations; Seeking God

References: Romans 3:9–20; 5:1–11; 6:1–14; Philippians 3:7–16

QUOTATION 995

Jesus is not repelled by us, no matter how messy we are, regardless of how incomplete we are. When we recognize that Jesus is not discouraged by our humanity, is not turned off by our messiness, and simply doggedly pursues us in the face of it all, what else can we do but give in to his outrageous, indiscriminate love?

Citation: Michael Yaconelli, *Messy Spirituality*

Topics: Brokenness; Human Condition; Limitations; Unconditional Love

References: Luke 19:1–10; Romans 5:1–11; 8:1–4

PHILIP YANCEY
AMERICAN WRITER (1949–)

QUOTATION 996

The Jesus I learned about as a child was sweet and inoffensive, the kind of person whose lap you'd want to climb on. Mister Rogers with a beard. Indeed, Jesus did have qualities of gentleness and compassion that attracted little children. Mister Rogers, however, he assuredly was not. Not even the Romans would have crucified Mister Rogers.

Citation: Philip Yancey, in the video *The Jesus I Never Knew*

Topics: Cross; Crucifixion; Gentleness; Jesus Christ

References: Matthew 23; Mark 11:12–18

QUOTATION 997

Faith during affliction matters more than healing from affliction.

Citation: Philip Yancey, *Prayer: Does It Make Any Difference?*

Topics: Affliction; Faith; Healing; Suffering; Trials

References: Romans 5:1–5; James 1:1–4; 1 Peter 1:3–16; 5:6–11

QUOTATION **998**

Some things just have to be believed to be seen.

> **Citation:** Philip Yancey, *Disappointment with God*
>
> **Topics:** Belief; Mysteries; Revelation; Skepticism; Trust
>
> **References:** 1 Corinthians 2:6–16; 1 Peter 1:3–16

QUOTATION **999**

We remain ignorant of many details, not because God enjoys keeping us in the dark, but because we have not the faculties to absorb so much light.

> **Citation:** Philip Yancey, *Disappointment with God*
>
> **Topics:** Knowledge; Limitations; Mind; Mysteries; Revelation
>
> **References:** Deuteronomy 29:29; Job 38:34–38; 40:1–5; 42:1–6; 2 Corinthians 12:4

QUOTATION **1000**

Faith is, in the end, a kind of homesickness — for a home we have never visited but have never stopped longing for.

> **Citation:** Philip Yancey, *Disappointment with God*
>
> **Topics:** Eternal Life; Faith; Heaven; Hope
>
> **Reference:** 2 Corinthians 5:1–10

QUOTATION **1001**

It is a terrible thing to be grateful and have no one to thank, to be awed and have no one to worship.

> **Citation:** Philip Yancey in the article "Open Windows" in *Marriage Partnership* magazine
>
> **Topics:** Atheism; God; Praise; Thanksgiving; Worship
>
> **References:** Luke 4:8; Acts 17:24; Revelation 14:7

SCRIPTURE INDEX

1001 QUOTATIONS THAT CONNECT

1001 QUOTATIONS THAT CONNECT

1001 QUOTATIONS THAT CONNECT

TOPICAL INDEX

160, 171, 278, 279, 282, 298, 306, 308, 315

death to self, 310

debt, 267

deceit, 26, 27, 44, 48, 55, 62, 91, 121, 136, 161, 168, 198, 208, 210, 217, 218, 222, 227, 227, 231, 234, 246, 265, 280, 295, 307

decisions, 12, 21, 28, 49, 51, 62, 105, 131, 146, 192, 194, 211, 228, 241, 244, 274, 279, 301, 314

dedication, 24, 32, 33, 35, 51, 53, 61, 63, 64, 71, 81, 81, 93, 93, 100, 104, 106, 113, 126, 176, 224

delight, 193

deliverance, 112

demons, 123

dependence, 98

depravity, 11, 12, 20, 21, 31, 36, 52, 57, 65, 71, 71, 84, 87, 156, 165, 165, 168, 169, 172, 184, 188, 192, 201, 203, 208, 217, 218, 223, 227, 227, 227, 227, 231, 259, 280, 296, 313

depression, 46, 258, 298

desires, 10, 11, 21, 21, 28, 30, 57, 71, 76, 79, 156, 202, 225, 226, 313

despair, 68, 223, 258, 261, 294, 298

destiny, 47

determination, 53, 70

Devil, 91, 104, 122, 146, 156, 218, 255, 278

devotion, 80, 100, 220, 257

devotional life, 10, 16, 25, 33, 33, 34, 75, 79, 82, 90, 101, 103, 111, 114, 119, 132, 133, 142, 143, 147, 151,

158, 180, 185, 211, 281, 282, 288, 288

difficulties, 48, 259, 295

dignity, 50, 188

direction, 44, 47, 49, 69, 86, 101, 105, 107, 111, 132, 143, 167, 199, 204, 209, 228, 247, 248, 282

disabilities, 302

disappointment, 176

discernment, 48, 54, 62, 65, 69, 122, 155, 156, 183, 192, 194, 200, 211, 215, 222, 228, 247, 252, 273

discipleship, 14, 25, 27, 76, 79, 80, 96, 96, 97, 104, 131, 137, 140, 140, 205, 222, 235, 236, 236, 262, 273, 277, 279, 282, 283, 284, 290, 293, 295, 314, 314, 314, 315

discouragement, 16, 176, 242

disease, 291

disobedience, 77, 137, 192

distractions, 10, 10, 19, 24, 33, 46, 54, 56, 59, 60, 64, 111, 122, 129, 132, 141, 161, 173, 178, 197, 226, 250, 251, 262, 268, 271, 288, 291, 292, 312

division, 18, 18, 30, 76, 119, 177

divorce, 71, 214

doctrine, 12, 14, 29, 125, 159, 194, 200, 202, 214, 293, 311

double-mindedness, 10, 24, 54, 64, 80, 105, 126, 221, 288, 292

doubt, 76, 108, 143, 193, 200, 206, 212, 214, 232

drugs, 75

drunkenness, 75

duty, 192

E

earthly concerns, 19

education, 201

egotism, 280, 286

emotions, 46, 174, 261, 280, 298, 303

empathy, 152, 153, 196

employees, 305

emptiness, 46, 46, 261

encouragement, 96, 193, 224, 265

endurance, 241

enemies, 55, 63, 64, 66, 76, 98, 104, 105, 109, 110, 121, 128, 164, 174, 201, 219, 239, 239, 248, 262, 266, 266, 270, 285, 302, 309

entertainment, 59, 119, 141, 220

enthusiasm, 280

envy, 30, 278

eternal and temporary, 40, 42, 47, 64, 67, 91, 102, 160, 247, 249, 265

eternal death, 40, 84, 141, 144, 171, 279, 298

eternal life, 22, 23, 25, 40, 47, 84, 102, 104, 107, 109, 125, 135, 136, 140, 141, 144, 161, 171, 179, 189, 193, 209, 257, 279, 282, 298, 302, 317

eternal perspective, 296

eternity, 22, 104, 111, 126, 135, 239

ethics, 12, 36, 44, 48, 99, 231, 274, 277

evangelism, 15, 17, 18, 24, 34, 81, 81, 100, 102, 108, 110, 110, 110, 115, 147, 173, 181, 185, 190, 210, 216, 216, 225, 226, 240, 243, 257,

271, 272, 277, 279, 290,
291, 300, 304, 306, 312

evil, 12, 13, 20, 23, 41, 54, 71,
76, 77, 81, 83, 91, 104, 109,
110, 122, 122, 128, 134,
146, 147, 157, 166, 168, 177,
184, 217, 218, 223, 227,
227, 256, 259, 278, 278,
296, 302, 306, 308

example, 100, 147, 157, 240,
250

excuses, 13, 13, 23, 53, 138,
231, 286

experiencing God, 20, 25, 34,
79, 79, 80, 83, 86, 94, 96,
103, 112, 114, 122, 124,
129, 130, 134, 138, 140,
142, 143, 145, 146, 151,
157, 158, 158, 160, 168,
192, 209, 213, 215, 220,
225, 232, 239, 254, 256,
257, 264, 270, 274, 287,
297, 299, 299, 305, 315

F

failure, 29, 32, 49, 53, 72, 99,
259, 262, 268, 288

faith, 13, 15, 26, 27, 28, 33, 58,
75, 76, 77, 79, 82, 106, 135,
138, 138, 158, 159, 160,
162, 166, 167, 168, 168,
186, 188, 193, 200, 200,
205, 212, 212, 215, 216,
217, 225, 232, 247, 251,
263, 270, 288, 295, 304,
308, 309, 310, 312, 316, 317

faith and circumstances, 300

faithfulness, 67

fall of humanity, 11, 12, 21,
192, 201

false teachers, 31, 44, 62, 65,
76, 86

family, 46, 71, 133, 153, 252,
254, 256, 274, 302

fasting, 129, 225, 281
fate, 47
fear, 17, 60, 63, 69, 70, 72, 83,
94, 127, 148, 160, 166, 175,
176, 184, 185, 190, 252,
253, 260, 265, 270, 271,
300, 304, 305, 311

fear of God, 15, 94, 126, 192,
200, 252, 293, 299

feelings, 46, 261

fellowship, 17, 18, 18, 20, 68,
86, 88, 96, 98, 98, 143,
145, 150, 153, 168, 196,
224, 233

feminism, 40

final judgment, 84, 97, 126,
144, 244, 262, 282, 298,
309

flesh, 25, 75, 296

focus, 10, 15, 19, 23, 24, 46,
49, 51, 53, 54, 57, 60, 64,
80, 93, 100, 114, 127, 132,
133, 155, 156, 178, 240,
250, 251, 262, 268, 269,
273, 291, 312

foolishness, 11, 27, 39, 44, 55,
63, 65, 67, 87, 122, 155,
172, 182, 188, 202, 207,
208, 216, 228, 266, 272,
294

forgiveness, 65, 76, 80, 121,
161, 164, 174, 183, 193,
236, 247, 253, 266, 267,
270, 271, 280, 302, 304,
309

free will, 179, 207

freedom, 36, 63, 145, 161, 164,
166, 179, 193, 198, 203,
207, 234, 286

friendship, 30, 46, 88, 121,
131, 138, 250, 258, 265

friendship with God, 160

fruitfulness, 16, 56, 289

fruit of the Spirit, 284

fulfillment, 49, 94, 193, 256
funerals, 308
future, 75, 107, 113, 131, 152,
161, 165, 189, 195, 209,
253, 304

G

generosity, 48, 56, 174, 188,
230, 298

gentleness, 29, 105, 135, 185,
199, 206, 206, 216, 231,
233, 240, 267, 290, 316

giving, 48, 56, 108, 146, 172,
174, 188, 194, 210, 230, 298

glory, 31, 74, 85, 108, 189, 193,
197, 241

goals, 19, 21, 53, 56, 61, 64,
94, 107, 127, 132, 143, 157,
186, 197, 202, 209, 211,
226, 258, 274

God, 38, 79, 86, 91, 101, 106,
114, 134, 140, 141, 148,
159, 159, 168, 199, 202,
205, 213, 255, 263, 270,
280, 292, 299, 299, 303,
314, 317

God as Father, 97, 220

God's glory, 119, 130, 140, 160

God's love, 17, 75, 80, 86, 107,
151, 156, 198

God's promises, 107

God's sovereignty, 10, 22, 25,
47, 58, 77, 86, 92, 101, 103,
104, 107, 109, 112, 131,
135, 135, 149, 166, 178,
184, 242, 242, 243, 245,
253, 260, 263, 269, 282,
288, 297, 300, 306

God's strength, 22

God's will, 21, 25, 51, 51, 69,
101, 130, 130, 130, 131,
131, 137, 146, 150, 166,
171, 179, 181, 277, 281,
289, 290, 301, 303, 310

God's wrath, 38, 92, 97, 170
godlessness, 192, 203
godliness, 20, 58, 82, 93, 137, 143, 147, 240, 246, 281, 287
Golden Rule, 144
good deeds, 50, 76, 82, 93, 99, 100, 108, 144, 189, 194, 216, 244, 257, 308, 308
goodness, 134, 134
gospel, 34, 136, 164, 200, 210, 216, 248, 277, 279
Gospels, 315
gossip, 44, 70, 112, 242, 307
government, 15, 15, 42, 175, 187, 195
grace, 24, 43, 84, 86, 109, 112, 119, 131, 135, 164, 174, 178, 179, 181, 184, 198, 221, 230, 230, 238, 247, 251, 253, 266, 266, 271, 277, 279, 280, 283, 288, 289, 299, 301, 303, 308, 314
Great Commission, 114, 164, 216
greed, 11, 39, 45, 46, 48, 49, 50, 52, 74, 91, 115, 127, 198, 202, 210, 230, 255
growth, 16, 34, 120, 127, 147, 151, 152, 153, 203, 211, 244, 253, 259, 262, 265, 297, 314
grudges, 260, 270
grumbling, 287
guidance, 23, 44, 47, 62, 69, 79, 86, 92, 101, 111, 125, 131, 132, 143, 143, 148, 156, 167, 168, 184, 195, 199, 204, 214, 217, 246, 247, 254, 274, 282
guilt, 31, 39, 55, 118, 149, 181, 233, 271

H

habits, 79, 229

happiness, 27, 56, 71, 87, 96, 100, 185, 190, 193, 202, 266, 279, 291
hatred, 98, 164, 174, 206, 221, 230, 232, 248, 262, 266, 266, 270
healing, 87, 108, 153, 258, 289, 316
hearing God, 129, 137
heart, 30, 36, 168, 194, 217, 256
heaven, 16, 19, 25, 47, 84, 104, 109, 122, 135, 141, 161, 171, 193, 195, 209, 225, 249, 255, 279, 282, 296, 302, 308, 317
hell, 47, 84, 141, 144, 171, 255, 279, 282, 294, 296
heresy, 86
hiding, 292
history, 202, 315
holiness, 10, 20, 24, 44, 59, 64, 66, 80, 89, 93, 106, 120, 122, 137, 151, 167, 171, 197, 198, 231, 240, 240, 243, 246, 266, 272, 277, 303
Holy Spirit, 24, 66, 69, 80, 86, 91, 126, 164, 168, 169, 173, 180, 199, 233
honesty, 11, 13, 46, 62, 193, 204, 208, 218, 234, 250, 258, 275
hope, 12, 23, 25, 31, 68, 77, 83, 98, 107, 109, 113, 127, 134, 134, 135, 136, 146, 148, 152, 153, 153, 154, 161, 166, 176, 178, 188, 193, 197, 215, 217, 225, 230, 235, 247, 258, 261, 265, 272, 302, 317
hospitality, 133
hostility, 121
human condition, 11, 12, 20, 21, 22, 36, 40, 71, 77, 77,

84, 156, 158, 159, 165, 165, 166, 169, 172, 182, 184, 188, 201, 203, 211, 217, 221, 223, 223, 223, 227, 227, 227, 227, 235, 280, 280, 283, 299, 315, 316
human nature, 11, 20, 21, 36, 47, 71, 84, 156, 158, 165, 169, 172, 182, 188, 192, 193, 203, 204, 206, 208, 231, 239, 283, 290, 296, 307
human will, 21, 25, 51, 53, 69, 101, 130, 130, 130, 131, 137, 150, 179, 181, 192, 203, 277, 281, 289, 301, 303, 304, 310
humanism, 41, 44, 80, 170, 202, 263, 285
humility, 12, 18, 20, 23, 45, 88, 89, 89, 93, 97, 101, 108, 110, 115, 120, 128, 137, 140, 149, 158, 162, 164, 165, 165, 167, 172, 178, 182, 185, 200, 220, 221, 233, 250, 269, 275, 278, 278, 280, 284, 297
hypocrisy, 29, 30, 31, 32, 60, 62, 62, 66, 68, 167, 167, 168, 171, 208, 210, 214, 217, 221, 223, 236, 240, 246, 262

I

identity, 41, 66, 220, 243, 286
identity in Christ, 94
idolatry, 30, 36, 41, 74, 80, 127, 169, 170, 170, 202, 225, 242, 260, 272, 285, 293, 299, 302, 309, 314
ignorance, 136, 166
illumination, 34, 69, 85, 99, 143, 166, 166, 166, 180, 194, 209, 213, 246, 255, 273, 285

M

malice, 121

marriage, 40, 46, 57, 61, 100, 133, 149, 153, 181, 182, 182, 186, 214, 244, 254, 254, 255, 263, 276

martyrdom, 78, 91, 104, 109, 110, 187, 210, 284, 310

materialism, 11, 20, 32, 39, 41, 52, 55, 74, 91, 97, 120, 127, 132, 154, 155, 170, 171, 173, 181, 188, 194, 198, 210

maturity, 14, 34, 35, 55, 99, 111, 120, 134, 139, 150, 151, 157, 161, 197, 219, 221, 230, 251, 252, 259, 275, 278, 283, 295, 311, 314

meals, 196

meaning, 42, 47, 50, 56, 57, 61, 66, 71, 87, 106, 124, 125, 126, 169, 189, 197, 202, 204, 205, 209, 211, 225, 248, 261, 305, 306, 312

media, 133

meditation, 146, 220

mentoring, 50, 102

mercy, 43, 43, 75, 83, 84, 86, 93, 105, 109, 109, 121, 135, 139, 160, 164, 174, 174, 178, 183, 186, 187, 198, 199, 231, 232, 240, 253, 266, 266, 266, 267, 280, 288, 308, 314

mind, 14, 30, 123, 125, 140, 166, 166, 169, 180, 194, 201, 201, 207, 207, 268, 317

ministry, 35, 61, 67, 82, 93, 114, 114, 151, 152, 153, 159, 164, 176, 179, 179, 212, 216, 232, 244, 251, 258, 261, 269, 276, 278, 289

misery, 170, 223, 229

mission, 81, 81, 84, 97, 101, 102, 106, 113, 114, 169, 173, 216

missions, 17, 41, 43, 106, 108, 110, 110, 113, 114, 114, 115, 115, 157, 190, 225, 226, 243, 277, 284, 291

money, 11, 32, 39, 41, 45, 46, 48, 49, 52, 55, 74, 91, 97, 120, 127, 154, 155, 170, 171, 188, 198, 202, 230

morality, 12, 13, 13, 13, 15, 29, 36, 41, 44, 48, 57, 65, 71, 90, 92, 154, 201, 212, 222, 231, 246, 261, 267, 300

mortality, 40, 171

motivation, 28, 42, 47, 61, 71, 81, 169, 209, 225, 226, 268, 307

motives, 47, 56, 61, 78, 113, 121, 169, 281, 306

murder, 221

music, 119, 119, 179

mysteries, 14, 15, 31, 44, 70, 79, 93, 103, 104, 106, 123, 124, 134, 136, 138, 140, 149, 159, 193, 193, 200, 206, 207, 212, 213, 215, 219, 242, 254, 260, 264, 282, 282, 299, 317, 317

N

narcissism, 147

needs, 79, 99, 135

neighbors, 40, 99

new covenant, 24

nurture, 168

O

obedience, 16, 21, 25, 51, 56, 57, 81, 92, 96, 98, 100, 118, 130, 137, 150, 186, 210, 211, 224, 229, 234, 277, 281, 290, 295, 301, 312

obstacles, 121

old covenant, 24

opportunity, 17, 34, 53, 72, 108, 156, 183, 195

opposition, 90, 176, 210, 219

oppression, 189, 201, 221

optimism, 235

original sin, 11, 12, 36, 169, 203, 208, 313

orthodoxy, 125

outreach, 15, 17, 24, 35, 62, 81, 81, 93, 97, 102, 109, 110, 114, 157, 164, 173, 179, 181, 276, 284, 300, 304, 306

overcoming, 48, 51, 54, 63, 63, 66, 72, 74, 104, 110, 121, 124, 127, 175, 176, 177, 215, 241, 245, 259, 265, 294, 300

overconfidence, 122

P

pain, 20, 38, 51, 100, 103, 104, 108, 138, 142, 143, 152, 153, 153, 156, 187, 196, 203, 215, 249, 302, 308

panic, 251, 270

paradoxes, 234

parenting, 254, 254

passion, 35, 57, 130, 131, 133, 183, 193, 209, 216, 243, 257, 280, 281

past, 11, 11, 31, 60, 65, 75, 113, 152, 155, 172, 225, 239, 253, 271

patience, 22, 123, 129, 134, 139, 265, 289, 289

peace, 30, 52, 75, 77, 83, 130, 153, 157, 166, 180, 189, 202, 230, 235, 251, 261, 264, 265, 301

perception, 165, 216, 300

perfection, 118, 151, 291

1001 QUOTATIONS THAT CONNECT

Z

NAME INDEX

1001 QUOTATIONS THAT CONNECT

Bonus CD-ROM with this book:

We have included in this book a bonus CD-ROM to facilitate your use of the 1001 quotations that are included in the text. The disk contains electronic files for the complete book. The disk can be used in Windows or Mac OsX systems. You will be able to use it with your word-processing software to do the following:

- Cut and paste quotations and insert them into your documents.
- Search to find a word, topic, name, or text.

Preaching That Connects

Using Journalistic Techniques to Add Impact

Mark Galli and Craig Brian Larson

Master the craft of effective communication that grabs attention and wins hearts.

Like everyone else, preachers long to be understood. Unfortunately, the rules first learned in seminary, if misapplied, can quickly turn homiletic precision into listener boredom.

To capture heart and mind, Mark Galli and Craig Brian Larson suggest preachers turn to the lessons of journalism. In *Preaching That Connects*, they show how the same keys used to create effective, captivating communication in the media can transform a sermon.

Amply illustrated from some of today's best preachers, *Preaching That Connects* walks through the entire sermon, from the critical introduction to the bridge to illustrations and final application. Key points include the five techniques for generating creative ideas, your six options for illustrations, and the ten rules for great storytelling—and why the transition sentence is the hardest sentence you'll write.

Preaching That Connects is for all who seek to hone their craft to communicate the truth of the gospel effectively.

Softcover: 978-0-310-38621-6

Pick up a copy today at your favorite bookstore!

The Art & Craft of Biblical Preaching

A Comprehensive Resource for Today's Communicators

Haddon Robinson and Craig Brian Larson, General Editors

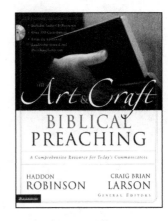

This extensive encyclopedia is the most complete and practical work ever published on the art and craft of biblical preaching. The eleven major sections contain over two hundred articles, which cover every possible preaching topic, including changing lives, sermon structure, "the big idea," introductions, outlining, transitions, conclusions, passionate delivery, application, leveraging illustrations, telling stories, preaching narrative texts, topical preaching, expository preaching, evangelistic preaching, preaching to postmoderns, using humor, speaking with authority, and many others.

Entries are characterized by intensely practical and vivid writing designed to help preachers deepen their understanding and sharpen their communication skills. The contributors include a virtual Who's Who of preaching from a cross section of denominations and traditions, such as John Ortberg, Rick Warren, Warren Wiersbe, Alice Mathews, John Piper, Andy Stanley, and many others. Haddon Robinson and Craig Brian Larson—two of today's most respected voices in preaching—provide editorial oversight.

Includes an accompanying CD with actual audio examples.

Hardcover, Jacketed: 978-0-310-25248-1

Pick up a copy today at your favorite bookstore!

ZONDERVAN®
.com

Movie-Based Illustrations

Movie-Based Illustrations for Preaching & Teaching

101 Clips to Show or Tell

*Craig Brian Larson & Andrew Zahn, Editors of
Leadership & Preaching Today.com*

Movies have become the stories of our culture. People love to
discuss favorite movies and actors, and this interest can help you communicate God's
Word with power—if you have exciting, movie-based illustrations at your fingertips.

This collection contains 101 complete illustrations straight from popular movies your
listeners can relate to. Each illustration is easy to use—you don't even have to be familiar
with the movie to share the truth it portrays.

- Complete indexes includes multiple keywords and relevant Scripture passages
  for easy selection.
- Each illustration provides plot summary and detailed description of the scene—
  you can tell the story well even if you haven't seen the movie.
- Exact begin and end times are given for each illustration if you wish to show
  the video clip.
- Each illustration gives background information on the movie—year created,
  MPAA rating, and more.

This handy, to-the-point resource will help you add dramatic muscle to your sermons
and lessons. Engage your listeners' imaginations through the power of movies—and drive
biblical truths home to their hearts.

Softcover: 978-0-310-24832-3

Pick up a copy today at your favorite bookstore!

ZONDERVAN®
.com

Movie-Based Illustrations

More Movie-Based Illustrations for Preaching & Teaching

101 Clips to Show or Tell

Craig Brian Larson & Lori Quicke, Editors of Leadership & Preaching Today.com

If you've used the original *Movie-Based Illustrations for Preaching and Teaching*, you know why this sequel is a must-have. If not, you're about to discover why *More Movie-Based Illustrations for Preaching and Teaching* is one of the most effective people reachers you can add to your tool kit. Movies have become the stories of our culture, and they can help you communicate God's Word with power—if you have exciting, movie-based illustrations at your fingertips.

This collection contains 101 complete illustrations straight from popular movies your listeners can relate to. Each illustration is easy to use—you don't even have to be familiar with the movie to share the truth it portrays.

- Complete indexes include multiple keywords, movie titles, and relevant Scripture passages for easy selection.
- Each illustration provides plot summary and detailed description of the scene— you can tell the story well even if you haven't seen the movie.
- Exact begin and end times are given for each illustration if you wish to show the video clip.
- Each illustration gives background information on the movie—year created, MPAA rating, and more.

Softcover: 978-0-310-24834-7

Pick up a copy today at your favorite bookstore!

1001 Illustrations That Connect

Compelling Stories, Stats, and News Items for Preaching, Teaching, and Writing

Craig Brian Larson and Phyllis Ten Elshof,
General Editors

Every preacher, teacher, or writer knows the value of a good illustration in helping connect the truth of the passage with the congregation or class—and how hard it is to come up with good illustrations week after week.

This book contains the cream of the crop: 1001 illustrations carefully selected from among thousands on Christianity Today International's popular website *PreachingToday.com*. These illustrations are proven, memorable, and illuminating. As the saying goes, they will preach! And they're fresh, all written within the past seven years.

Of course, the best illustrations are no good if you can't find the right one. These illustrations have been arranged according to thirty-seven master topics. In addition, they've been indexed according to both Bible references and key topics. A searchable CD-ROM is included, allowing you to get the illustration into your lesson or sermon with ease.

Softcover: 978-0-310-28037-8

Pick up a copy today at your favorite bookstore!

Share Your Thoughts

With the Author: Your comments will be forwarded to
the author when you send them to *zauthor@zondervan.com*.

With Zondervan: Submit your review of this book
by writing to *zreview@zondervan.com*.

Free Online Resources at
www.zondervan.com/hello

 Zondervan AuthorTracker: Be notified whenever your
favorite authors publish new books, go on tour, or post
an update about what's happening in their lives.

 Daily Bible Verses and Devotions: Enrich your life
with daily Bible verses or devotions that help you start
every morning focused on God.

 Free Email Publications: Sign up for newsletters on
fiction, Christian living, church ministry, parenting, and
more.

 Zondervan Bible Search: Find and compare
Bible passages in a variety of translations at
www.zondervanbiblesearch.com.

 Other Benefits: Register yourself to receive online
benefits like coupons and special offers, or to participate
in research.